Robert Grant Watson

Spanish and Portuguese South America

During the colonial period. Vol. 2

Robert Grant Watson

Spanish and Portuguese South America
During the colonial period. Vol. 2

ISBN/EAN: 9783337150808

Printed in Europe, USA, Canada, Australia, Japan

Cover: Foto ©ninafisch / pixelio.de

More available books at **www.hansebooks.com**

SPANISH AND PORTUGUESE
SOUTH AMERICA

DURING

THE COLONIAL PERIOD.

BY

ROBERT GRANT WATSON,
EDITOR OF "MURRAY'S HANDBOOK OF GREECE," FOURTH EDITION, 1872.

IN TWO VOLUMES.

VOL. II.

LONDON:
TRÜBNER & CO., LUDGATE HILL.
1884.
[*All rights reserved.*]

Ballantyne Press
BALLANTYNE, HANSON AND CO.
EDINBURGH AND LONDON

CONTENTS OF VOL. II.

CHAPTER I.
BRAZIL; THE DUTCH WAR: 1623-1637 . . . 1

CHAPTER II.
BRAZIL; THE DUTCH WAR. GOVERNMENT OF COUNT MAURICE OF NASSAU: 1638-1644 . . 22

CHAPTER III.
BRAZIL; THE DUTCH WAR; RISING OF THE PORTUGUESE: 1644-1645 42

CHAPTER IV.
BRAZIL; CONCLUSION OF THE DUTCH WAR: 1646-1661 53

CHAPTER V.
JESUIT MISSIONS IN NORTHERN BRAZIL: 1652-1662 . . 76

CHAPTER VI.
ESTABLISHMENT OF THE FRENCH IN SOUTH AMERICA: 1657-1696 95

CHAPTER VII.
BRAZIL; ITS PROGRESS DURING THE SEVENTEENTH CENTURY: 1600-1700 112

CHAPTER VIII.
PERU; PROGRESS OF THE VICEROYALTY: 1551-1774 . 126

CONTENTS.

CHAPTER IX.
Viceroyalty of New Granada: 1535–1790 . . 146

CHAPTER X.
Chili; Progress of the Colony: 1604–1792 . . 159

CHAPTER XI.
Brazil; Discovery of the Mines; Attempt of the French on Rio de Janeiro: 1702–1720 . 169

CHAPTER XII.
Brazil; Discovery of the Diamond District: 1724–1749 186

CHAPTER XIII.
Progress of Buenos Ayres: 1580–1800 . . . 203

CHAPTER XIV.
Brazil; The War of the Seven Reductions: 1750–1761 218

CHAPTER XV.
Expulsion of the Jesuits from Portugal and Brazil: 1759–1767 232

CHAPTER XVI.
Expulsion of the Jesuits from Buenos Ayres and Paraguay: 1749–1805 247

CHAPTER XVII.
Brazil in the Eighteenth Century; Arrival of the Braganzas: 1776–1806 256

CHAPTER XVIII.
English Expeditions to La Plata, under Beresford, Auchmuty, and Whitelocke: 1806–1807 . . 271

Appendix 295

SOUTH AMERICA.

Book II.

CHAPTER I.

BRAZIL; THE DUTCH WAR.

1623-1637.

THE appearance of the Dutch as actors on the Brazilian stage arose, as might be expected, from the connection of the Low Countries with Spain and from that of Spain with Portugal. Their success in attacking the sources of their enemy's supplies in the East led to the establishment of a West Indian Company, the chief object of which was to make conquests in *Brazil*. A fleet was fitted out under the command of Willekens, who had under him the celebrated Peter Heyne. The religious intolerance from which the Dutch had themselves so terribly suffered at the hands of their Spanish rulers had taught them to be tolerant in such matters towards others, and to this circumstance they were now indebted for much valuable information respecting *Brazil*, which they received from the Jews who had taken refuge amongst them.

The Dutch fleet sailed at the close of 1623, and when they had crossed the line, the commander found that his sealed instructions directed him to attack *S. Salvador*. A storm, however, interrupted this programme; and Willekens, on reaching the neighbourhood of *Bahia*, was compelled to delay for some days, awaiting his comrades. On the news of his approach being communicated to the governor, it was received at first with Brazilian apathy, which, however, was succeeded by alarm on his strength being correctly reported. The colonial forces were mustered for the defence of their possessions; but, as no immediate attack was made, alarm in time again gave way to apathy, and the colonists dispersed to attend to their individual concerns. When Willekens had collected his fleet, he found *S. Salvador* undefended; and on the following day he took possession of the place without opposition. In this easy manner the Dutch, without having had to strike a blow, became masters of the capital of *Brazil*.

Willekens had with him a soldier of experience, Van Dort, who now took the command on shore. The fortifications were repaired, and proclamations were issued offering full possession of their property and freedom of worship to all such as would submit. Amongst those who were thus brought under Dutch rule were two hundred Jews. The Brazilian authorities, who imagined that this was merely a predatory expedition on the part of the Dutch, such as they had become more or less accustomed to on the part of Englishmen or Frenchmen, were astonished to find that the Hollanders meant to keep possession of what they had taken. Their national spirit revived with the realization of this fact; and as a consequence measures were concerted to recover their honour and their property. The governor having been taken prisoner, the bishop and other chief persons opened his succession papers, by which they found that their obedience was now due to the governor of *Pernambuco*. Messengers were accordingly sent to advise him of his new position, and meanwhile the command was vested in the bishop Teixeira. His force consisted of fourteen hundred Portuguese and two hundred and fifty natives, with which he established a fortified camp about a league from the city, procuring three guns from a vessel which had taken refuge in one of the rivers of the *Reconcave*.

The bishop, who was at least energetic, if not otherwise qualified for a military command, was so fortunate at the outset as that the Dutch general, Van Dort, fell at the hands of one of his skirmishing parties, while the officer who succeeded him was shot. In the midst of this undecided situation it seems strange indeed that the invaders should have been so confident as to admit of Willekens sailing for Holland with eleven vessels. A few days after his departure, his next in command, Admiral Heyne, sailed in turn with the remaining vessels for *Angola*, his object being to secure a supply of negroes for the Dutch colony in *Brazil*. The admiral was, however, baffled in this object; and, returning to South America, he met with no more good fortune in an attempt upon *Espirito Santo*. Proceeding from there to *Bahia*, he found the Spanish and Portuguese fleets in possession, and, being unable to oppose them, made sail for Europe.

The loss of *Bahia* had fallen like a thunderbolt on the court of Madrid; and orders were given to have a great fleet equipped for the purpose of recovering that city, whilst immediate succours were sent to such other ports as were supposed to be most in danger, namely, to *Pernambuco*, *Rio de Janeiro*, and *Angola*. The Spanish Government showed on this occasion the spirit by which it was chiefly animated, by ordering all sorts of religious exercises to be undertaken in connection with the recent calamity. The authorities of Portugal were instructed to inquire into and punish the crimes which had drawn down so marked a manifestation of the Divine vengeance as the delivery of the capital of *Brazil* into the hands of heretics. Special prayers, to be repeated during nine successive days, were ordered throughout the kingdom, whilst a litany was composed for use at daily mass. In addition to this, a solemn religious procession was ordered in every town and village. The Portuguese, to whom the loss of their chief Brazilian town came more immediately home, showed their concern at the intelligence in a more worldly fashion; the city of Lisbon giving a donation of one hundred thousand crowns to the Government towards its recovery, and the Dukes of Braganza and Caminha twenty and sixteen thousand, respectively. The nobles generally offered their persons and property in the public service, whilst men of the highest rank embarked as volunteers,—amongst them Noronha, who had been Portuguese Viceroy in India. The armament now sent out to *Brazil* was so thoroughly a national one on the part of Portugal that it is said there was not one noble family in the country which was not represented in it. It consisted of six-and-twenty vessels, bearing four thousand men, and they were to join the Spanish fleet at the Cape *de Verds*. The latter fleet, however, had not been equipped with the breathless haste displayed in the case of that of Portugal; and the Portuguese had thus to wait during nine weary weeks at the place of rendezvous for the arrival of the Spaniards. Of the proportions of the Spanish fleet, however, nothing could be said, since it consisted of forty sail, bearing eight thousand men.

Albuquerque, the governor of *Pernambuco*, and who was now governor of *Brazil*, being unable to muster a sufficient force to cope with the Dutch, contented himself with harassing them by attacking their outposts and cutting off their supplies. In March 1625 the united fleets of Spain and Portugal appeared off *Bahia*, and so intoxicated were the Brazilians at the sight that they forthwith made an attack on the Dutch entrenchments. The attack, however, was premature, and they were repulsed with loss. The city had been fortified with careful science, and was defended by ninety-two pieces of artillery. The Spanish commander, *Don* Fadrique de Toledo, who knew that reinforcements were expected from Holland, proposed to land three thousand men leaving the rest on board to intercept the enemy's succours. It was resolved, however, to land half of the army; whilst the fleet, by stretching across the entrance to the bay, should, at the same time, blockade the ships in port and cut off supplies.

The besieged Hollanders first made a bold attempt with six hundred men to surprise the camp, by which they effected considerable slaughter; and next, by means of two fire-ships, to burn the blockading fleet. The latter attempt, however, recoiled upon themselves, for the Spanish were so alarmed at the possibility of danger such as that which they had escaped, that they resolved without loss of time to destroy the Dutch ships. The Dutch drew their vessels under the forts; but a way was hewn through the rocks which exposed them to artillery fire, and the greater number were sunk. Meanwhile a portion of the garrison became mutinous; the French and English mercenaries, who were sure of quarter, refused any longer to fight, and nothing was left for the Dutch commander but to capitulate. He and his men were to receive shipping and stores to convey them to Holland, and sufficient arms for their defence by the way; but the city of *Bahia*, which was given up on the 1st of May, suffered considerably at the hands of those who had come to expel the invaders. There was, however, some difficulty in executing the terms of capitulation, for the country round *Bahia*, having been taxed beyond its resources, was now destitute of provisions, and before these could be procured from the neighbouring captaincies the state of affairs had assumed altogether a new aspect.

Tidings at length arrived that the long-expected Dutch fleet, with reinforcements, had passed the *Canaries;* and a Portuguese prisoner who had escaped brought intelligence of its approach. Thereupon the two thousand prisoners were placed on board of dismantled ships, which were drawn under the guns of the fortress; and it was determined to await the enemy's approach within the harbour. On the 22nd of May the Dutch fleet of thirty-four sail stood into the bay, under the delusion that *S. Salvador* was still held by their countrymen. The admiral, Henrik, however, was soon undeceived; but in his confusion he lost the opportunity of attacking the Spaniards and Portuguese with advantage. He stood off to the north and passed *Olinda* during a gale which carried him on to the Bay of *Traiçam*, where the natives were disposed to welcome any one who might deliver them from the hands of the Portuguese. Here he landed his sick and fortified himself; but he was disturbed by an expedition from *Pernambuco* and *Paraïba*, upon which he thought it better to re-embark his men and depart. Henrik's fleet met with no further success. He himself died, and the remains of his unfortunate expedition found their way back to Holland.

The Spanish general, leaving a sufficient garrison in *Bahia*, now sailed for Europe, taking the Dutch troops with him. The fleet encountered storms, and three Spanish and nine Portuguese vessels foundered; another sank on reaching the island of St. George; whilst two were taken by a Dutch squadron. Another vessel caught fire from a captured Dutch ship, together with which it was burned. In short, Menezes, who had sailed out of the Tagus with six-and-twenty vessels, returned to that river with his own alone. The Dutch prisoners had parted from the fleet early enough to escape its disasters.

In Holland, the recovery of *S. Salvador* by Spain and Portugal, and the bad fortune which had attended the expedition of Henrik, had naturally the effect of considerably damping the public ardour on behalf of the West India Company; but, the Prince of Orange steadily adhering to a war policy, his views prevailed. The Spanish Government, warned by their repeated losses at sea, resolved at length to keep up a strong naval force in

America; but, as was usual with them in all questions great or small, lost a considerable amount of valuable time discussing whether it would be better to equip the intended fleet in Europe or in *Brazil.* Whilst this point was being decided on, the Dutch admiral, Heyne, in 1627, once more entered *Bahia.* As it was known that 1627. he was off the coast, the governor, Oliveira, had made every preparation for its defence. In particular, two-and-forty large pieces of cannon were placed so as to bear upon the Dutch should they attempt to enter. In beating up against the wind, Heyne was so unfortunate as to run his own vessel between the two largest of the enemy's floating batteries. But, on the other hand, he was so placed that the Portuguese could not fire upon him without endangering their countrymen ; and in the course of half an hour he had sent one of the batteries to the bottom; whereupon the others struck. The Dutch, coming in boats, cut the cables of the smaller vessels and carried them out, blowing up Heyne's ship and another. The admiral now sent four of his largest prizes to Holland, adding four others to his own fleet, and destroying the rest.

Heyne, indeed, was as fortunate as Henrik had been the reverse. After a cruise to the southward he returned to *Bahia,* when he undertook a most perilous enterprise in attempting to cut out four ships from one of the rivers of the *Reconcave.* They were some miles up the river, and although preparations had been made to intercept his return, he brought one vessel back with him and the lading of the other three. After this exploit, Heyne, having taken his departure, fell in with and captured the Spanish fleet from *Mexico,* thereby securing the greatest prize which has ever been made at sea, and by which the West India Company were amply reimbursed for all their former losses. As might be expected, their schemes of conquest now revived. One of their captains took possession of the island of *Fernando Noronha,* near *Pernambuco ;* but before it was effectually fortified, the Portuguese took the alarm and sent a sufficient force to crush the new settlement.

1629. The West India Company lost no time in preparing fresh enterprises against *Brazil*. This time their efforts were directed on *Pernambuco*, from which province they estimated that one hundred and fifty vessels might annually be freighted with sugar; whilst its harbours were conveniently situated as points of departure whence their cruisers might sail to intercept more rich prizes from the Spanish Main. In order to ensure secrecy as far as possible, the preparations for their fleet were distributed over several ports, and the ships were to rendezvous at the *Cape de Verds*. Nevertheless, information of what was going on was brought to Lisbon, and the court of Madrid was duly warned. The governor of *Brazil* was accordingly instructed to place both *Bahia* and *Olinda* in a state of defence; whilst Mathias de Albuquerque was sent out from Madrid, with some men and stores, to the assistance of his brother, the captain of *Pernambuco*.

On his arrival at *Olinda*, Mathias found the place almost utterly undefended; nor did he himself do much to make things better. He had brought out the news of the birth of a prince and heir of Spain; and whilst *Olinda* was occupied in merry-making over this joyous event, a pinnace arrived from the *Cape de Verds* announcing the assemblage there of the Dutch fleet and its departure for *Brazil*. That fleet consisted of fifty sail, under Henrik Loncq as general and Peter Adrian as admiral. Eight of these had driven off the Spanish

1630. fleet near *Teneriffe*. On the 15th of February they appeared before *Olinda*, having on board about seven thousand men. The whole force of the town, such as it was, was collected to oppose them, and the summons which Loncq sent in was answered by a discharge of musketry. The entrance to the harbour had been blocked by sunken vessels, and the sea was so rough that the Dutch could not use their guns with effect.

But whilst a harmless cannonade was being carried on, Colonel Wardenburg, taking sixteen ships some miles to the north of the town, was able to land without opposition. Retaining only a few gunboats with eleven pieces of artillery, he divided his troops into three divisions, and on the following morning began his march towards *Olinda*. The news of his landing had already produced a panic, and all were anxious that their families and portable property should be placed in security in the country. Under these circumstances, Wardenburg advanced without any serious opposition, although it would have been easy in a wooded country to impede his progress. Indeed, the river *Doce* was itself an obstacle, and the Dutch had to delay its passage until low tide, when they forded it breast-high. At this point some shots from the gunboats caused a general stampede. The redoubt at the entrance of *Olinda* checked the invaders for a moment; but it was soon overcome, and the town was given up to be plundered.

The Portuguese governor had retreated to *Recife*, which place, however, he had now not sufficient men to defend. As there was no hope of preserving it, he set fire to the ships and warehouses, which contained much valuable property; and there remained only for the invaders to reduce the two forts of *St. Francisco* and *St. George*, which commanded the entrance to the harbour. Five days were suffered to elapse before the latter was attacked. It was defended by Vieira and a band of young men who had volunteered with him, with a courage and pertinacity which formed a bright contrast to the confusion and pusillanimity displayed by their countrymen. The two forts, however, could not hold out long, and the Dutch fleet entered the harbour in triumph. Their hold upon *Pernambuco* was still further confirmed by the arrival, nine days later, of another fleet with reinforcements.

When the fugitive inhabitants of *Olinda*, relieved from

the actual presence of the invader, found themselves unpursued in the country, they began to collect their reason and to recover their composure. Their general now pointed out to them that the object of the Dutch was gain rather than glory; that they coveted the sugar and tobacco which *Pernambuco* could produce, and that the surest way to frustrate their plans was to prevent them from cultivating these articles. Works were accordingly begun at a distance of three miles from *Olinda* and *Recife*, and were prosecuted with the utmost alacrity by the population in general, whilst four pieces of cannon were procured from the wreck of a Dutch ship. Indeed such was the speed with which the camp was constructed that it was already in a state of defence when the knowledge of its existence first came to the ears of the invaders; and an attempt to gain it by surprise was frustrated by the vigilance of Mathias de Albuquerque. On this occasion the Dutch fled, leaving forty slain.

Emboldened by this success, the Portuguese now assumed the offensive and laid an ambush for the Dutch general, who with six hundred men was proceeding from *Recife* to *Olinda*. He was taken by surprise, and owed his safety to the flight of his horse. The danger of passing from one of these towns to the other was so considerable, and afforded so good an opportunity for Portuguese attack, that it gave rise amongst these to the enrolment of a force who from the nature of their duties were called bush-rangers. They consisted, for the most part, of peasants, who came to the camp when they could spare time from their proper occupations. These men, who were only occasional visitors to the camp, were well off; but the fugitives from *Olinda*, some fifteen thousand in number, who dwelt at *Bom Jesus*, as the camp was called, suffered excessively from lack of provisions.

In the above respect the Dutch were no better off, for they could only hope for relief from the sea, whilst the only water to be found at *Recife* was collected from pits dug in the beach, and was scarcely fit for use. And although forests were before them, these were so well guarded by the Portuguese that their only fuel was that which they had brought with them. So pressing were the necessities of the Dutch, that the high prices which it was worth their while to offer were sure to tempt some of their mongrel opponents, three of whom were hanged by Mathias after having been detected in a forbidden traffic with the invader. The Dutch had nothing better to do but to endeavour to extend their conquests by sea. Their first expedition was against the island of *Itamaraca*, which contained twenty-three sugar-works, and was situated eight leagues to the south of *Olinda*. They did not succeed, however, in conquering it, and contented themselves with building a fort opposite the neighbouring shore commanding the entrance of a port. In Fort *Orange* they left eighty men with twelve guns before returning to *Recife*.

Whilst these events were passing, information of which was, of course, conveyed to the court of Madrid, that Government was not wholly idle. Nine vessels were despatched for the relief of the camp of *Bom Jesus*, some of which fell into the hands of the enemy's cruisers, so that but little good resulted from their expedition. The inhabitants of the province of *Pernambuco* were on the whole left to defend their own interests, it being hoped that the harassing warfare which they were prosecuting would prove the best means of inducing the Dutch to withdraw from the country. When it appeared, however, that the Low Countries were fitting out a strong fleet to be sent to *Pernambuco* under the command of Admiral Hadrian Patry, who was to take out with him many Dutch families as settlers, the Fabian policy of the court of Madrid was no longer pursued. Again a fleet was equipped at Lisbon, the command of which was given to *Don* Antonio Oquendo. Of this force, which was ultimately to proceed to Spanish America, ten vessels, with one thousand men and twelve pieces of cannon, were destined for *Pernambuco*.

The fleet which sailed under Oquendo's flag, besides the ten vessels with troops for *Pernambuco*, consisted of twenty ships of war; whilst four-and-twenty merchantmen, laden with sugar, joined him for the sake of his convoy at *Bahia*, at which port he had been instructed to call. This latter instruction gave the Dutch admiral time to reach *Recife*; and, having landed his troops, he sailed out again, with sixteen ships, in quest of the enemy. When the fleets came in sight of one another Oquendo ordered his transports and merchant vessels to fall to leeward. His own ship then engaged in a desperate struggle with that of his opponent, whose vessel it grappled. Ere long the Dutch vessel was on fire, and that of Oquendo narrowly escaped the same fate. It was, however, towed away in time. The renowned admiral Patry, disdaining to attempt to save his life, determined at least to preserve his colours from falling into the hands of the enemy, and plunged with them into the sea. In this fierce action, which was splendidly fought on both sides, about three thousand men fell, the loss being pretty equally distributed. On the morrow, Oquendo, having given orders to the Count of Bagnuolo to take the succours into *Pernambuco*, proceeded on his way to the Spanish Main to convoy the homeward-bound galleons.

Bagnuolo gained the port of *Barra Grande*, thirty leagues from the camp of *Bom Jesus*. The troops were safely landed, and after a difficult march joined Mathias de Albuquerque. The Dutch commander, knowing that the Portuguese had received reinforcements, thought it necessary to concentrate his troops at *Recife*, upon which he set fire to *Olinda*, the entire city being consumed. But it was not long before the Dutch discovered the impolicy of this latter measure, for, being concentrated at *Recife*, the whole Portuguese force was brought to bear on that one point. In order to make a diversion, three thousand men were despatched to attack *Paraïba*. This place was defended by a fort which commanded the bar, and the Dutch therefore determined to attack by land rather than to enter the river. There was some severe fighting; but *Paraïba* being reinforced from the camp, the invaders were at length constrained to retire, leaving their stores behind them. The next attempt of the Dutch was upon *Rio Grande*, at the entrance of the river *Potengi ;* but here too they were unsuccessful.

Whilst *Olinda* remained closed, the trade between the province of *Pernambuco* and Portugal passed for the most part through a port, about seven leagues to the north of *Recife*, called *Pontal de Nazareth*, so named from a celebrated church on a mountain, possessing a miracle-working image of the Virgin. It was fortified with four guns, and had a garrison of nearly two hundred men. On this place the Dutch directed their next attempt; but, not liking its appearance, they coasted along, meaning to land in a creek some distance beyond. It so happened that they were received by a sharp fire from a party of soldiers who were escorting some treasure, and whose numbers were concealed by the thicket. Thinking that a strong party had been sent thither from *Nazareth*, the Dutch commander now doubled back on that place. He was, however, mistaken, and his attack on it was repulsed with a loss of seventy men.

The Dutch had now been for two years at *Recife ;* but their conquests were confined to the possession of that place and to a fort on the island of *Itamaraca*. A gleam of good fortune, however, now awaited them. A mulatto named Calabar, a native of *Pernambuco*, for some reason not known, deserted to the invaders. He was possessed of such sagacity and enterprise, and moreover was so well acquainted with the country, that his assistance was invaluable. Although he had been the first to

1632.

desert, he was soon the means of inducing others to follow his example. His earliest exploit was to lead the Dutch on an expedition to *Garrasu*, which place he surprised whilst the inhabitants were at mass. They plundered and burnt the town, treating the people with much cruelty.

Before the alarm occasioned by the fate of *Garrasu* had cooled down, Calabar next led the Dutch on a second expedition to the south, where they destroyed another settlement. He then guided them to the river *Fermoso*, and surprised five ships nearly laden. On the Portuguese building a little fort here to prevent the recurrence of a similar disaster, Calabar once more attacked the place, when the commander and nineteen out of the twenty men of the garrison fell in its defence. Indeed, Calabar completely embarrassed his late commander, whose every plan was thwarted, and who was utterly at a loss what to do. His measures were so uniformly unsuccessful that he did not escape from his countrymen the suspicion of treachery, though he may be acquitted of anything further than incapacity.

The results of this warfare were so meagre and its progress so slow, that the West India Company now resolved upon the step of sending out two commissioners with full powers to decide as to its continuance or otherwise. They brought with them fresh stores and three thousand men. As the chances of the war were now in their favour, they resolved to pursue it. They did so with vigour; and, having gained some successes, determined to attack the camp. The attempt was made on Good Friday, when it was supposed that the Portuguese would be employed in religious ceremonies. Three thousand men advanced under the Dutch commander Rimbach; but they were received by a hot fire, by which Rimbach himself fell, and were forced to retreat in great disorder. The next attempt of the invaders was upon the island of *Itamaraca*, in which they were this time successful.

The loss which the Portuguese thus repeatedly sustained was not made up to them by reinforcements, and their whole force had now dwindled to twelve hundred men. This state of things suggested to the Dutch commissioners the idea of winning the camp by siege. The natural difficulties of the country, however, put an end to this plan so soon as it was attempted to put it into execution.

The indefatigable Calabar next projected an expedition to a greater distance, namely, to some lagoons forty-six leagues to the south of *Recife*. The object appears to have been merely to create terror amongst the inhabitants; and the Dutch ere long perceived the impolicy of ravaging a country which it was their object to possess. It was their good fortune to intercept a small squadron and a supply of stores, sent from Lisbon to the relief of the Portuguese. After a struggle, one of the Portuguese men-of-war was driven on shore, the men, the guns, and part of the cargo being saved; but the other man-of-war was sunk. The commander of the first Portuguese vessel received orders to embark his men at *Cunhau*, where four vessels would be ready to receive them. These, however, had scarcely got under weigh when the Dutch were upon them. Three were burnt; the fourth was taken. This affair proved one of the greatest losses which the Portuguese suffered during the entire expedition. Of the six hundred men sent out, but one hundred and eighty reached the camp.

The next attempt made by the Dutch was against *Rio Grande*, their guide, as usual, being Calabar. The fortress was defended by thirteen guns; but it was commanded by a sand-hill, to which Calabar led the besiegers. *Rio Grande* fell almost immediately; and five hundred men, who arrived from *Paraïba* to its assistance, had the mortification of seeing the Dutch flag flying over its walls. Indeed, the Dutch were now victorious on all sides; for they had, by means of emissaries, been able to rouse against the Portuguese the *Tapuyas*, a barbarous tribe who had been driven by the latter into the interior, and who now took a merciless vengeance upon their women and children; and the Portuguese were still further harassed by a collection of negroes, who had from time to time escaped from slavery, and who had settled in a tract of country called the *Palmares*.

1634.   In February 1634 the Dutch commander quitted *Recife*, leaving that place with so diminished a force that Albuquerque determined to attempt to surprise it— an attempt which only failed owing to the lukewarmness with which it was carried out. The Dutch had gone in force to *Paraiba*, their object being to get possession of *St. Augustines*, the point at which stores and troops for *Brazil* usually landed, and whence much of the produce of *Pernambuco* was shipped. Having thrown the Portuguese off their guard by a feint, the Dutch proceeded along the coast to a place called *Pedras*. Eleven of their vessels ran in across the bar, whilst they were followed through an opening in the reef by the launches with Calabar and a thousand men on board. The port of *Pontal* was now in the possession of the Dutch, but as the bar was still commanded by the Portuguese, the former could only communicate with their main force outside by means of the opening in the reef by which Calabar had entered.

Albuquerque and his general arrived ere long from the camp with three hundred men, and, having collected a force of eight hundred, proceeded to attack the Dutch in the town. The latter were thrown into confusion, and the Portuguese would have easily regained *Pontal* but for a party of their own men who were sent to surprise the Dutch by attacking them on the flank, but who surprised their comrades instead. The Portuguese, however, were in such strength that their opponents could not push their advantage against them. Indeed, the Portuguese general felt confident that the Dutch ships in port must fall into his hands; but he had not realized the resources of their ingenuity. Although it was impossible for them to escape without loss over the bar as they had entered, they were yet enabled to enlarge the opening in the reef sufficiently to admit of the egress of their vessels. They, however, left a garrison of two thousand men to defend the town of *Pontal*.

The Dutch at this time were still further reinforced by three thousand five hundred men, the first use made of which was to make a renewed attack upon *Paraïba*, a flourishing town of about a thousand inhabitants, and having twenty sugar-works in its neighbourhood. *Paraïba* is situated some three miles up the river of the same name, the entrance of which was commanded by Fort *Cabedello*. Before this place the Dutch appeared with two thousand four hundred men, and effected their landing without loss. As they were vastly superior to the Portuguese in numbers, they carried all before them, although much bravery and devotion was shown on the side of their opponents. Fort *Cabedello* fell, and with it Fort *St. Antonio* on the other side of the river. The inhabitants of *Paraïba* were now advised to lose no time in retiring with their families. Some of them did so, but the greater number remained, willing to submit to any authority that could protect them, and thus the province of *Paraïba* fell into the hands of the invaders.

Following up this success, the Dutch commander next reduced the captaincy of *Itamaraca*, lying between *Paraïba* and *Pernambuco*. Both the camp of *Bom Jesus* and the port of *Nazareth* were now simultaneously attacked. The former, being inland and cut off from communication with the latter, suffered greatly from want of provisions. After a three months' siege the camp surrendered, on the condition that the garrison should march out with the honours of war and have a free passage to the Spanish Indies. No terms were granted to the provincial force, who now became Dutch subjects, and whose first experience of their new rule was that they were shamefully ill-used until they paid the life-ransom which their conquerors demanded. The fortifications of the camp were razed.

The siege of *Nazareth* was now pressed. The place was so closely beset that no supplies could be introduced into it excepting by sea. The Dutch scoured the country in all directions; but Albuquerque was enabled to introduce some provisions by means of three dismantled barques. These stores, however, could only put off the evil day for a time, and the garrison were reduced to great distress. Many died at their posts from want of food, and at length Albuquerque, who had taken up his post at *Villa Fermosa*, about six leagues to the south, determined to give up the fort, which accordingly capitulated upon the same terms as had been granted to the camp.

Notice was now given to the inhabitants of *Pernambuco* of the intention on the part of the Portuguese authorities to evacuate the portion of the captaincy which was situated round the capital. Such of the people as might choose to emigrate were offered protection; but the greater number preferred to submit to the Dutch. About eight thousand persons emigrated, not including Indians or slaves. Their way led past *Porto Calvo*, which was in the hands of the Hollanders. Albuquerque took precautions against an attack, and a native of the place, who had submitted to the Dutch, was allowed to go out to reconnoitre. He contrived to drop a letter in the sight of the sentinels. This was conveyed to Albuquerque, and informed him that the dreaded Calabar had entered *Porto Calvo* on the previous evening with two hundred men. On the report of the same informer the Dutch commander was easily persuaded to attack the Portuguese. He fell into an ambuscade, and had to retreat, leaving fifty men on the field. The victors pursuing, entered the fortified place and won it after a desperate struggle, more than half of the garrison being slain. The Portuguese, too, lost heavily; they were not, however, discouraged, and secured every pass by which the enemy might send for succours. The Dutch were now deprived of water, and were closely besieged. After six days they were forced to surrender, and were offered good terms, namely, to be sent by way of Spain to Holland. *Porto Calvo* was the native place of Calabar, and here he ended his career by being hanged.

Albuquerque now razed the fortifications of *Porto Calvo* and buried the guns which he had taken. He then conducted the emigrants to the *Lagoas*, where they dispersed, some going to *Bahia* and others to *Rio de Janeiro*. The Portuguese military force now left at the *Lagoas* consisted of four hundred men, besides Indians, and it was determined to fortify the southern settlement.

The Dutch meanwhile were giving the court of Madrid serious cause for alarm, by building naval arsenals at *Recife*, such as made them no longer dependent on Europe for the repairs of their fleet. Cornelis Jub, with fourteen vessels, took possession of *Fernando Noronha*. He thence sailed to intercept the Mexican fleet, and came up with it at the *Bahamas*. Owing to the misconduct of some of his captains, he failed to capture it; but the danger to which it had been exposed caused the king of Spain to give orders that no efforts should be spared for the recovery of *Pernambuco*. A force was accordingly prepared for this purpose, and seventeen hundred men were sent forward in advance under *Don* Luiz de Roxas, who was to supersede Albuquerque. Roxas was landed at the *Lagoas* with his stores and men. 1635.

The new Spanish commander displayed no small amount of self-sufficiency, choosing to disregard the advice given him by those who were acquainted with the country. The Dutch, finding great inconvenience from the communication, which it was impossible to prevent, between the Brazilians who had submitted and the

SOUTH AMERICA.

1636.

Portuguese authorities, now ordered all who dwelt in the district of *Porto Calvo* to move towards the north. Leaving seven hundred men at *Lagoa* under the Count of Bagnuolo, Roxas at the beginning of the year began his march northwards with twice that number. He was no sooner on the move than information reached him that the Dutch general had retaken *Porto Calvo*. Upon this, Rebello was sent forward with two companies to occupy the enemy until the whole should come up. Schoppe, however, did not wait for their appearance, but retreated to *Barra Grande*. Roxas then learned that another Dutch general was advancing to Schoppe's assistance, and, having weakened himself by leaving five hundred men at *Porto Calvo*, he set out in quest of him. The two forces were not long in meeting, but they had to lie on their arms for the night. In the morning, Roxas, who had meanwhile sent for his troops from *Porto Calvo*, did not wait for their arrival, and in the fight which immediately ensued he was himself slain. The Dutch commander did not pursue his success, but returned to *Peripueira*.

The command now devolved upon the Count of Bagnuolo. He advanced to *Porto Calvo*, where eighteen hundred men were collected, and from which place the portion of the country in the hands of the Dutch was now molested. The condition of the inhabitants was indeed deplorable, for they were called upon to serve two masters, whose service was as difficult to reconcile as that of God and Mammon. They were not even allowed to practise their religion in peace, for the Dutch did their best to bring them over to the reformed faith. The conquerors are stated to have treated the colonists with inexcusable cruelty. They were not only liable to death on the slightest suspicion of communicating with the enemy, but were not unfrequently tortured to make them discover their wealth.

Nor was the position of the Dutch a very happy one.

They had won three captaincies; but it was their object to develop the resources of these, and as the Portuguese were now in sufficient strength to assume the offensive in a harassing predatory warfare, this was not very easily effected. It is not to be wondered at that the inhabitants of Pernambuco should desire to emigrate, and that four thousand of them should put themselves, with this end in view, under the convoy of the native chief Cameram. They were conducted in safety over seventy leagues of a country subject to the Dutch. Many more, who were unable to join this convoy, attempted to follow and were cut off in so doing.

It being now evident that it was impossible to develop the resources of the country until it should be completely subjected, representations were addressed to Holland with this object in view. The fame and fortune of the war had for the moment turned in favour of the Portuguese. It is interesting to know that up to this date the expenses of the Dutch West India Company amounted to forty-five millions of *florins*. They had taken from the enemy no fewer than five hundred and forty-seven vessels. More than thirty million *florins* of prize-money had gone into the public stock; and they had brought home from Africa merchandise to the amount of almost fifteen millions more. Their receipts thus balanced their expenditure, not to mention, their colonial possessions, and the fact that they estimated that they had put the Spaniards to an outlay of nearly two hundred millions. They now resolved to send out Jan Maurice, Count of Nassau, as a general with unlimited powers, and with a force sufficient to complete and secure their conquests. He reached *Recife* in January 1637.

CHAPTER II.

BRAZIL; THE DUTCH WAR; GOVERNMENT OF THE COUNT OF NASSAU.

1638-1644.

THE Count of Nassau arrived in *Brazil* at a critical moment, for the Portuguese were so emboldened by success that even the road between *Recife* and *Olinda* was not safe, and the sugar-works, whose existence was of such vital importance, were placed in danger. The tenths of these were at this time farmed for no less a sum than two hundred and eighty thousand *florins*. Nassau distributed two thousand six hundred men among the garrisons; whilst he formed an army of three thousand, and assigned six hundred for predatory warfare. The stores had run so short that it was difficult to supply the garrisons and at the same time to provide the troops with provisions for a two months' expedition. Dutchmen, like Englishmen, fight well when well fed, but grumble sadly when put on reduced rations. Such, however, was now their fate.

After a day of general prayer, Nassau began his march. The Dutch had advanced unmolested to within two leagues of *Porto Calvo* before the Portuguese were informed of their movements. A sally was then made, but without effect, and the same evening Nassau pitched his camp under the fort. The Portuguese general, Bagnuolo, had retreated during the night, and the Dutch could now communicate with their fleet at the mouth of the river of *Pedras* on which *Porto Calvo* is situated. After fifteen days, the fort, which had suffered greatly, surrendered on honourable terms, the garrison being promised a passage to the Spanish Indies. Bagnuolo retreated to the town of *San Francisco*, on the river of the same name. His force, however, was totally disorganized, and had lost all confidence in its general. Without waiting for the Dutch, he quitted this position and fell back on *Seregipe*.

Having secured *Porto Calvo*, the Count of Nassau lost no time in pursuing. He crossed the *Piagui* river upon rafts, a passage of much danger. He, however, did not think fit to pursue Bagnuolo beyond the *San Francisco*. The Portuguese were now driven out of the province of *Pernambuco*, and his object was to secure this river against them. The town of *San Francisco* having yielded, Nassau there built a fort, which he called after his own name, Mauritz; and having crossed the river, he made the inhabitants of the further shore, with their effects, pass over to the northern bank. He then explored the river for about fifty leagues upwards, finding magnificent pasturage with countless herds of cattle. Delighted with the land, he wrote to his relative the Prince of Orange, urging him to use his influence with the Company to induce them to send over German colonists; he would even be glad of convicts, to develop by their labour the resources of this region of plenty. He likewise asked for more soldiers, and for provisions fitted for storing a fleet.

Whilst Nassau was occupied at the south, his countrymen were busily engaged in the re-organization of *Olinda* and *Recife*. All persons there engaged in trade were formed into companies; the Jews were permitted to observe their own Sabbath day; measures were taken to convert the natives, and schools were opened for their children. The rebuilding of *Olinda* was encouraged in every way. Search was made for mines, but for the most part in vain. At the commencement of the rainy season, Nassau, leaving Schoppe with sixteen hundred men at Fort *Mauritz*, returned to *Recife*, where his presence was much needed. The weight of his position and authority, together with his strict justice, overawed his countrymen, who had given a-loose to every kind of lawlessness. Great irregularities, which had hitherto prevailed, were now put a stop to; and from the tenths of the sugar, the flour, and other duties, the government began to derive a considerable revenue. The sugar-works which had been deserted were sold for the public benefit; and some idea of their importance may be gathered from the fact that they produced no less a sum to the West India Company than two million *florins*.

Nor did Count Nassau overlook the advisability of inducing the Portuguese to return to their possessions in the province, but on such terms as might render them safe subjects. They were to be under the Dutch laws and taxes; they were to possess entire liberty of conscience, their churches being kept in repair by the state; but they were not to receive any visitors from *Bahia*, nor were any fresh monks to be admitted so long as a sufficiency should remain for the service of religion. Two days of each week were to be set apart by the supreme council for the administration of justice amongst them.

On these terms it was permitted to the exiles to re-enter into possession of their property; and they were considered so fair, whilst Nassau's treatment of his prisoners was so generous, that the odium against the Dutch was thereby sensibly diminished. Nassau also established a beneficent system to be observed by his countrymen towards the indigenous Brazilians.

The Count of Bagnuolo had established himself at *Seregipe* or *St. Christovam*. This small captaincy, which extends only for forty-five leagues of coast, separates *Bahia* from *Pernambuco*, being bounded on the south by the *Tapicuru*, and by the *San Francisco* on the north. Thence Bagnuolo sent advices of his situation to all quarters; and thence he renewed his system of predatory warfare. Three times did the adventurer Souto, who had betrayed Calabar, cross the *San Francisco* on rafts and harass the unguarded Dutch, carrying devastation almost as far as to *Recife*. To such an extent were these incursions carried, that Nassau, who was at this time disabled by illness, had to send Giesselin with two thousand men to strengthen Schoppe, with a view to driving Bagnuolo out of *Seregipe*.

It was now a question with the Portuguese of making a stand at the last-named place; but the arguments of prudence or of timidity prevailed, and Bagnuolo once more retreated, having first sent a party to lay waste the country behind him. The unhappy fugitives were dogged by the revengeful natives, who had such long arrears of wrongs to repay. In their misery many resolved to submit to their pursuers; but the greater number still held on their melancholy way. In the meantime, Schoppe advanced to *Seregipe*, which province he laid bare before his return to Fort *Mauritz*, thus counteracting the prudent policy of Nassau in respect to conciliating the Portuguese, who were now driven onwards by despair towards *Bahia*.

The course of the war between Spain and Holland now takes us for a moment from *Brazil* to the coast of Africa; for, since the operations on the latter continent were conducted under the orders of the Count of Nassau, they must be connected with Brazilian history. Information was sent to the Count by the commander of the Dutch fort of *Mouree* on the Gold Coast, that a well-directed attack on the important Portuguese settlement of *St. Jorge da Mina* would probably lead to the capture of that place. Details as to its condition had been communicated to the governor, who had further tampered with the garrison. The place had once before been unsuccessfully attacked by the Dutch, and on this occasion the remembrance of their former defeat called for the greater caution. Eight hundred men were sent in a squadron of nine vessels under the command of one of the Supreme Council. After a brief siege of four days, and without the death of a single Portuguese, the place fell into the hands of the Dutch. The invaders had, however, suffered considerably at the hands of the negro allies of Portugal. Having left a garrison in *St. Jorge*, the Dutch commander returned to *Recife*.

In the meantime Nassau was not idle in *Brazil*. The province of *Ceará* fell into his hands; and he himself made a journey through the captaincies of *Paraïba* and *Potengi*, with the object of putting such places as had suffered into due repair. He now received intelligence from Lisbon that another large fleet was being equipped for *Brazil*, and he took the precaution of soliciting reinforcements from the West India Company. On his return from *Paraïba*, although he had only received an addition of two hundred troops, he resolved to undertake an expedition against *San Salvador*. The people of *Bahia* were far from expecting any such attack, but, fortunately for them, Bagnuolo, who had been made wary by disasters, took precautions for them. By means of spies he was made aware of the movements of Nassau, and took up his quarters at *Villa Velha*, close to *San Salvador*. The chief of the Portuguese intelligence-department — the active Souto, who had betrayed Calabar—was despatched to *Pernambuco* to gain more precise information. He was not long in obtaining it; for, after having gallantly attacked a Dutch force superior in numbers to his own, a letter fell into his hands detailing the intentions of Nassau.

1633. The people of *Bahia* were now awake to their danger; and, after a hurried preparation of five days, the Dutch appeared off the bay. Having landed in the afternoon at *Tapagipe*, they advanced on the following morning against the city, which was defended by a garrison of fifteen hundred men, in addition to a thousand or more from *Pernambuco*. The first day the forces on either side faced each other in the open without advancing to the attack; but, as these prudent tactics on the part of their defenders did not suit the taste of the townspeople, Bagnuolo on the following morning marched out to give the Dutch battle. The enemy had, however, altered their position, and he had nothing better to do than to return.

Nassau now commenced to attack the forts and to take possession of the heights around the city; and the Portuguese in their hour of danger had the good sense to concentrate the military command in one person, Bagnuolo, whose zeal and activity at this critical moment justified the confidence reposed in him. An attack made on the trenches of *San Antonio* by fifteen hundred Dutch was repulsed with the loss of two hundred. The Dutch general was thwarted in his efforts, mainly through want of local knowledge respecting the country in which these operations took place. The intelligence-department of the Portuguese, on the other hand, was admirably served, and the besieged were amply provided with provisions, whilst there was a scarcity in the Dutch camp.

On the 1st of May the Dutch batteries were opened; but as fast as the walls of the town disappeared before them, fresh works arose within. Days and weeks went on, and Nassau began to experience much inconvenience from the scarcity of provisions, an evil which his foraging-parties were unable to remedy. He now resolved to carry the trenches by storm, and on the evening of the 18th three thousand men were ordered to the assault. The ditch was easily won; but a fierce fight took place at the gate. All the forces were brought up to this spot on either side. At length the Dutch gave way, notwithstanding all the efforts of their general, and when darkness came on the knowledge of the locality which the Portuguese possessed gave them a still further advantage. Next morning Nassau asked for a truce for the purpose of burying the dead. The Dutch had lost five hundred men slain, whilst fifty others were made prisoners. The loss on the side of the Portuguese was less than half the above number, but it included the indefatigable Souto. For another week the besiegers continued a useless fire upon the city, at the end of which time they abandoned their enterprise, having suffered much from sickness during the six weeks' siege. The Dutch returned their prisoners, leaving sixty of their own, but they carried away with them four hundred negroes.

Notwithstanding his repulse, Count Nassau did not abandon the hope of taking *San Salvador* at a more convenient season, and with this object he now reiterated his request to the Company for reinforcements. That body, after much deliberation, now resolved to throw open the trade with *Brazil*, which had hitherto been their monopoly. Nassau, whose opinion was asked, gave his advice in favour of this measure. He urged that the only hope of creating a successful colony was by offering inducements to Dutchmen to emigrate to *Brazil*, and that, were the trade not thrown open, such inducements could not exist. His word carried the day; and the monopoly of the Company was for the future confined to the traffic in slaves, in implements of war, and in Brazilian woods.

The remembrance of the capture of the Mexican fleet by Heyne now induced the Company to send out a large squadron, under the experienced Jol, to attempt a similar feat. The old captain set out from *Recife* in great hopes, which were, however, doomed soon to disappointment. He indeed met the Mexican fleet, which he resolutely engaged; but his captains did not support him, and so the Spaniards escaped. This futile attempt, by drawing away men at a moment when Nassau was sorely in want of succours, was the cause of much embarrassment to that general in the execution of his plans. Early in the following year [1639], Artisjoski brought out a small reinforcement; but he himself soon returned to Holland, after having brought some absurd charges against Count Nassau, which were at once refuted.

At this period the West India Company were in possession of six provinces in *Brazil*, extending from *Seregipe* in the south to *Ceará* in the north. Of these the first had been laid waste, whilst their hold on the last-named was confined to one small fort. Nevertheless the natives were friendly allies of the Dutch. The important captaincy of *Pernambuco* contained five towns, namely—*Garassú, Olinda, Recife, Bella Pojuca,* and *Serinhaem;* it likewise possessed several considerable villages. Previously to the Dutch invasion there had been one hundred and twenty-one sugar-works, of which thirty-four were now deserted. In *Itamaraca* fourteen works still survived, of three-and-twenty which had existed before the conquest. *Paraïba* still possessed eighteen works out of twenty; whilst *Rio Grande* had one out of two. In the whole Dutch dominion one hundred and twenty survived. The tenths of their produce were leased—in *Pernambuco* for 148,500 *florins;* in *Itamaraca* and *Gojana* for 19,000; and in *Paraïba* for 54,000. With other items, the whole tenths amounted to 280,900 *florins.*

Whilst the country had suffered severely from the Dutch invasion, the city of *Recife,* being the seat of government and of commerce, had thriven. Colonists were greatly wanted; more especially there was a constant demand for skilled labour,—three, four, and six *florins* a day being given as wages to builders and carpenters. The Portuguese inhabitants of these provinces were held in subjection only by fear, with the exception of the Jews, who were excellent subjects. With the native Brazilians the Dutch had considerable trouble; whilst negroes were more scarce, and consequently more dear than before, some having followed their Portuguese masters in their emigration, and others having joined the black community at the *Palmares.* The military force of the Dutch amounted to rather more than six thousand men, and they reckoned on a thousand native auxiliaries; but all this force was required for garrisons. On the whole, the colony could scarcely be pronounced flourishing. Without supplies from Holland it could hardly furnish its own food, since so many cultivators had been driven away. All possessors of land were compelled under heavy penalties to devote a certain portion of it to the cultivation of mandioc.

Count Nassau, who took a large-minded view of the future of his countrymen in *Brazil*, now set about building himself a palace, which he called *Friburg*, on an island near *Recife*; and to his gardens on this spot he transplanted seven hundred full-grown cocoa-trees, as well as lemons, citrons, and pomegranates. In order to relieve the crowded state of *Recife*, he proposed to build another city on this island; the marshy ground was soon drained by canals; streets were laid out, and houses rapidly arose in *Mauritias*, which was to be connected by a bridge with *Recife*. After the expenditure of a hundred thousand *florins*, the contractor gave up the attempt in despair; but what could not be effected by means of stone pillars was possible with the aid of wood, and in two months the bridge was completed by Count Maurice himself. On the success of this undertaking, Nassau next built another bridge over the *Capivaribi*; thus connecting *Recife* with the opposite country through *Mauritias*. It is remarkable, if it be the case, as stated, that these should be the first bridges erected in a region so well watered as Portuguese America.

Nassau's measures, showing as they did that the Dutch fully believed in their power to retain what they had taken, were not a little calculated to dishearten the Portuguese. But all hope was not lost at Lisbon. One of the ministers obtaining an audience of the king, so forcibly represented the ruinous consequences of the manner in which Brazilian interests were treated, that the favourite, Olivares, found himself compelled to make an effort for their relief. A grand fleet was equipped, the command being given to the Count Datorre, who was named governor of *Brazil*. This fleet, like so many others coming from the same country, was destined to misfortune, its first calamity being to be sent to the *Cape de Verds*, there to await its Spanish consorts, and where it endured a terrible mortality, more than a third of the men being cut off. When it had reached *Recife*, instead of being in a condition to blockade that place, and so to reduce it by famine, its commander was compelled by the numbers of sick on board to proceed to *San Salvador* [*Bahia*] as to a sanatorium. In this healthy climate his men recovered, but a whole year elapsed before he was again in a position to put to sea.

Meanwhile, before starting, the governor sent forward troops divided into small parties, who were to carry fire and sword into the enemy's provinces, and finally to unite in one body and join operations with the fleet when it should appear in sight. Nassau, however, had time to prepare, and the opposing forces met at sea on the 12th of January 1639 near *Itamaraca*, when the Dutch admiral fell. Three more naval actions ensued, —the last off the *Potengi*, so far had the Portuguese been driven by the winds and currents beyond their destination. Thus by superior manœuvering and by the advantages of weather, was a very inferior force enabled to baffle a fleet consisting of no less than eighty-seven vessels, and carrying two thousand four hundred pieces of cannon. Once beyond *Recife* at that season, that place was perfectly secure for the meantime; for it was hopeless for the fleet to attempt to retrace its way against the currents and the prevalent winds.

Under these circumstances the military force of thirteen hundred men, together with the native allies, landed north of the *Potengi*. These troops had before them the terrible task of finding their way by land to *Bahia* over a distance of three hundred leagues, through such a country as is *Brazil*, and without any stores beyond what each man could carry. After this the Count Daborre went before the wind to the West Indies and thence to Europe. We are not surprised to learn that on reaching Lisbon he was thrown into prison. His subordinate, Vidal, who was at the head of the land forces, had no choice but again to break them up into small parties. These being joined by the troops from the north, made their way back, as well as was possible, to *Bahia*, which place the fugitives reached in safety, having meanwhile subsisted, as it is said, mainly upon sugar.

Nassau was not slow in pursuing the work of retaliation for the havoc committed by the Portuguese. Two thousand *Tapuyas*, in alliance with the Dutch, were let loose upon *Bahia*, their families being meanwhile kept as hostages in the island of *Itamaraca*. Admiral Jol was next sent to the *Reconcave* to lay it waste with fire and sword. The whole of the sugar-works in that extensive bay were destroyed. But ere long both parties saw the folly of this desolating warfare, and the new Viceroy, the Marquis of Monte Alvam, entered into negotiations with the Dutch for suppressing it; but these bore no fruit until the province of *Pernambuco* had been by his secret orders in turn laid waste. His predatory bands, however, were so well acquainted with the country that they eluded the vigilance of the Dutch, and their proceedings were publicly disowned by the Viceroy.

An important change in Europe at this time altered the face of affairs in *Brazil*. In 1640 the Duke of Braganza recovered the throne of Portugal. On information of this event reaching the Viceroy, measures were at once taken for disarming the Spanish portion of the garrison; after which King John was proclaimed. This news was received with enthusiasm throughout *Brazil*, as it had been throughout Portugal. It had an important bearing on the relations between Portugal and Holland, inasmuch as either country was now at enmity with Spain, and it was accordingly duly communicated to Nassau. A strange turn now took place in the fortunes of the Viceroy himself. Two of his sons, it appeared, had deserted the cause of their country and fled to Madrid, with the result that Vilhena, a Jesuit, was sent to *Bahia* with conditional instructions to depose the Viceroy, in case he too should have followed the same party. Although he had behaved most loyally to Portugal, he was now improperly and outrageously superseded and sent a prisoner to Lisbon.

Meanwhile the news of the revolution in Portugal had been received with great joy at *Recife*, as well by the Pernambucans as by the Dutch, though for very different reasons. The inhabitants of *Pernambuco*, who were anxious to shake off the foreign control, expected to receive more effective aid in doing so than they had met with from Spain; whilst the Dutch looked forward to securing their own conquests during a period when their enemies were divided against themselves. Nor were the latter mistaken in their calculation. Whilst general rejoicings were in progress, a ship arrived from Holland announcing that a truce for ten years had been agreed upon between the States and Portugal. Owing to circumstances, however, which it requires some little attention fully to appreciate, this truce proved wholly illusory.

1641.

Immediately after the revolution, the King of Portugal found himself in a position demanding the utmost circumspection. His first object was to secure the allegiance of the powers at enmity with Spain; that is to say, of England, France, and Holland. His next object was to procure for Portugal a supply of arms and ammunition, of which he had been in great measure deprived by Madrid. With these objects in view, ambassadors were at once despatched from Lisbon to the three countries above-named. The Portuguese court contended that as their country had merely become involved in hostilities with Holland as being an appendage of Spain, they were, on becoming again independent, entitled to regain the possessions which had been taken from them. The Dutch, on the other hand, argued, with better reason, that as the resources of Portugal had been employed against them, they were fully entitled to retain the possessions which it had cost them so much to conquer and to hold. These questions were for the meantime set at rest by the conclusion of a ten years' truce.

But the Dutch negotiators showed a Machiavellian spirit. A year's time was given for notifying the truce to the Dutch authorities in the Indies, and with this proviso arms and ammunition were supplied to Portugal, whilst troops and ships were sent to Lisbon to be employed against the common enemy. The Dutch meanwhile treacherously required Nassau, who had requested to be recalled, to seize the opportunity of extending their conquests, more especially in reference to *Bahia*. The only excuse which is put forward for this conduct on the part of Holland, is that they did not believe that the separation between Spain and Portugal would be lasting, and that in despoiling the latter country they thought they were merely injuring their sworn enemy.

On the departure of the Viceroy from *Brazil* the government had fallen into the hands of a commission of three persons, who now sent Vilhena the Jesuit, with another, to *Recife* to establish a friendly intercourse between the two colonies. Vilhena took advantage of the opportunity to recover a considerable quantity of plate and other treasure, which had been buried by the brethren of his order and by the Albuquerques. Laden with this he sailed from *Brazil* in a small vessel, in which he duly reached *Madeira*. There, however, he became oppressed with the apprehension of trusting his wealth once more to the small ship which had carried him safely so far. It accordingly sailed without him, and duly reached its destination. He himself was not so fortunate. Thinking to provide himself the better against attack, he transferred his person and his riches on board a large Levant ship bound for Lisbon. It was taken by Algerian pirates, who fell heirs to the treasures of the Jesuits and of the Albuquerques, and who sold Vilhena into slavery.

The orders of the temporary government at *Bahia* to the Portuguese freebooters to withdraw their forces within the Portuguese territories were now obeyed, and the leaders were invited to *Recife*. During their stay there, the Portuguese commissioners saw grounds for suspicion in the attitude of Count Nassau, and they warned their superiors accordingly. It is scarcely to be believed by those accustomed to our modern ideas of international good faith, that Count Maurice of Nassau, after his public professions, and after having entertained not only the emissaries of the Brazilian Government, but likewise the commanders who had recently been in arms against him, should now have acted as he did. But it is nevertheless the case that he prepared to extend his conquests on all sides, even venturing, on the strength of the confidence which the government of *Bahia* placed in his good faith, to withdraw the larger portion of his garrisons for the purpose of attack. The inhabitants of *Seregipe* were surprised by a squadron carrying a flag of truce, and *St. Christovam* was thus taken possession of.

Another of the results of the cessation of Portuguese hostilities was that Nassau now sent Admiral Jol, with two thousand troops, against *St. Paul de Loanda*, the most important Portuguese possession in Africa. It fell into the hands of the Dutch without much opposition, thus causing a grievous loss to the Brazilians, whose entire supply of negro slaves came from this source. It was not solely a loss to them as slave-traders; but without a supply of slaves their Brazilian possessions were almost worthless. The Dutch Company established a government in *Angola* independent of that of *Recife*. From *Loanda* Admiral Jol proceeded against the island

1641. of *St. Thomas*, which place, after a siege of fourteen days, surrendered. The climate, however, made the Dutch pay a severe penalty. It is said that but a tenth of the invading force escaped death or disease, Admiral Jol himself being one of the victims.

It is now necessary to revert to the northern portion of Brazil, which, being separated by the scene of the Dutch conquests from the seat of government at *San Salvador*, had hitherto remained unaffected by the war. In this part of the world some English adventurers endeavoured unsuccessfully to obtain a footing; but the chief incidents to be related are an endeavour to discover the sources of the *Amazons*, and a slave-hunting expedition of the younger Maciel, as great a villain as his father, and who was now governor of *Pará*. The origin of the former expedition was a voyage of some missionaries who had been sent to the natives from *Quito*, and who had been taken to the river *Napo*. Down this stream they were, like Orellana, carried to the *Amazons*, and like him they were borne on that river to the ocean. Soon after their arrival at *Belem*, an expedition was concerted to explore the river upwards, taking the missionaries as guides. Of this exploring party Teixeira took the command, with seventy soldiers and twelve hundred natives, 1637,1648. and in due time he arrived at *Quito*, where he was received with great rejoicings.

The *Conde* de Chinchon, who was at this time Viceroy of *Peru*, thought this expedition of so much consequence that he ordered Teixeira to return by the same route, taking with him two persons who should proceed to lay his report and surveys before the court of Madrid. Christoval d'Acuña was chosen as the chief of these. On their way downwards, amongst many discoveries, the chief of which are to be found on the early maps of *Brazil*, they made one of an object which is to us in Europe of familiar acquaintance from our boyhood upwards, namely, the *Caoutchouc* or India-rubber plant.

It is stated that the Portuguese of *Pará* were in the habit of employing it for shoes, hats, and garments, its impenetrability by water making it invaluable. When the Portuguese, on their downward voyage, came into familiar regions, their slave-taking instincts came strongly upon them. They were restrained for some time by their commander, Teixeira, and by the Jesuits who accompanied him.

Further on their course, however, Teixeira and Acuña had the mortification to find the Portuguese established in a fort collecting for a slave-hunting expedition. These were headed by young Maciel, who by treachery and great excesses contrived to procure a booty of two hundred slaves. The consequence of this and other such like barbarous practices was that the natives along the banks of the *Amazons* became so hostile to the Portuguese that the latter, even up to the middle of the eighteenth century, had not been enabled to explore that river thoroughly farther than to the first falls. It was not until the 12th of December 1639 that Teixeira and his party arrived at *Belem* or *Pará*.

The Dutch Company had sent Count Nassau directions to take possession of the island and province of *Maranham*; being masters of which they could at their ease prey upon the Spanish Main. Of the island in question the elder Maciel was now governor, and although he was warned to beware of Dutch aggression, he remained in a state of blind confidence until a Dutch squadron of fourteen guns appeared in the channel which separates the island from the mainland. Maciel, after having protested that his government was at peace with Holland, came to terms with the Dutch commander. It was agreed between them that Maciel should continue in his government until the arrival of instructions from the Netherlands, and that meanwhile the Dutch should be quartered in the city. They, however, were not acting in good faith. Owing to Maciel's cowardice, rather than to anything else, they obtained possession of the place and made the governor a prisoner. He was shortly afterwards removed to *Recife* and sent a prisoner to the fort of *Rio Grande*, where he died at the age of seventy-five years.

1642.

The court of Lisbon naturally protested to the Hague against the conduct of Nassau, whose proceedings against their colonial possessions were in direct contrast to the assistance which Portugal was meanwhile receiving from Holland against Spain. The only satisfaction, however, which they received, was an evasive and untrue reply to the effect that Nassau had acted as he did in ignorance of the ratification of the truce. The Dutch were determined to retain what they had won, and the Portuguese were equally determined to recover what they had lost. A new governor was appointed to *Brazil*, with orders to proceed against the commission of three who had wrongly superseded the Marquis of Monte Alvam. Two of them were sent home as prisoners, one of them being allowed for years to remain in the jail of Lisbon; the bishop, who was the third member, was compelled to refund the emoluments which he had received during his co-administration.

The new governor of *Brazil* now imitated the insincere conduct of which Nassau had set him the bad example. He professed to be friendly with the Dutch, but awaited the first opportunity to act against them. Nassau was not allowed to enjoy at peace the possessions which he had gained. An unusually wet season caused the rivers to overflow, sweeping away men and cattle, and destroying much vegetation; in addition to this, great ravages were produced by the small-pox. The people were unable for these reasons to pay the usual taxes; and yet the Dutch Company, in reliance on the truce which they had so disregarded, instructed the Viceroy to reduce his military expenditure, a measure against which he strongly protested. He naturally pointed out that the Portuguese would await an opportunity to recover their losses.

BRAZIL; THE DUTCH WAR.   39

Count Nassau was at this time meditating extensive plans of conquest. He intended an expedition against *Buenos Ayres;* but the force reserved for this service was now needed for the protection of *Maranham* and *St. Thomas.* Indeed so great was the risk of insurrection as well in these places as in *Angola* and *Seregipe,* that, in order to have a force at hand, Nassau was compelled to defer an expedition against the negroes in the *Palmares.* Before this necessity occurred a squadron had sailed, which was destined to act against *Chili.* It was commanded by Brouwer, whose name is remarkable as being one of the earliest navigators who doubled Cape *Horn.* He had intended to pass through the Straits of *Magellan,* but was driven southward by storms. He reached *Chiloë,* and stormed some Spanish forts. But intelligence of his coming had been received at *Lima,* and the Spaniards were prepared to resist his further progress. Brouwer died at *Castro.* His successor, Herckmann, reached *Valdivia;* but, being unable to establish himself there for want of supplies he returned to *Pernambuco.*

The ambition of the Dutch was out of proportion to their population and their resources; whilst their system of government was far from being a conciliatory one. In *Maranham,* as in *Bahia* and *Pernambuco,* the people now began to work for their own deliverance. In *Maranham* a conspiracy was formed to free the place from foreign rule. The sugar-works on the river *Itapicuru,* where there were collected three hundred Dutch, were the object of attack. The first one assailed was easily carried, and the Dutch found in it were slain. In the second the Dutch were likewise either cut down or shot, or consumed in the flames. In like manner fell the other three, and it was only at the last that any quarter was given. Fort *Calvary* next fell, which was garrisoned by seventy Dutchmen. Moniz Barreiros, the leader of the insurrection, now crossed over to the island of *Maranham.* Here the Dutch were no more fortunate than they had been on the mainland.

After an engagement in which they were totally defeated, Moniz and his adherents attacked the fort of *St. Luiz.* The Dutch garrison despatched vessels to *Recife* for assistance, whilst Moniz applied to his countrymen at *Pará.*

1643.

Such are the immense distances between different localities in *Brazil* that a considerable time elapsed before either party had received the reinforcements asked for. On their arrival hostilities were forthwith resumed, to the disadvantage of the Dutch, who were repelled with loss. After this success Moniz died, being succeeded by Teixeira, who, after having waited for months in the hope of receiving succour and ammunition, abandoned his present position and recrossed to the mainland. He was reduced to great straits, being deserted by his allies, who returned to *Pará.* He had still, however, with him sixty Portuguese and two hundred natives, and he was opportunely aided by the arrival of some ammunition from *Belem.* The Dutch likewise at this time received reinforcements, which made them superior to any force that could be brought against them in the field; but they were disheartened by the general feeling against them.

They were now confined to the fort of *St. Luiz;* whilst the island, outside the fort, was held by the Portuguese. On one occasion the garrison sallied out with the hope of surprising the Portuguese whilst dispersed at their harvest operations. In this they were successful; but they were in the end utterly defeated. Of all who had quitted *St. Luiz,* ten French mercenaries alone re-entered, and these were hanged as traitors. After a time Teixeira was about to be reinforced by the arrival from Portugal of one hundred men with stores, under Pedro de Albuquerque, who was appointed governor of *Maranham.* Albuquerque, however, not knowing the state of things on the island, and having no pilot on board, fired his guns off to announce his presence. His signals not being answered, he proceeded to *Pará,* where the ship struck on a sandbank, the greater part of those

1643.

on board being lost, including Luiz Figueira, the Jesuit, with eight of his brethren. Notwithstanding the loss of this expected succour, Teixeira held his own in *Maranham* so effectually that the Dutch found it necessary to evacuate *St. Luiz* by sea. Including their native allies, they had still nearly five hundred men. They made for the island of *St. Christopher*.

The latter period of Count Nassau's eight years' residence in *Brazil* was clouded by misfortunes, the direct result of the treacherous policy which he had been instructed to pursue on the acceptance of the ten years' truce. The Dutch had not only been driven out of *Maranham*, but had further been cut off in *Ceará*, where the natives had risen as one man against them, surprising them at their different posts. The fort of *Ceará* was now again in the hands of the Portuguese. At *St. Thomas* too the people were in arms, the Dutch being confined to the citadel. It was at this time that Nassau again sought his recall, which was now granted. He made over the military command to Henrik Haus, and the civil government to the Great Council, with much apprehension for the future which awaited the transatlantic dominions of Holland. For the guidance of his successors he left elaborate and judicious instructions; but, so confident did the Dutch in general appear to be in the continuance of the truce which they themselves had so wantonly violated, that the fleet which bore Nassau to Europe took likewise away no fewer than fourteen hundred of his countrymen.

1644.

CHAPTER III.

BRAZIL; THE DUTCH WAR; RISING OF THE PORTUGUESE.

1644-1645.

IT is satisfactory to know that the treacherous policy which the Dutch had thought themselves strong enough to pursue toward Portugal in her hour of weakness, was followed with the worst possible results to themselves. They had at no time been so completely masters of *Pernambuco* as to be able to supply *Recife* with provisions for the country; and, when an honestly-observed truce might have enabled them to consolidate their conquests, they set the Portuguese an example of practices which speedily recoiled on their own head. The pecuniary resources of the Company were exhausted by the various expeditions to *Seregipe*, *Maranham*, *Angola*, and *Chili*. Money became scarce at *Recife*. Hitherto all transactions had been carried on on credit; but now credit was stopped, and money had to be borrowed at the ruinous rate of 3 or 4 per cent. interest per month. Many of the planters were ruined by the floods and the subsequent ravages of the worm; whilst the small-pox committed great havoc amongst the valuable negroes imported from *Angola*. So great was the pecuniary distress that the most desperate measures were resorted to, and which only made matters worse. Some creditors endeavoured to procure payment of their debts by means of large abatements; others threw their debtors into prison; whilst the government felt itself compelled to exact its dues by seizing the sugar produce at harvest time. Thus a conflict arose between the government and the public as to the priority of their respective claims, and the result was embarrassing and ruinous.

In this state of things it was suggested that the Company should contract with the owners of the sugar-works for a certain number of years, receiving the whole products of the works and satisfying the demands on the estate. The plan was approved by the Home Government; but it only proved a partial remedy to the disorder. Many of the Portuguese in *Pernambuco*, being now deeply indebted to the Dutch, had a greater interest than ever in inciting insurrection. They had further cause of complaint in the insolence and brutality of their conquerors. An edict was passed inviting slaves by the promise of reward to give notice if any of their Portuguese masters should have concealed arms. This measure, as may be believed, led to intolerable abuses, certain Dutchmen going to the length of tampering with slaves to hide arms, in order to have their masters condemned. On one occasion two Dutchmen were informed upon by a slave upon whom they had thus practised, and having confessed their guilt, were deservedly put to death.

The departure of Count Maurice of Nassau was a real loss as well to the Portuguese as to his own countrymen. He had systematically endeavoured to repress the excesses of the latter, and had so far won the affections of the former that they looked upon him as their special protector. They respected his high birth and his princely manner of life, which stood out in contrast to that of his countrymen about him. His successors sent deputies to *Bahia* to compliment the new governor on his arrival. They were charged, ostensibly, with certain proposals respecting extradition, and, secretly, with instructions to espy the condition of the Portuguese at that place. They learned that the number of troops at and near *San Salvador* was about two thousand five hundred. A new system had been adopted of sending out men-of-war from Portugal to convoy the Brazilian merchantmen home; and the deputies concluded that the price of Portuguese imports into Europe would be thereby so increased that Holland could undersell them.

This report of their deputies had the effect of making the Dutch more suspicious than before of the Pernambucans, and, as it shortly proved, not without reason. They were not fortunate, however, in the measures they adopted to allay discontent. The Portuguese inhabitants of *Pernambuco* had petitioned for the intercession of the King of Portugal towards securing them freedom of religious worship. This step was so highly resented by their Dutch governors that the public funds which had hitherto been appropriated to religious purposes were now declared government property, to be applied to the support of schools, churches, and hospitals. All priests were imprisoned who entered the conquered provinces without a safe-conduct; and such of them as chose to reside there were required to take the oath of fidelity, and were prohibited from receiving ordination from the bishop of *Bahia*. It was discovered that some of the priests with the Dutch and French Catholics had refused to give these absolution whilst serving against Christians, that is to say, Portuguese; and, in retaliation, the Dutch now ordered all priests and monks to quit their dominions within a month. They were shipped from the island of *Itamaraca* and landed on the Spanish Main.

We now come to a remarkable epoch in the history of *Brazil*. Joam Fernandes Vieira has already been mentioned as having distinguished himself in the defence of Fort *St. George* after the loss of *Olinda*. He was a native of *Funchal* in *Madeira*, and at a very early age sought his fortune in *Brazil*. He was found to be so able and honest that he was soon put in the way of setting up in trade for himself. In the course of some years he became one of the wealthiest men in the country; and, as he had so much to lose in case of troubles, the Dutch looked upon his fidelity as assured. He was noted for his liberality and his fair dealings. Whether his patriotism alone would have led him to risk all his worldly possessions by taking the lead in a revolt can only be conjectured; but the main principle of his life was devotion to the Catholic faith, and his main object was to do what he could towards the suppression of heresy.

So long as Count Maurice of Nassau remained in South America Joam Fernandes took no step which could place him in danger; but the vexatious system of government which ensued ripened his designs. Taking counsel with Vidal, who had been appointed to the captaincy of *Maran-ham*, he addressed a memorial to the Governor of *Brazil*, pointing out that the Dutch were weak and were off their guard, that the fortifications were neglected, and that many of the best officers had departed with Nassau. He did not ask for advice, for the die he said was cast; he merely prayed the governor for assistance. The grievances and outrages which he and his compatriots had to endure were such as to force them to take up arms in self-defence, despite of any truce or treaty. Open assistance the governor could not, of course, give; but he now took advantage of the lesson which the Dutch had taught him. Sixty chosen men were placed under the orders of Antonio Cardozo, who was to act under the instructions of Fernandes. In order to avoid suspicion they made their way, unarmed, and in small parties, to *Recife*, near which place they were quartered in the woods, on the estates of Fernandes, and supplied with arms and food. At the same time the native chief, Camaram, and Henrique Diaz, the two partisan chiefs, set out by land to join in the enterprise.

Joam Fernandes now determined to open his designs to his kinsmen and friends, whom he assembled at a banquet for this purpose. In reply to his inspiriting harangue there was apparently an unanimous consent on the part of his hearers; but there were traitors amongst them, who, on reflection, did all they could to discourage his patriotic scheme, and who even went the length of secretly denouncing him to the Dutch. Such, however, was the credit which Fernandes enjoyed, that, calling all those in whom he had confided together, he defied the traitors and bade them beware of themselves or he would denounce *them* in turn to the Dutch as impostors. Cardozo likewise declared, that were he taken he would denounce the traitors as having invited him, and affirm the innocence of Fernandes. Cardozo, however, was not taken, although the Dutch had full information of his presence and that of his men in the country.

The Dutch Council was now considerably embarrassed as to the course of action which it should pursue. They had information of an intended Portuguese revolt, which they were aware their system of government was only too likely to bring about; and likewise, that Joam Fernandes and his father-in-law were the heads of the conspiracy; but, as they stated in their despatches to the Company, they had not sufficient evidence to warrant the committal of these to prison. They did not venture on a search and on disarming the Portuguese, lest it should provoke the insurrection which they dreaded, and against which they were so ill-prepared. Their magazines and store-houses were ill-secured; and, as they could not withdraw from the garrisons a force sufficient to protect the open country, the Dutch living outside the forts would certainly be cut off.

Joam Fernandes conducted the revolution of which he was the moving spirit with all the foresight and precaution which he would have employed in conducting a great commercial enterprise. In his capacity of president of many religious fraternities he had ventured, openly, on the purchase at *Recife* of considerable quantities of powder, under the pretext of using it for fireworks on saints' days; and he had procured more powder by land from *Bahia*. This was carefully concealed in his woods, where he had likewise collected stores, of various descriptions. He had sent off the greater part of his herds to his grazing farms, under the pretence that in the plain near *Recife* many animals had been stolen by negroes, and that many more had died from eating a plant called *fava*. At length, however, the time came when his practices could no longer be ignored by the government, who were set on their guard against him chiefly by the Jews. These are certainly not to be blamed for wishing a continuance of the *status quo;* since, in the event of an outbreak, they were certain to be plundered by both parties with complete impartiality; whilst, in the event of a victory on the part of the Portuguese, they had before them the image of the fiendish agents of the Inquisition.

The Government at last resolved to seize Fernandes; but it was considerably easier to resolve to do this than it was to execute the resolution. As he was engaged in a contract with them, they sent to desire his presence, on the pretext of concluding the contract in question. But the wary and wealthy conspirator was well informed by his spies of what passed, and, when the Government's broker arrived at his *fazenda*, he pleaded that urgent business prevented his repairing in person to *Recife*, but that he had given full powers to his man of business to execute the contract, on his behalf. His house was surrounded by sentries, who kept a constant look-out; his servants were prepared for resistance or for flight; one hundred armed negro slaves guarded his person, whilst a secret mode of escape from his house was ready in case of emergency. His horse was kept always saddled, and each night he retired to sleep in the woods.

When news reached *Recife* that Camaram and Enrique Diaz had passed the *San Francisco*, both parties felt that the time for action had arrived. An attempt made by Dutch troops on the eve of St. Antonio's Day, to surprise

Fernandes in his house failed. They found the place deserted. Nor were the Dutch more successful in their endeavours to secure the other leaders of the conspiracy. Fernandes took up his position on an eminence in the woods from which a good look-out could be observed, and he was there joined by his retainers and by slaves from his various estates. Thence he issued a proclamation to the people, summoning them to arms, and offering pay and freedom to all slaves who should join in the cause. Many obeyed the call, and fell upon such Dutchmen and Jews as happened to be within their reach. But it is not to be supposed that the spirit of patriotism pervaded the whole population. Many persons looked upon the insurgents' cause as hopeless, and, wishing to be allowed merely to live in peace, only prayed for its speedy collapse.

The measures which the Dutch Council at this time adopted served only to extend the limits of the insurrection. Not being able to lay hands on the actual rebels, they commenced a system of general arrests amongst the inhabitants of the provinces who had stayed at home. These had given the best possible proof of their being peaceable and inoffensive subjects; but it suited the authorities—or at least their subordinates—to pretend to suspect them; and, in order to obtain their liberty, they were required to pay for it. Another source of extortion was found in compelling all Portuguese to take the oath of allegiance and to provide themselves with a pass; for which, of course, fees were exacted. The authorities, after having in vain tried, by means of an enormous bribe, to induce Fernandes to return into the paths of peace, now offered the sum of four thousand *florins* for his person, dead or alive,—a compliment which was reciprocated on his part by an offer of twice that amount for the head of any member of the Council.

Hostilities first broke out at *Ipojuca*, a small town near Cape *St. Augustine*. A free mulatto, named Fagundes, took advantage of a passing affray to fall upon the

Dutch; their garrison took to flight, leaving their arms to the insurgents. Fagundes next attacked three vessels laden with sugar, and massacred the Dutch on board. On this the whole neighbourhood took to arms, and the land communication between the Dutch at Cape *St. Augustine* and all to the south was cut off. This news arrived at *Recife*, together with the intelligence that *St. Antonio*, a town to the north-west of *Ipojuca*, was besieged, and that Camaram and Diaz were devastating the neighbourhood of the *Lagoas*, the garrison of which place had now to be withdrawn. On the appearance of a force of two hundred Dutch and four hundred natives at *Ipojuca*, Fagundes and his men retreated to the woods.

The Dutch now prepared to attack Joam Fernandes, whose small force consisted of not more than four hundred men. A call, however, was made in the name of religion upon the inhabitants for assistance from themselves and their slaves, with the result that in five days eight hundred volunteers flocked to the meeting-place. They were but indifferently off for arms; but their leader had the good fortune to capture a quantity of flour which was being conveyed under an escort to *Recife*. The country was flooded; but this was a disadvantage which told equally against the operations of either party. In point of intelligence, however, the Portuguese had a great advantage. It was the object of Fernandes to delay fighting as long as possible, in expectation of the arrival of Diaz and of Camaram. With this view he crossed the *Capivaribi* and proceeded to the *Tapicura*, over which latter river his men were ferried, eight at a time, on a small raft.

The chief of the Portuguese forces had now to deal with considerable discontent amongst his own men, who, as was natural, felt the depressing influence of the weather, and of the hardships they were enduring, without the excitement of being brought into contact with the enemy. He showed considerable prudence in dealing with the dangerous spirit which had arisen; and ere long he was joined by the insurgents from *Maribeca* and elsewhere,—a force of four hundred men. Some Indians sent in advance likewise brought him the glad tidings of the approach of Camaram and Diaz. The Dutch Council now issued a proclamation requiring the families of all such persons as were with the insurgents to leave their homes within six days, under pain of being declared rebels. The fate of these poor people, who had to take to the woods at such a season and under such circumstances, was indeed pitiable; and the reasons assigned for this cruel measure, namely, that the women supplied the insurgents with information, and that the latter would be embarrassed by their presence with them, cannot justify so inhuman a proceeding.

Joam Fernandes again retorted by a counter-proclamation, which he contrived to have posted in all the most frequented parts of *Recife*. The Dutch, he said, had, contrary to the law of nations, made war upon that sex which was exempted from all acts of hostility; and he, as general of the Portuguese, ordered all his countrywomen to remain in their houses, under his protection, adding that he would exact rigorous vengeance for any injury offered to them. On this, the Council forbore to repeat the proclamation or to enforce it; and such persons as had not already fled were no further molested. But at this time a massacre of about seventy Portuguese occurred at *Cunhau*, at the hands of the *Pitagoares* and *Tapuyas* from the *Pontengi*. This measure, doubtless, arose from the instincts of the savages; but it was represented as having taken place by order of the Council, and it inflamed the insurgents to fury.

The Dutch general, Haus, having ascertained the locality where Fernandes and his men were concealed, now advanced against them. They removed to the *Monte das Tabocas*, about nine leagues to the westward of *Recife*. The Dutch commander had with him fifteen hundred well-armed European troops; he had likewise a considerable native force. An engagement was soon brought on. Failing to surprise the enemy, Haus, in his disappointment, set fire to a sugar-factory, the smoke of which gave Fernandes the alarm. The Portuguese outposts were soon in conflict with their opponents, and, by their knowledge of the country, were able to hold their own, notwithstanding their inferior numbers. Cardozo had cut three openings in the cane-wood which surrounded the position on the *Monte*, and when the outposts were driven in a number of his men were posted in ambush hard by. Fagundes and his followers were ordered to dispute the passage of the *Tapicura*, a small stream which the Dutch must pass; and when he could no longer withstand them, he was to fall back in such a manner as to decoy them towards the ambuscades.

Before commencing the passage of the *Tapicura*, Haus directed a heavy fire into the wood on the further side, and then immediately advanced under cover of the smoke. As was foreseen, the Dutch were led on, step by step, into the cane-wood. They were received at the first ambush with a discharge, every shot of which took effect. They pushed on to the second; but at the third their loss was so great that they were compelled to fall back. They were not, however, disheartened, and, having re-formed into three bodies, they again advanced through the canes. They were visibly gaining ground, when, in a panic caused by the fear of another ambuscade, they were a second time repulsed.

The engagement now lasted for several hours; but the Dutch had not yet brought their entire force into action. After a short breathing-time they returned with fresh troops to the attack. It was now that the exhausted Portuguese were indebted to the priests amongst them for enthusiasm which supplied the place of strength. They were exhorted not to give way to heretics; and many were the vows offered to Christ and the Virgin by those who besought their help in this their hour of need. Fernandes in particular promised a church to the latter; whilst he appealed to his slaves to distinguish themselves, by the promise of immediate freedom. His guard rushed down the hill, blowing their horns, and charged the heretics with such spirit that the latter were driven back through the canes. Haus made one more attack; but this, too, was in vain, and the Portuguese remained masters of the field.

1645. The fight had lasted the entire day [August 3rd]. On the stormy night which followed, the Dutch, under cover of darkness, recrossed the *Tapicura*. The Portuguese passed the night in preparations for a renewal of the attack on the morrow; but daylight showed them the extent of their victory. A messenger arrived from Haus, requesting quarter for the wounded, when Fernandes, according to his promise, immediately emancipated fifty slaves. Three hundred and seventy Dutch were found dead upon the field; whilst about four hundred wounded had been carried away. Of the Portuguese the loss is said to have been under forty, not, however, including the negroes or natives. So important a success, and one obtained at so small a cost, was, of course, ascribed to supernatural assistance; many persons affirmed, and perhaps believed, that in the hottest hour of the battle a woman and a venerable man were seen amongst the combatants distributing powder and bullets, and dazzling the eyes of the heretics. These were the Mother of Mercies, whom they had invoked, and the good St. Anthony, the hermit, the favourite protector of the Portuguese.

CHAPTER IV.
BRAZIL; CONCLUSION OF THE DUTCH WAR.
1646-1661.

HAUS, with the wreck of his army, continued his retreat throughout the night, never halting until seven leagues' distance lay between him and the scene of his defeat. He then awaited his wounded and stragglers, whilst he sent to *Recife* for immediate assistance. Succours reached him the same day, sufficient to secure his further retreat, but not to enable him to resume offensive operations. The Council now distinctly perceived their danger; and they had reasons to distrust the professions of the governor of *Bahia*. Three weeks before the battle Hogstraten and another deputy had been sent to *Bahia* to express the belief of the Dutch Government that Camaram and Diaz were not authorized in their proceedings by the Portuguese governor, and to request that they might be recalled, or, in the event of their disobedience, be declared enemies of the Portuguese Crown. Telles persevered in his previous line of conduct, putting off the Dutch with vague professions. He taunted them in turn with their acts of aggression at *Angola*, at *St. Thomas*, and at *Maranham*. He further indicated that Camaran and Diaz were not men to be restrained by any words of his; and he pleaded that the Portuguese had been driven into insurrection by false accusations on the part of untrustworthy persons. Finally, he offered to act as mediator.

Hogstraten now repeated his offer to deliver *Nazareth* into the power of the governor, a proposal which he said he had already imparted to Joam Fernandes. His offer was accepted; and as he was somewhat afraid lest his conference with the Portuguese authorities might excite suspicion in the breast of his fellow-deputy, he had the audacity to tell him that they were tampering with him for the betrayal of his fort, and that he pretended to listen to them in order the better to thwart them. On his return to *Recife* he repeated the same tale, adding that the governor merely awaited some ships from *Rio de Janeiro* before attacking the Dutch possessions. Two regiments were now embarked at *Bahia*, and were to be landed at *Tamandare*. They were to be escorted by the homeward-bound fleet of thirty-seven ships.

It was arranged that, on the two regiments being landed at *Tamandare*, their commander, *Payva*, should proceed to *Recife* with letters for the Council, in which the Governor-General should state that he had sent two officers to remonstrate with the insurgents, and that, should remonstrances fail, he would compel them to return to their duty. Whilst this farce was being enacted, the Dutch commandant at *Serinhaem* had received instructions to disarm the Portuguese in that district. The Portuguese, however, declined to be disarmed, and the fort being surrounded and its water cut off, was compelled to surrender, the Indian allies of the Dutch being given up to the Portuguese.

Joam Fernandes had remained for seven days upon the scene of his victory at the *Monte das Tabocas*, when he was informed of the arrival of the troops from *Bahia*. Camaran and Diaz, the two partisan leaders, likewise reached the *Monte das Tabocas* about the same time. On meeting the troops from *Bahia*, after some formal words, Fernandes was joined by the whole Portuguese force; after which his first act was to send a detachment to reduce the fort of *Nazareth*.

Blaar was now sent to take possession of all the Portuguese women who might be found in the *Varzea* or

BRAZIL; CONCLUSION OF DUTCH WAR.

open country behind *Olinda*, to hold as hostages. A number were taken, and were conveyed to the headquarters of Haus. This intelligence was speedily conveyed by a chaplain to Fernandes, and the army, being naturally roused by a desire to rescue the women, was put in motion for this purpose. By midnight they reached some sugar-works. Remaining there for three hours, they were roused by Fernandes, who announced that the wonderful *St. Anthony* had appeared to him, and had reproved him for his ill-timed delay. Once more being put in motion, the troops at daybreak reached the *Capivaribe*, which they crossed with considerable difficulty.

Having accomplished this passage without opposition from the enemy, they ere long came in sight of the headquarters of Haus, when they sent forward a party who succeeded in capturing some Dutch sentinels. From those they learned that the officers were at their morning meal, on the conclusion of which they were to march off with their prisoners. They were roused by the dread signal by which Camaram summoned his Indians. Their men were driven in, and no way of retreat was left to them, whilst the Portuguese poured in a steady fire upon them from their shelter. In this emergency the Dutch brought out the Portuguese women, and exposed them at the windows to receive the fire. This artifice brought a flag of truce from the assailants; but the besieged were so confident in their newly-found resource that they fired upon the flag, killing the ensign who bore it; they at the same time took aim at the Portuguese general, Vidal, who had approached under the protection of the flag. Enraged at this conduct, the Portuguese forgot the women, and proceeded to set the whole place on fire; which brought the enemy to their senses. It required all the authority of Vidal to induce his soldiers to spare the cowards who had so nearly taken his life.

The enemy now surrendered on the bare condition that their lives should be spared; they were not, however, able to procure the same terms for their Indian allies. More than two hundred Dutch were made prisoners in this affair, which, according to the Portuguese writers, was, of course, not accomplished without the aid of miracles. Joam Fernandes was now master of the field; and he conducted a triumphal procession to one of his own chapels to return thanks to his patron saint. The prisoners were sent to *Bahia*, Blaar being assassinated on the way. About the same time *Olinda* fell into the hands of a party of Pernambucan youths; whilst the traitor, Hogstraten, was as good as his word in delivering *Nazareth* to the patriots. The Dutch regiment which had garrisoned it entered the service of the Portuguese.

Whilst the troops sent from *Bahia*, nominally to aid in suppressing the insurrection, were thus taking an active part in extending it, the farce which the governor had commenced to play was continued by the Admiral Correa, who, according to his instructions, proceeded to *Recife* with the homeward-bound fleet. The Dutch authorities at that place, who may be excused for preferring to judge of the Governor-General's intentions by acts rather than by words, were naturally not a little alarmed at the arrival of a fleet of such formidable dimensions. Correa, however, who was unaware of the recent occurrences on land, proceeded to execute the instructions which had been given him at *Bahia*, and with the utmost courtesy not only placed his own services at the disposal of the Council, but likewise offered them those of Vidal and his troops, which were at that moment most actively employed against them.

The Council, naturally enraged at this transparent duplicity, at first proposed to arrest the messengers of Correa; but, on the reflection that their own fleet was not in a condition to meet that of the enemy, they wisely sent a courteous reply, declining the services of the Admiral; on receiving which Correa, still wholly unaware of what was passing on shore, immediately set sail for

Europe. Relieved from this danger, the Council lost no time in ordering Lichthart to get his ships ready with all speed, and to do the utmost damage to the Portuguese, an order which he obeyed to the letter.

Meanwhile Payva was with his two regiments on board of eight ships in the Bay of *Tamandare*. Letters had been written to advise him to put into the port of *Nazareth*, since it was known that the Dutch fleet was in search of him; but these warning despatches were intercepted, and he fell an easy prey to the squadron of Lichthart. Of his eight vessels one reached *Bahia*; two were abandoned and set on fire; two others ran aground, whilst three were taken by the enemy. The Portuguese are said to have lost seven hundred men in the action.

Whilst these events were passing in *Pernambuco*, the Portuguese were not less active in the other ceded provinces. Fernandes and Vidal sent officers to *Paraïba* to head the insurgents; whilst the Indians and Negroes were headed by officers sent respectively from the regiments of Camaram and Henrique Diaz, the result being that the Portuguese were soon masters of the captaincy. The Dutch were likewise in turn compelled to abandon Fort *Mauritz* on the *San Francisco*. It was soon razed to the ground, there being then no obstacle to prevent the free passage of the Portuguese from *Bahia* into the province of *Pernambuco*.

Fernandes now pitched his camp upon the neck of sand which divides the river from the sea about a league from *Recife*, commanding the communication of that place with *Olinda*, and on this locality he erected a fort to secure his ammunition and stores. To this fort was given the name which had been applied to the camp, *Bom Jesus*, and a small town soon grew up under its shelter.

The Dutch beheld with consternation the near approach of the enemy; and the splendid out-houses and gardens, which had been laid out by Nassau, as well as the bridge of *Boavista*, were destroyed by the people of

Recife, in order to facilitate the defence of that town. The new town of *Mauritias* was likewise demolished. So great was the anxiety of the people that the Council found it advisable to communicate to them the contents of their latest despatches to Amsterdam, in order to convince them that their critical situation had been duly represented.

On the advice of Hogstraten an expedition was now organized against the island of *Itamaraca*, on which the enemy had to rely for grain. After three attacks, the assailants, under Fernandes and Vidal, forced their way into the town, and had actually secured their victory, when it was lost through their rapacity and cruelty. The troops from *Bahia* showed an example of plundering which was not thrown away upon the Dutch deserters of Hogstraten's regiment; and Cardozo had given orders to put all the Indians to the sword, the result being that the Portuguese had to retire with loss and disgrace. They, however, fortified *Garassu*, and secured all the roads by which the enemy from *Itamaraca* could molest them.

For some time after this expedition the Portuguese were kept inactive by a strange infectious disease, which seemed only to yield to the treatment of bleeding, and which filled the hospitals, until Joam Fernandes hit upon the expedient of setting up certain images of saints, before whom mass was daily performed. To their intercession the cessation of the scourge was ascribed. At the same time that the main body of the Portuguese insurgents were suffering from this cause, their countrymen in *Rio Grande* were massacred by the *Tapuyas*, in revenge for the execution of the Indians at *Serinhaem*. This slaughter had, however, the effect of convincing the Portuguese who had not yet taken up arms of the uselessness of neutrality.

Meanwhile the action of the two forces at *Recife* was confined to isolated attacks, the besiegers not being provided with the means either of properly besieging the place or of blockading it. Every day or night witnessed some sally or skirmish, and many dashing but unimportant deeds are recorded. The general conviction, however, gained ground that the Portuguese would eventually win the day; and many slaves deserted to them whilst there was still some merit to be gained by doing so.

The Dutch at this time hoped to effect a diversion in their favour by means of Hogstraten's regiment of deserters. Although he himself was a traitor beyond redemption, it was rightly believed that most, if not all, of his men had taken service with the Portuguese on compulsion, and would be glad of an opportunity to return to their natural service. In this belief, communication was opened with the regiment; and it was arranged that a sally was to be made from the city in order to facilitate their desertion. This measure was only thwarted by a chance movement of the Portuguese commander. The backwardness of the would-be deserters, however, could not escape notice. Their captain, named Nicholson, demanded an opportunity of clearing their fame, which, being granted, he and seventy of his men succeeded in effecting their purpose, and reached *Recife* in safety. After this, the remaining Dutch were disarmed and sent to *Bahia*.

Meanwhile massacre and counter-massacre, on the part of the respective Indian allies on either side, took place in the captaincy of *Paraïba;* and the Dutch became seriously alarmed for their supplies. They resolved, in desperation, to make a vigorous attack against Camaran. They were no match, however, for that active and able leader; and the Dutch commander was compelled to retreat, with the loss of many men, besides the whole of his baggage. The Portuguese cause at this time suffered a serious loss, in consequence of an ill-timed order from *Bahia* that the sugar-plantations of *Pernambuco* should be destroyed. The Governor-General, when issuing this edict, was not aware that these plantations were now in the hands of his countrymen. The unhappy Fernandes, while protesting against this measure, had to destroy his own canes to the value of two hundred thousand *cruzados.**

The Dutch now became so greatly distressed for provisions that the Indians were only kept in their service by the opinion which was propagated, that every deserter to the enemy met with torture and death. The besiegers, too, began to suffer from want of provisions; but the form which discontent took in this case was desertion to *Bahia*, and severe measures had to be adopted by the Governor-General to put a stop to this practice. The Dutch, having made an attempt in force to intercept a convoy of cattle from *Paraïba*, were defeated with considerable loss at *S. Lourenço.*

Shortly after the above-mentioned event, there arrived at the camp two Jesuits, sent by the Governor-General, and who were the bearers of an astounding mandate from the King of Portugal, to the effect that his generals, Vidal and Martim Soares, should retire forthwith to *Bahia*, leaving *Pernambuco* in the possession of the Dutch. The reason of this order will presently be explained. In the meantime it is to be shown in what manner it was received. The two generals, or camp-masters as they were called, were at first so taken aback that they knew not how to reply. To yield up the country which they had won step by step with such difficulty, and to leave in possession a heretical enemy whom they detested, was naturally abhorrent to their feelings as soldiers, as patriots, and as Catholics. On Joam Fernandes, who had risked all on the insurrection, the blow fell yet more heavily. He was, however, the first to rally; when he declared that the King's orders, having been issued in ignorance of the actual situation, ought not to be obeyed without a further reference to his Majesty.

This opinion prevailed, and was accordingly referred

* About £50,000.

to the Governor-General at *Bahia*. He, however, having received positive orders, declined to take any responsibility upon himself should they be disobeyed. Upon this Martim Soares gave up his command, and sailed soon afterwards for Lisbon. Vidal and Joam Fernandes, however, remained true to their first resolution.

The orders from Lisbon had not been issued without great reluctance. The Duke of Braganza did not feel secure of his throne, and was apprehensive lest Holland should ally herself with Spain against him. He was at this time represented at The Hague by Francisco de Sousa Coutinho, an ambassador of great ability, which was in no small degree essential to his country, seeing the difficult part he had to play. De Sousa saw from the first that the West India Company were not equal to carrying on the expensive war in which they were embarked; and he accordingly advised his master to give the insurgents effective though unavowed assistance. When it became evident in Holland that the Portuguese authorities of *Bahia* put forth no effort to suppress the insurrection, the States retaliated by giving orders to seize all vessels coming from *Pernambuco*, a measure which was made a pretext for seizing Portuguese shipping in general. In short, Holland and Portugal were gradually drifting into open war; and, as has been said, the fear of an alliance being formed between the States and Spain had weighed with the King to send orders for the evacuation of *Pernambuco*.

It will be remembered that at the commencement of the insurrection there were many murmurs and menaces directed against Joam Fernandes; it had been even necessary to take special precautions against his being assassinated. In face of his brilliant successes, all murmurs against him had been silenced, and he was rightly regarded as the hero of a successful revolution for the liberation of his province. Now, however, that he was known to be acting in contravention of the express orders of his sovereign, the clamour against him recommenced.

He was repeatedly warned that his life was in danger, and he received the names of nineteen persons who were engaged in a conspiracy against him. These communications producing no effect, the writer called upon Fernandes, and remonstrated with him; but he had the mortification of finding himself looked upon as a calumniator. With Vidal, however, he had more success; in so far that his story was at least believed, and an attempt was made to bring the conspirators to reason.

Not long afterwards, however, Fernandes, in coming from one of his sugar-works, having outridden his bodyguard, was attacked by three *Mamelucos*, one of whom shot him through the shoulder. One of the assassins was cut to pieces by his guard; the other two escaped through the canes. Fernandes, although he was aware of the conspirator who had set on the assassins, was magnanimous enough not to denounce him.

After this escape, Fernandes and Vidal organized a daring expedition against the island of *Itamaraca*. It was not successful in winning Fort *Orange;* but the rest of the island fell into the hands of the Portuguese, the Dutch having previously expelled from it their Indian allies.

The distress in *Recife* now reached the length of famine. The city was searched for food, and all that could be found was put into a common stock, one pound of bread per week being allowed for each soldier and citizen. But even this scanty allowance had soon to be withheld from the townspeople, in order that that of the soldiers might be doubled; for the latter now began to listen to the suggestions of the enemy. Horses, dogs, cats, and rats were greedily devoured; and many slaves died of inanition. Neither courage nor ingenuity could avail to procure food; whilst to venture beyond the works was certain death at the hands of Diaz and his negroes.

Months had elapsed since the dangerous position of the city had been known in Holland, but still no reinforcements arrived. Things had now come to such a pass that a capitulation or a complete surrender could no longer be delayed; for there was but food left for two days more. It is strange that at this critical moment the stoutest defenders of *Recife* should have been the Jews. Were the place rendered up to the Portuguese, they could hope to avoid death by apostasy alone; they had resolved, therefore, to perish by the sword rather than to surrender, and they had even induced the Council seriously to consider a plan for a general sally of the whole besieged population. Such was the result of the intolerant bigotry of the Portuguese.

At this supreme moment what were the feelings of the starving crowd when they beheld two vessels bearing towards the port under full sail, and carrying the Dutch colours? Casting anchor, they saluted with three guns, thus denoting that they were from Holland. They were the advanced guard of a convoy which might hourly be expected. It is here necessary to state the circumstances under which this fleet sailed, and also those which led to its tardy arrival.

It has been mentioned above that the interests of Portugal were at this time watched over at the Hague by a most astute diplomatist. The professional morality of European diplomacy has become considerably stricter in the course of late years than it was in the year of which we write, namely, 1646. Francisco de Sousa must be judged, therefore, as to his diplomatic conduct, by the ethics of his own age rather than by those of the present time. He had a most difficult part to play; and, being a thorough patriot as well as doubtless a devout Catholic, he held that the interests of his country, if not those of his faith, justified him in any amount of dissimulation, in order to secure them. His judgment both as to the importance of the Portuguese settlements in Northern *Brazil* to his country and as to the practicability of recovering them, was sound, as was proved by the event; but, as has been said, there were imperious reasons to make the court of Lisbon dread an open rupture with Holland. Under the circumstances the ambassador had the courage to take upon himself the entire responsibility of negotiating with the Dutch, leaving it to his master to disavow his proceedings should it prove necessary for the public wellbeing so to do. He was well aware that he was fully trusted; but he could not foresee all the possibilities of the future.

The Dutch statesmen, although they were slow at arriving at conclusions, could not but perceive that the Portuguese diplomatist had been merely seeking to gain time. They therefore called upon him to give a categorical statement of the intentions of his government with reference to *Brazil*. He replied in a note, in which he asserted that he had instructions to treat with them respecting the affairs of *Pernambuco;* and he requested that a conference might take place in time to save them the expense of fitting out an unnecessary armament. The Dutch Government, perceiving that he was only renewing his former practices, declined his proposal; whereupon De Sousa, being hard pressed, offered to communicate the instructions on which he was to act. This was a bold step; for it required the exercise of some creative genius on his part. He had, however, with him some blank despatches from his Government already signed, and one of these he filled up so as to suit the moment. The result was that the Dutch, being deceived, suspended their naval preparations.

The ambassador, however, although he had tricked the States, was perfectly open in his communications with his own Government; and he suggested to his sovereign to order his own disgrace or punishment should it be necessary to disavow the act which, according to his knowledge of the existing circumstances, he had judged best for the public interests. His action was secretly approved; but the Portuguese Government had sufficient decency to refrain from any open commendation of the ambassador's conduct, nor did they confer upon him any reward. The King now assured the States that the insurgents in *Pernambuco* disregarded his authority, and that, therefore, they were justified in making war upon them. The Dutch naval preparations were therefore resumed; but they had been delayed for several months. It was November 1645 before the fleet was ready to sail; the frost delayed it at Flushing three months longer, and six months were consumed upon the voyage. Had the insurgents possessed the means of pressing the siege of *Recife* with vigour, the convoy would have arrived to find that place in the possession of the Portuguese.

As it was, the arrival of the fleet had the effect of prolonging this lingering war for years still to come. With the fleet arrived five new members of the Council, with six thousand troops, besides seamen and volunteers, all under the command of the experienced Schoppe. The first attempt of the new general was to regain possession of *Olinda;* but in this he was defeated. As, however, he had now a superior force in the field, the insurgents thought it advisable to evacuate *Paraïba*, and accordingly sent orders to Camaram to withdraw from that captaincy.

The Dutch leader next made a descent upon the northern captaincies, in which he made preparations for the future supplies of provisions for *Recife*. He sent also a considerable force to the river *San Francisco* for the purpose of cutting off the source from which the Portuguese were nourished; but in this latter attempt he was not so successful, and lost a hundred and fifty men. He next secretly fitted out a naval expedition with which he set sail to surprise *Bahia*. Landing upon the island of *Itaparica*, he established himself upon a commanding position, which he fortified. The Governor-General, being taken completely unawares, thought only of protecting the city; and meanwhile the invaders devastated the

Reconcave unopposed. On this the Governor-General determined to attack the Dutch position—an unsuccessful enterprise—in which six hundred men were sacrificed. After this, Schoppe, who had only meant to effect a diversion in favour of *Recife*, returned to that place.

The Portuguese were now, in turn, considerably straitened for supplies; and Vidal had to proceed on foraging expeditions to *Paraïba* and to the *Potengi*. The insurgent leaders, however, were buoyed up by the hope which they entertained of assistance from Portugal. So strongly indeed did they entertain this hope that they concerted measures for the co-operation with them of the fleet which was to arrive; and a battery which was now erected caused much trouble to *Recife*. As it commanded the harbour as well as the streets, the Dutch were compelled to remove their vessels. In one of the sallies made by the Portuguese, the palace built by Count Nassau was sacked.

The convenient pretence that Portugal and the States were still at peace was abandoned, in so far as South America was concerned, after the attack by the Dutch on *Bahia*. The order of the Jesuits in *Rio de Janeiro* contributed to the insurgent cause a ship-load of supplies.

1647. A new Governor-General now arrived at *Bahia* in the person of the Count of Villa Pouca, who brought out with him reinforcements in twelve ships, three of which were unsuccessful in a conflict with the Dutch. The arrival of this fleet without any considerable succours for *Pernambuco* was a sore trial to the patriots of that province. The fleet brought them, however, a new commander, Francisco Barreto, with the rank of Camp-master-General. He had with him an escort of three hundred men, together with arms and ammunition. The Dutch, having information of his sailing, intercepted his ships off *Paraïba*, and Barreto was carried prisoner into *Recife*. After nine months' captivity he effected his escape and joined the insurgents.

It certainly seemed a measure little calculated for insuring success to supersede at this juncture two such capable and efficient commanders as Fernandes and Vidal, who had hitherto headed the insurrection with such vigour, and who were so thoroughly acquainted with the country in which they had to operate. Such, however, was their thorough loyalty, and such the good sense of Barreto in conforming to their advice, that no ill effects resulted from this change in the command. In the course of the insurrection, Vidal and Vernandes had overrun one hundred and eighty leagues of country, from *Ceará* to the *San Francisco*; they had captured eighty pieces of cannon; and they now delivered up to the new commander two months' provisions for the army, twenty-four *contos* * in specie, and the value of eighteen thousand *cruzados*.†

Soon after this event a fresh fleet arrived from Holland, 1648. bringing out six thousand men, which placed the Dutch at an unmistakable advantage in the field, compelling the Portuguese to contract the limits of their operations. The insurgent leaders, with this view, called in their troops from various out-stations, and evacuated *Olinda*, confining themselves between *Serinhaem* and *Moribeca*. All of the inhabitants of the *Varzea*, capable of bearing arms, were ordered to repair to the camp. Upon a muster being taken, the entire insurgent force was found to number only three thousand two hundred men. Its quality, however, made up for its deficiency in quantity.

In describing the details of this long and tedious colonial war, one is glad to arrive at a point which, though it did not mark its conclusion, was nevertheless decisive as to its result. Such a point is the first battle of *Guararapes*. The Dutch commander had determined to take possession of the small town of *Moribeca*, from which place he could co-operate with the fleet destined for *Nazareth*. With this view he attacked the *estancia* of *Barreta*,

* = £240,000.   † = £4500.

making prisoner of Soares, the officer in command. A range of hills, called the *Guararapes*, rises between three or four leagues south of *Recife*, its skirts extending to within three miles of the sea, the intervening space being swampy. Where the range most nearly approaches the ocean there is only a narrow slip of land between the hills and the swamp—the entrance to the pass being between a lake and a thicket. Of this pass the Portuguese took possession, being protected by the wood from the view of an approaching enemy.

On the morning on which the Dutch were to enter the pass, the officer above-named, who had been captured at *Barreta*, contrived to make his escape, and his countrymen were thus well informed as to the disposition and strength of the enemy. A skirmishing party was sent out to decoy them onwards; and the Dutch thus suddenly found themselves in a position where their numbers were of little avail. After the first discharge of firearms the fight was hand to hand. It was well contested. Vidal had two horses killed under him; whilst the charger which Joam Fernandes rode on this decisive day had one of his ears perforated by a bullet. A Dutch soldier, who aimed a blow at the rider, lost his arm by a stroke from the sabre of Fernandes. As was to be expected, in spite of their inferiority of numbers, the patriots won the fight. The enemy left twelve hundred dead upon the field, of whom it is said one hundred and eighty were officers. Amongst the fallen was Haus, who had returned to *Brazil*; amongst the wounded was Schoppe.

After this victory the insurgents once more took possession of *Olinda*; but their joy was somewhat damped by the loss of their fortified battery, called the *Asseca*, which had so long annoyed *Recife*, and which, during the absence of the commanders, had been yielded without a struggle. At this time they likewise sustained a severe loss by the death of their Indian ally, Camaram. He was a man of much ability, and although a typical Indian warrior, was of such dignified and courteous manners that he obtained the love and respect of all. We are somewhat surprised, however, that he is claimed by the Church as a model convert, who every day heard mass and repeated the office. He invariably bore upon his breast a crucifix and an image of the Virgin. The Dutch were still masters of the sea; and in consequence the Portuguese suffered much damage. By means of cruisers the Dutch carried on a tolerably lucrative war; whilst *Recife* offered a ready market for produce, and a ready means of sending remittances to Europe.

Meanwhile a blow was struck at the supremacy of the States in a quarter in which it was little expected. A member of the family of Correa de Sa, by whose means the French had been expelled from *Rio de Janeiro*, now projected an expedition for the recovery of *Angola*. Under pretext of erecting a fort on that coast to secure a supply of negroes, he set out from *Brazil*, having obtained a large amount subscribed for the purpose. Arrived on the coast of Africa, he set sail for *Loanda*, and was there informed that a detachment of Dutch was acting against the Portuguese at *Massangano*. On this information, he sent a flag to the governor, stating that, although he had not come with a hostile purpose, he felt it his duty to defend his oppressed countrymen, and he allowed the Dutch two days in which to surrender. The latter, at the end of this time, made a show of resistance, but soon fled; after which, by great address, Correa de Sa effected the relief of *Massangano*, taking prisoners the entire Dutch force of over two thousand men, whom he caused immediately to embark for Europe. The city of *St. Thomas* was likewise abandoned. The tidings of this success reaching Portugal about the same time as those of the battle of *Guararapes*, had no small share in deciding the government of King Joam to take the course which, after long hesitation, they ultimately adopted in their negotiations with the Dutch respecting *Pernambuco*.

The councils of King Joam were now not a little distracted. The Dutch were fully aware of the value of the possession which was the subject of contention between them and Portugal; and they were fully determined not to yield *Pernambuco*. Their demands were that Portugal should cede to them the whole of the provinces which they had occupied at the conclusion of the truce, with the third part of *Seregipe* in addition; that the island and port of the *Morro* of *St. Paulo*, opposite *Bahia*, should be given to them, likewise, for twenty years, until the terms of the treaty should be fulfilled; that they were to receive 100,000 *florins*, yearly, for twenty years; and likewise one thousand oxen, one thousand cows, four hundred horses, and one thousand sheep, yearly, for ten years, and a thousand chests of sugar, yearly, for twenty years. All their slaves were also to be restored.

Although these exorbitant terms were subsequently somewhat lowered, the Portuguese nation had still sufficient pride not to submit to them. The King placed the matter before the members of his Council, from each individual of whom he required a separate written opinion. The result was that a memorial was laid before His Majesty, stating that however desirable might be a peace with Holland, yet that religion and honour alike necessitated the rejection of the terms proposed. The King had, however, one adviser who took an opposite view. This was Vieyra, the Jesuit, who proceeded to expose the weakness of the several arguments which were adduced by the Council. This able statesman looked not to the Portuguese possessions in *Brazil* alone, but to the imperial position which Portugal occupied in the world. He met the religious objection by the argument that there was nothing to prevent the Portuguese of *Pernambuco* from emigrating elsewhere. Since the very existence of Portugal was at stake, it was before all things the King's duty as a Catholic sovereign to look to the safety of that stronghold of the faith. The captaincies which the

Dutch required, were after all only about a tenth part of the country.

Sixty ships, he pointed out, had been captured during that year. The Dutch, he declared, possessed fourteen thousand vessels against one hundred and fifty belonging to Portugal. They had in India more than a hundred ships of war, and more than sixty in *Brazil*. But it was on the state of India that Vieyra rested his main argument, and on the certainty of the Portuguese losing their possessions on that continent should they persist in war with the States. Thus was the King left in as great perplexity as ever, since his Council advised him in one sense, whilst the statesman whom he most trusted took an opposite view of the situation. One suggestion of Vieyra's was, however, complied with, namely, a Portuguese *Brazil* Company was established, and this had a notable effect in bringing the war to a conclusion.

The necessity for the above-named measure had long been represented to the King by this sagacious Churchman. It was indeed an imitation of the Dutch East and West India Companies. Individual interest, he argued, would create exertion and enterprise; whilst foreign capital would be attracted by so promising an adventure. There was one condition absolutely needed, however, to insure its success, namely, that all capital embarked in this adventure should be free from confiscation. It is necessary to explain that this *proviso* referred to the Inquisition, the political evils of which institution had been ably exposed by Vieyra. Were the property of merchants engaged in this Company liable to be seized at the instance of the Holy Office, the Company would, of course, cease to command public confidence. As a matter of course the Holy Office denounced the proposed measure. They objected even to the use of money belonging to suspected persons. It required the losses of eight successive years and the threatened ruin of the trade of Portugal to induce the Government to put down this obstacle raised by interested bigotry. But at length the Company was formed, and the King's eldest son became Prince of *Brazil*.

1649.

To return to *Pernambuco*. The *Guararape* hills were once more the scene of a battle between the parties who contended for the mastery of this fertile province. On this occasion the relative position of the combatants was reversed, the Dutch being the defendants and the Portuguese the assailants. The former had sallied from *Recife* with a force of some five thousand men, and had taken possession of the pass between the sea and the hills of the above name. Here they were attacked by the Portuguese, and, after a struggle of six hours, were routed with a loss of eleven hundred men, nineteen stands of colours, with the whole of their artillery and ammunition. Prink, the Dutch commander, fell, as did the chief of the naval forces which assisted him. Joam Fernandes, the hero of the insurrection, had, as usual, several narrow escapes with his life. On the side of the victors fell Paulo da Cunha, who had taken a prominent part in the war.

Shortly after this battle the first fleet sent out by the new Company arrived at *Brazil*, the Dutch being unable to oppose it. There is not much, however, to record respecting the proceedings of the contending parties during the next three years. Holland, being engaged in war with the Protector of England, left the West Indian Company to provide for *Pernambuco* as best it could; but the means of the Company were exhausted, and their naval force at *Recife* became unfit to go to sea. Schoppe, indeed, made one attempt to intercept the homeward bound fleet of 1652; but he was beaten off with loss.

1653.

The conclusion of the struggle for the independence of *Pernambuco* was due, as had been its commencement, to the initiative of Joam Fernandes. To his intelligent and patriotic mind two considerations presented themselves, namely, that the Pernambucans must rely for their freedom on themselves alone ; and that the expulsion of the

Dutch could never be secured while *Recife* remained open to their ships. Taking these as his principles, it occurred to him that although there was no hope of obtaining direct succour from Portugal, yet that the Company's fleet might be made use of to obtain the desired end. His commander, Barreto, entering into his views, the camp-masters met in council in *San Gonzalo's* chapel, and agreed to endeavour to carry out the scheme.

The annual fleet was to sail from Lisbon early in October, with Pedro de Magalhaens as general and Brito Freire as admiral, the latter being the well-known historian. Barreto had been desired to have the ships in the ports of *Pernambuco* ready to join the fleet on its way to *Bahia*. The advice was received on the 7th of December, and on the 20th the convoy came in sight of *Recife*. After beating off some Dutch frigates, the general and the admiral landed at the *Rio Doce*. This scheme was then opened up to them, and they were requested to block up the harbour whilst the insurgents should make a last and desperate attempt to effect the capture of *Recife*.

As was to be expected, the commanders were not a little startled at the part which had been assigned to them. Magalhaens represented that his instructions from the King did not authorize him to engage in any act of hostility; nor had he permission from the Company to divert the fleet from its destination. He further intimated that were he to involve his country in war with Holland, the penalty would be his head. To this Fernandes replied by the argument once used by John Knox, that all temporal penalties, which at least ended with this world, could not outweigh in the scale the value of a soul which was to exist to all eternity; and that were the general to fail in carrying out the part which Providence now assigned to him, the souls of all those who would be thus exposed to renunciation of the faith would be required at his hands. It was an age of deep religious conviction, and both Magalhaens and Freire yielded to the arguments of Fernandes.

The result is soon told. The Dutch fleet, perceiving the intentions of the Portuguese, stood out to sea whilst they were able to do so. Their disappearance set at liberty the merchant ships along the coast, which were employed under the orders of Barreto. A line was drawn across the harbour of *Recife*, and strict precautions were taken that no relief should reach the city by sea or by land. The besieging force consisted of three thousand five hundred men. The indefatigable Fernandes led the first assault; and he was good enough to promise a separate mass for the soul of each of his men who should fall. On the morning of the 15th of January, the besieged were astonished to find themselves cannonaded by a battery of twenty-four pounders, and the fort of *Salinas* surrendered on the same night. One post gave in after another, and at length the inhabitants compelled the General to treat for a capitulation. The Dutch, having surrendered their arms, might remain for three months at *Recife* to settle their affairs; but all their possessions on the coast of *Brazil*, without exception, were to be surrendered to the Portuguese.

1654.   Fernandez entered the city and received the keys of the magazines and forts, seventy-three in number, which he proudly delivered to Barreto. Twelve hundred regular troops laid down their arms at *Recife*. The Portuguese likewise gained possession of two hundred and seventy-three guns; the Indians had retired toward *Ceará*. Some of the distant garrisons, having received timely warning of the loss of *Recife*, succeeded in effecting their escape; but at *Itamaraca* four hundred men were taken. The General and the Admiral now proceeded with the convoy to *Bahia;* whilst Vidal set out to announce the glad tidings in Portugal. But in this intention the commander was anticipated by a Benedictine priest, who, arriving at

Lisbon on the same evening, proceeded at once to communicate the information to the King.

The news of this event reached Holland at a time when the Dutch, however much they might feel disposed to do so, were by no means in a position to take revenge. Their arms were not just then successful against England. But they succeeded in recompensing themselves for the loss of *Pernambuco* by wresting Ceylon from the Portuguese. They did not, however, immediately resign the hope of recovering their possessions in *Brazil*. Although Louis XIV. was accepted as mediator between Holland and Portugal, the States nevertheless sent a fleet under De Ruiter to the Tagus and attempted some reprisals. In the end, Holland yielded to circumstances. Charles II. of England, while treating for his marriage with the Portuguese princess, intimated to the Dutch that if they should persevere in the contest he would become a party to it. France likewise interfered energetically on behalf of Portugal; and at length 1661. the negotiations were concluded, the latter country consenting to pay a certain amount in money and commodities to Holland, and to restore her captured cannon.

CHAPTER V.

BRAZIL: JESUIT MISSIONS IN NORTHERN BRAZIL.

1652-1662.

MENTION has more than once been made in the preceding chapter of Antonio Vieyra, the Jesuit, a man of singular ability, who was destined to play a distinguished part in the history of his time, both as a statesman and as an ecclesiastic, and who has left behind him one of the foremost names in the splendid literature of his country. Before proceeding to relate the part which he took in the affairs of *Brazil*, it may be well to give a sketch of his remarkable career up to this time.

Vieyra was born at Lisbon in the year 1608, but when in his eighth year he emigrated with his parents to *Bahia*, where he was brought up at the Jesuits' school. In his early youth it is said that his intellect was clouded. Being aware of this fact, he earnestly prayed to the Virgin to remove the cause, and he himself records that something seemed to give way in his head, causing him violent pain, from which hour his intellect shone out in all its exceptional clearness. When in his fifteenth year, a sermon which he heard on the glory of the Beatific Vision determined him to select a religious life. The provincial of the Jesuits in *Brazil* was a frequent visitor at his father's house; and the youth, knowing it to be in vain to seek his parents' consent, fled to the Jesuits' College, the doors of which were gladly opened to receive him. His parents remonstrated, but without effect; and, at the age of sixteen he was permitted to take the vows which bound him to the Order for life. A year later he was employed to write the yearly letter from the province to the general at Rome, and in the following year he lectured on rhetoric at *Olinda*.

Vieyra's tastes inclined him to abandon his studies and to devote himself entirely to the Indians; but his far-seeing superiors discerned too well his remarkable talents to permit them to be devoted entirely to such a purpose. After some years spent in ministering amongst Indians and negroes, and in the acquisition of the *Tupi* language, for the benefit of the former, and of that of *Angola*, for the benefit of the latter, he was, in 1635, ordained a priest. He now lectured on theology at *Bahia*, and, sometime later, he accompanied the agent sent to Portugal to congratulate the King on the recovery of his rights. Arriving at Peniche in company of *Dom* Fernando Mascarenhas, whose brother had adhered to the king of Castile, he was arrested by the people and narrowly escaped being put to death. The populace were, however, persuaded to deliver him over to justice. Reaching Lisbon as a supposed criminal, he obtained an audience of the King, upon whom his remarkable talents produced an instant effect. He was appointed preacher to Joam IV., who continued ever afterwards to regard him with the affection of a father to a son. In his sermons he expressed himself with such freedom as well as eloquence that he was at one time brought under the notice of the Inquisition.

The favour which Vieyra enjoyed at court created the jealousy even of his own order, and it was once feared that they were about to expel him. In anticipation of this, he was offered by the King a bishopric, which offer, however, was declined. The jealousy of Vieyra's superiors was at length, happily, removed, and he was employed during several years in the most important diplomatic service, including a mission to the Hague at a critical period. About the year 1652, after the *Brazil* 1652.

Company had been established owing to his representations, the fleet of which Company was the means used by Fernandes to complete the reduction of *Recife*, the thoughts of the Jesuit Father began to be powerfully attracted towards the land of his early education. From the possession of his special gifts, more particularly his knowledge of the Indian and *Angola* languages, he probably felt that there was work to be done which he was likely to perform better than any living man. But there was a strong obstacle in the way. This was the favour with which he was regarded both by King Joam and by his son, Prince Theodosio, from both of whom he felt it would be useless to solicit permission to depart on his proposed voyage.

This being the case, as it was a matter of conscience, Vieyra determined to set out clandestinely, that is to say, without the royal permission. A strong succession of circumstances now occurred. Vieyra had made up his mind to set out for *Maranham*, and there was but one vessel in the *Brazil* fleet which was bound for that State. It was arranged that Vieyra and his companion, Ribeiro, should accompany the last Jesuits on board, as if to take leave of them. As they were on the way, they learned that the ship was detained for a royal officer. Vieyra therefore returned to the King, and obtained permission for the vessel to depart without this person. But now the captain was compelled to wait for the morning tide, and Vieyra and his companion returned on shore for the night. Their purpose being now suspected, the captain of the ship received notice that he would be hanged were he to convey Vieyra away; and notice was likewise given to the masters of all the other ships in the river forbidding them to give the two Jesuits a passage, Vieyra being at the same time summoned to the palace.

Upon this Vieyra went to the Prince, and told him that he must go to *Maranham*; but he was answered that nothing would induce the King to consent to his going. The Jesuit then endeavoured to escape in a vessel bound to *Madeira*, from which place he hoped eventually to be able to proceed to *Brazil;* but this vessel, too, lost the tide, and as Vieyra had been seen to go on board, he was again commanded to return. He was cordially received by the King and Prince, with whom, however, he argued as to the superior authority under which he was prompted to proceed to South America. The Prince was in ill-health, and it was probably owing to this circumstance that the royal consent to Vieyra's departure was now obtained. The King having once yielded, now entrusted Vieyra, as Superior of the Mission, to found such churches and missions in the interior as he might think fit, and enjoining all persons in authority to render him every assistance for this purpose.

It was arranged that Vieyra and a brother missionary should proceed in a *caravel* to their destination; but whilst they were waiting the King and the Prince, with whom Vieyra was now living in daily intercourse, repented of the permission which they had given. Vieyra, too, felt more than ever reluctant to quit his royal master, to whom he was bound not alone by ties of the deepest loyalty, but likewise by those of the utmost personal affection. The services, too, which he might render to his country in Europe at that critical time were suggested to him; and the result was that his missionary projects were abandoned. So much publicity had, however, been given to them, that both the King and Vieyra were somewhat afraid of ridicule on the announcement of their relinquishment. It was therefore determined for the present that nothing should be given out on the subject, and that when the time should come for his departure he should be summoned back from on board ship as if on a sudden impulse from the King. When the time came, however, for the Jesuit's departure, and he had gone through the form of going on board ship, owing to some accident the royal mandate for his return never reached him; and thus it happened that after all he unintentionally sailed, and touched at the *Cape de Verde* Islands, where his vessel remained for four days.

Vieyra must have been a very Chrysostom; for we read that he preached twice at *Porto Praya* with such effect that the people first petitioned him and his companions to remain with them, and then offered a large bribe to the master of the vessel to sail without them. At *Maranham* Vieyra was welcomed by his brother, when he lost no time in setting about the duties of his mission. It is almost needless to say that he was greatly shocked at the low moral and religious condition in which he found the community. It was in fact Christian in name alone, and was destitute even of the elements by which Christian instruction might be imparted. The zealous missionary lost no time in communicating his impressions to the King and to the Prince, whom he implored to send out suitable assistance. The harvest he said was great, but the labourers were few.

Maranham was in truth in a far worse condition than that of the older captaincies, the inhabitants of which had by this time acquired the customs of civilized life. In them had long been established the forms of municipal government. They were likewise communities which subsisted by regularly-established commerce; whilst they enjoyed regular intercourse with the mother country, and were presided over by men of position and character. But *Maranham* and *Pará* were, so to speak, back-settlements. It was exile for a governor of position to go to them, and they were consequently ruled either by men who went thither for a short time on promotion or who accepted the post of governor in order to make money in the only way by which it could be made—that is to say, by slave-dealing. It is to be remembered, too, that at this period *Maranham* and *Pará* were separated from the Portuguese settlements in Southern *Brazil* by the presence of the Dutch in the intervening provinces adjoining *Pernambuco*.

In the older presidencies the supply of Indians available for slaves was by this time so exhausted that the slave market had to be stocked from *Angola;* but at *Maranham* the native population, being newly brought into contact with the Portuguese, afforded an ample field for the energy of the slave-hunter and those who were interested in his operations, in which latter category were included officials of every rank. In fact, Vieyra found *Maranham* a huge Augean-stable, the proportions of which would have made a man of less energy stand aghast in despair.

The Portuguese race has unquestionably filled a most distinguished part in the world. At the period of which we write it had gloriously recovered its national independence, and was renowned alike for its splendid literature, its famous geographical discoveries,—more especially those of Bartholomew Diaz, Vasco de Gama, Cabral, and Magalhaens,—and its magnificent colonial possessions in the east as well as in the west; and that the race has not lost all its energy is proved by such exploits of the present day as those of Serpa Pinto and others. But in two respects, as well to-day as two centuries ago, the same race is less honourably remarkable, namely, in addiction to the more superstitious adjuncts of Catholicism, such as worship of images, belief in everyday miracles, etc., and in addiction to every form of the slave-trade. The former may be considered an indication of puerile ignorance; the latter is a national disgrace.

There seems indeed something peculiarly ingrained in the Portuguese race which makes them take to slave-dealing and slave-hunting as naturally as greyhounds take to chasing hares; and this observation applies not to one section of the race alone, but to Portuguese wherever they are to be found beyond the reach of European law. No modern race can be cited as slave-hunters within measurable distance of the Portuguese. Their exploits in this respect are written in the annals not only of the whole coast of *Brazil* from *Pará* to *Uruguay* and along the *Misiones* of *Paraguay*, not only on the coast of

Angola, but throughout the interior of Africa. We may take up the journals of one traveller after another, of Burton, of Livingstone, of Stanley, or of Cameron, and, in whatever respect their accounts and opinions may differ, on one point they are one and all entirely agreed, namely, as to the pestilent and remorseless activity of the ubiquitous Portuguese slave-catcher.

Nor does the eminence of the Portuguese race as purveyors to the slave-market end at the dark continent. In India, it is true, their activity in this respect is restrained by the presence of a paramount power; but further east their national character has found ample scope for its development. In the nineteenth century a Christian country of Europe has shown an example to such nations as China and Japan by maintaining at *Macao* an emporium of coolies destined for *Peru* and elsewhere, and sent out under conditions differing from those of slavery in name alone, and the records of which traffic are a *pendant* to those of "the middle passage." Finally, a branch of the Portuguese race has at this moment the unenviable distinction of possessing the only civilized country in which slavery is acknowledged by law.

To return to *Brazil*: the kings of Portugal had, it is true, been individually ever desirous of mitigating the conditions of slavery to which their Indian subjects in South America were subjected; but circumstances were ever too strong for them. The wealth of *Brazil* was only to be obtained by agricultural labour; and so long as Indians were to be captured or reared for the purpose, the cupidity of the colonists devoted their Indian fellow-subjects to this end. The native races, however, were not used to such hard labour as was imposed upon them, and they gradually sank and died away beneath it. They were then replaced by Africans, whose descendants are now the means of producing the sugar-wealth, coffee-wealth, and tobacco-wealth of *Brazil*. Various enactments were from time to time passed by the Government at Lisbon to restrain their colonial subjects in their dealings with the natives; but all were of no avail. In the first instance the colonists were permitted to enslave them without control; but a law was passed by King Sebastian, declaring that no Indians should be considered slaves, excepting such as should be taken in war made by command of the King or Governor, or such as were aggressive cannibals; but this regulation was invariably made to suit every individual occasion.

By a second law, it was provided that the Indians who worked for the Portuguese should not be regarded as slaves, but as free labourers. King Phillip II. decreed that none should be considered slaves excepting those taken in hostilities for which he should have issued orders. Philip III. forbade that any Indians should be made slaves; but the evil had gone too far for his edict to be attended with any good result, and he was induced to revoke it, and to permit the enslavement of Indians taken in war. In short, so general was the interest amongst all classes of the Portuguese in *Brazil* in encouraging slavery, that every well-meant edict and regulation of the Portuguese Crown was evaded. The same law provided that in each village of the "reduced" Indians there was to be a captain, who should hold office for three years. The Indians were to be settled in villages of about three hundred houses. Lands were to be allotted for their use and a church built in each village. These Indians were to be considered free, and were paid for their labour.

Joam IV. renewed the law of Philip III., and Sousa Pereira, going out as governor of *Maranham*, took with him orders emancipating all Indians then enslaved. These orders produced an insurrection, which was only quelled by a promise of the Governor that the law should not be enforced, pending an appeal to the King. The same occurrence took place likewise at *Pará* when the law was announced at that place. Such was the state of things in Northern *Brazil* at the date of Vieyra's coming.

Much as the Jesuit Father had been shocked on his

arrival at *Maranham* by the low religious and moral condition of that dependency, his convictions on the subject were much intensified as his opportunities of observation increased. Many of the colonists troubled themselves neither with mass nor with church throughout the year, and it was a common thing amongst them to die without confession. In the whole captaincy there were but two churches with resident priests; the one on the island, the other on the mainland. The Portuguese of *Maranham* and *Pará* were pursuing the same course towards the Indians which had resulted in their extermination along the sea-coast of the other captaincies. The law permitted that Indians taken in war should be made slaves, and likewise that such prisoners as were rescued by the Portuguese from other tribes, and who were thus saved from being eaten, should be devoted to slavery. These two regulations were made to cover the most iniquitous transactions. Every captain of a fort could at any time provoke his Indian neighbours into war; whilst Indian captives were habitually threatened or tortured into the confession that they had been rescued or purchased by the Portuguese from other Indians.

In the general system of oppression the Indians who had voluntarily submitted to the Portuguese bore their full share. Indeed they were perhaps, if possible, in a worse position than their brethren. The captain for the time being, holding his office merely for three years, looked upon them in the light of so many animals out of whom he was to extract as much benefit for himself as he could during that period. They were chiefly employed in raising and preparing tobacco; whilst their families were left to starve. Some Indians thought it better to quit this "free" condition and voluntarily to become domestic slaves. Others preferred to die.

It is not surprising that such a state of things should have worked up Vieyra's indignation to the boiling point. He had soon an opportunity of venting his most righteous wrath from the pulpit. It was the season of Lent, and as his reputation for eloquence had preceded him, the church was, for once at least, filled to overflowing. In a discourse which has been preserved, he acted on the command given to the Prophet Isaiah, "Cry aloud, spare not, "lift up thy voice like a trumpet, and show my people "their transgressions." In a passage which might perhaps be addressed from the pulpit to the Brazilians of to-day, he observes, " But you will say to me this State cannot " be supported without Indians. Who is to plant our " mandioc ? Must our wives do it ? Must our children " do it ? If necessity and conscience require it, I reply, " ' Yes ; ' for better it is to be supported by the sweat of " one's own brow than by another's blood." He had no difficulty in touching by his impassioned eloquence the consciences, if not the hearts, even of the hardened congregation whom he addressed ; and on the same afternoon a meeting was held, in which it was agreed to go into the history of each individual Indian who was detained in a state of slavery, and to leave each case to be decided by the Senate. A deed expressing the consent of the people to this arrangement was immediately drawn up and signed by all the chief persons of the place.

Vieyra now undertook the task of instructing the Indians each Sunday ; and after a time he made plans for a missionary expedition amongst the tribes. In this project, however, he had to encounter the selfishness of the governor, who could not spare from his own plantations the Indians whom Vieyra required to accompany him. Disappointed in this quarter he turned to another, only to meet with a like repulse. The results of his efforts convinced him that it was impossible to proceed with the conversion and civilization of the Indians, so long as the civil authorities should have any power over them. He accordingly wrote to the King his opinion that the governors and chief-captains should possess no authority over the Indians excepting in time of war, when a certain number should be allotted for military service; that the Indians should have an advocate in each captaincy, annually elected, and independent of the governor; that the natives should be governed by religioners; that at the beginning of each year lists should be made of the Indians in each captaincy, and likewise of the settlers, and that the former should then be divided amongst the latter by their own advocate and by the superior of the religious order; that no Indian should work for a settler for more than four months in a year, in terms of two months, their wages being deposited in advance. He added other excellent suggestions; but so urgent was the case that it was thought better that he should himself proceed to Europe vividly in order to plead in person.

On his homeward voyage Vieyra encountered a tempest near the *Azores*, from which he owed his deliverance to the crew of a Dutch privateer, who took him from his ship after its masts had been cut away. He and his companions, after having been plundered of all they possessed, were landed on the island of *Graciosa*. Vieyra's credit, however, was sufficient to procure for himself and his forty companions the means of subsistence during two months, and likewise a passage to Lisbon, which he thus vividly describes:—

"The ship belonged to heretic owners, and the pilot and the sailors were heretics; we passengers were some religioners of different orders, and a great quantity of those musical islanders who come here to compose a choir of four voices with their nightingales and goldfinches, canary-birds and blackbirds. The weather was worse than ordinary, and the effects which I observed in it were truly admirable. We religioners were all employed in prayers and litanies, making vows to Heaven and exorcisms to the waves, throwing relics into the sea, and above all in acts of contrition, confessing many times, as if at the point of death. The sailors, like the heretics, when the hatches were lying at the feet of the masts, ate and drank more merrily than ever, and mocked at what they called our ceremonies. The little birds at the same time, at the sound which the wind made in the rigging, as if those cords had been the string of some musical instrument, exerted their strength in singing. God, help me! if labour and fear had not taken off all attention, who would not in this situation have admired effects so various and so opposite, the cause being the same? What, . . . all in the same ship, all in the same storm, all in the same danger, and some singing, some mocking, some praying and lamenting?" It is interesting to see this great man, who in following his duty shrank neither from labour nor from any kind of danger, ingenuously confessing the effect which a storm at sea had upon him in common with other bad sailors.

It is needless to add that the Portuguese Government were now faithfully and fully informed of the condition of things in the northern provinces of *Brazil;* but although the King was most desirous to do what was right and just, his power in the matter was limited. Deputies from *Maranham* and *Pará* were in Lisbon, and neither gold nor falsehood was spared on behalf of the slaveholders.

The King ordered that a *junta* should be convened of theologians and lawyers under the guidance of the President of the Palace. After eight days' discussion, Vieyra having pleaded his own cause, the *junta* gave their opinion in favour of his system being adopted. This step was followed by a direction from the heads of the other orders established in *Maranham* and *Pará* that the members of their respective communities should act in conformity with the decisions of the *junta*. Vieyra's next object was to establish a missionary board, which should at all times supervise the interests of the missions. A decree was issued declaring that all the Indian settlements in the State of *Maranham* should be under the direction of the Jesuits; that Vieyra, as superior of the mission, should direct all expeditions into the interior, and settle the "reduced" Indians as he might think fit; that the chief of every ransoming party should be approved by the Jesuits, who should have a vote upon the examination of the ransomed Indians; and that these should not be slaves for longer than five years. The free Indians were not to work for the Portuguese for more than six months in the year.

1655. *Recife* being now once more in the hands of the Portuguese, the services of Vidal were at the disposal of the King, and were suitably employed in the government of *Maranham*. His Majesty would have prevented Vieyra from returning; but, as he was unwilling to decide so important a point on his own judgment, he referred to the triennial meeting of the Jesuits of the province the question whether a man whose services were so important at home ought to be sent as a missionary among savages. Vieyra demanded to be heard before them. It may well be conceived that he had many reasons to urge why he should not abandon the mission he had chosen. He pointed out the scoffs that would be uttered were he who had incited others to go to *Maranham* to prefer for himself the rest of Europe. What would the Indians say as to his having left them to seek relief, and forgetting his promise of speedily returning? What an example would his turning aside from the path of difficulty present to the youth now growing up in the colonies? Some of the Fathers, being in despair that the Company should lose the advantage of Vieyra's talents at headquarters, nobly kneeling at the Provincial's feet, offered to take Vieyra's place abroad, provided he might remain at home. The votes were given secretly; but the majority agreed that Vieyra ought to go upon the mission. The King submitted to this decision; and, after a residence of only four months in Portugal, Vieyra again embarked for *Maranham*.

When the terms of the new law became known, such

discontent was occasioned that a popular tumult sprung up; but it was sternly repressed by Vidal. The new governor soon afterwards proceeded to *Belem*, accompanied by Vieyra, in order to give effect to the King's decrees in the province of *Pará*. The utter contempt of law displayed by the condition of that province was startling. It was known that the slave-dealers had brought down with them not less than sixteen hundred Indians; yet, after every person had made oath that he had presented all whom he had brought or received, the whole number fell short of eight hundred, the rest having been concealed. One man presented eight-and-twenty Indians, who, being examined, replied individually that they had been rescued from other tribes. They were accordingly passed as lawful slaves. A week later, the chiefs of some allied Indians arrived at *Belem* to request that the governor would release some of their people, whom the Portuguese had stolen. On being told to point them out, they selected the twenty-eight above-mentioned. The poor wretches, who were subjects of the King of Portugal, had been threatened to be flogged to death, unless they should answer that they were rescued prisoners of war. The above are mere samples of the wholesale villany which was practised.

The ecclesiastics who were members of the board upon whom it devolved to determine the lawfulness of the capture of Indians, were too anxious on all occasions to bring them by any means within the pale of Christianity to be at all scrupulous in deciding in favour of the slave-dealers when there was the least opening for doing so. Vieyra, too, was most anxious to bring within the King's protection, and within the fold of the Church, as many Indians as might be induced by fair means to come, but this without violence or injustice. He insisted that, before Indians were brought from their own country, provision should be made that they might not perish from want, as so many had already perished. One governor coolly replied, when the probability of a great mortality was pointed out to him, that the death of such people was of no consequence; but it was better for them to die amongst the Portuguese, as they would then be baptized.

Wherever Vidal had the power to do so he acted in the spirit as well as according to the letter of the King's instructions; and under his protection Vieyra diligently pursued his schemes. The chief settlements of the "reduced" Indians were to the north of *Maranham*, where fifty villages were established along the coast. Vieyra's desire was to form a line of stations in like manner towards the south, as far as *Ceará*, thus connecting the Jesuit stations of *Maranham* with those of Southern *Brazil*. He desired likewise to continue the same connecting system up the great rivers. With the latter object in view, two Jesuits, with a Portuguese surgeon and a hundred Indian boatmen, went for a distance of three hundred leagues up the river to the *Tocantins*. The Fathers were successful in persuading about a thousand persons to follow them on their return down to *Belem*, where they were received by Vidal and Vieyra. Many Indians were likewise brought from other quarters, and for some time the success of the missionary work, aided as it was by the strong arm of the civil authority, was all that could be desired.

But a period came to this prosperity. In the year 1657, Vidal was promoted to be Governor of *Pernambuco*. About the same time, Vieyra sustained a severe, and indeed an irreparable, loss by the death of the Prince of *Brazil*, which was soon followed by that of King Joam. He had still, however, a powerful and steady friend in the Bishop of *Japan*, who was the Queen's confessor; and he was appointed Visitor and Superior in that part of America. The new Governor, *Don* Pedro de Mello, however, who succeeded Vidal, displayed a great falling-off from his predecessor. He lost no time in engaging

1657.

in a serious war with the inhabitants of the islands at the mouth of the *Amazons*. He had brought out with him the news that Holland and Portugal were then at war; and it was apprehended that the Dutch might renew their operations in this quarter. The new Governor, therefore, was urged to attack the Indians with all his force before the Dutch could arrive to help them. Vieyra alone advised that conciliatory measures should at first be used; and he offered to undertake the task of negotiating. Being permitted to try what he could do, he wrote to the tribes, informing them that the new laws which he had gone to Portugal to procure had put an end to the wrongs and grievances of which they complained. He pledged his word that the old unjust system was prohibited, and said that he was ready either to receive them or to go amongst them. His messengers could give them full information of the actual state of things.

The messengers departed, fearing the worst, and telling Vieyra that should they not return by the next moon he might give them up as being dead or in slavery. The next moon came, and all had given them up for lost; but, to the surprise of every one, the messengers returned, bringing with them a party of Indians with seven chiefs. They said that they had come simply on the faith of the paper from the Great Father, who for their sakes had crossed the deep and obtained for them so many benefits. Vieyra would have returned with them to the island; but they preferred that they should first have an opportunity of making preparations for his reception, when they should come for him with a larger escort. They accordingly came at the date appointed, arriving in seventeen canoes. They found Vieyra so ill that he was then unable to accompany them; but he followed them as soon afterwards as his health permitted, taking with him another Father, the chiefs of all the "reduced" Indians, and only ten Portuguese.

On the fifth day of their voyage they were met by the chiefs of a tribe who had promised to make a settlement, and the Fathers were led to a church which had been constructed in anticipation of their visit. A house had likewise been prepared for them close by. The neighbouring hordes had been summoned by their chiefs to assemble, when they took the oath of obedience, which was administered by the missionaries with much ceremony. On the right of the church stood the chiefs of the converted Indians, in their best attire. On the left were the savage chiefs, naked and feather-adorned, and with bows in hand. Vieyra performed mass, after which he addressed them through an interpreter; when they submitted themselves to the King of Portugal, and accepted the true faith. The chiefs approached the altar one by one, laid down their weapons, and took an oath of obedience. It is estimated that the number of islanders who submitted to the Portuguese on this occasion was not less than forty thousand.

Vieyra's next task was to regulate the mission amongst the tribes of *Ibiapaba*, which place he reached, footsore and weary, after a painful journey of three weeks from *Maranham*. Having arranged the affairs of this mission, he returned to *Belem* by sea.

Hitherto no open opposition had been attempted to the laws under which the missions were making such progress; but the jealousy of the settlers against the Jesuits was gaining head. The Chamber of *Belem* now wrote to that of *St. Luiz*, proposing that they should unite with the object of depriving the Jesuits of their temporal power over the Indians; and, the proposal having been acceded to, the Chamber actually addressed a remonstrance to Vieyra, representing the distress to which the State was subjected in consequence of the restrictions on slavery. The King's tenths, they said, were so diminished that no person would farm them. Men of noble lineage could not bring their children to the city, because they had no slaves to row their canoes; their daughters could not appear at mass for want of fit clothing; many persons in *Belem* had no one to fetch them wood or water, and were perishing for want of slaves to cultivate their land. In his reply, Vieyra observed that the evils imputed to the want of slaves arose from other causes,—from the nature of the country, from the scarcity of grain, and from the want of combination amongst the people. As for slaves, he said, experience had shown that however great was the supply, the mortality was in excess thereof.

The discontented party received encouragement from *Don* Pedro de Mallo, the governor of *Maranham*, to whom they sent deputies with copies of the correspondence. That functionary, being afraid of the people, had secretly fomented their feeling against the Jesuits. He had, however, been kept in restraint, as were the colonists, by the consideration that Vieyra's patron, the Bishop of *Japan*, possessed supreme influence with the Queen-Regent. This restraining motive was removed by the news which now arrived of the bishop's death. Some letters, which had been written by Vieyra to the bishop, had fallen into the hands of the mendicant friars, who now gratified their jealousy of Vieyra by making them public. Not being meant for publicity, they were in Vieyra's usual graphic style; and the picture which they exhibited of colonial morality now raised a storm against him and his order. A tumult occurred. The mob dragged the Jesuits from their cells, and compelled their superior to resign his authority over the Indians into the hands of the Chamber. He and his brethren were then forced on board ship, there to await the arrival of the Jesuits from other quarters, prior to their all being deported.

Vieyra was at this time on his way from *Belem* to *Maranham*. On hearing of the tumult, he returned to the former place, when he addressed a memorial to the

Chamber, requiring them to continue in obedience to the laws, reminding them of the services which the Jesuits had recently rendered to the State, and pointing out the evils which would ensue were public faith broken with the Indians. His reasoning, however, produced no effect. When the news of the insurrection at *St. Luiz* was made public, the people of *Belem* arose and surrounded the college. Vieyra himself was seized and insulted, and was imprisoned in the chapel of St. John the Baptist, where he was supplied with food by the devotion of an Indian woman. He was sent to *St. Luiz*, where he was closely confined, his despatches to Lisbon being taken possession of. The dwelling-house and church of the Jesuits were destroyed, and their property sequestrated. Of the two vessels in which the Jesuits were deported, one was seized by a privateer; the other, with Vieyra on board, reached Lisbon in safety.

The Queen-Regent received the news of the rising with indignation. A new Governor was on the point of setting out for *Maranham*, who was directed to restore, if possible, the authority which had been set aside, without an appeal to force. Sequeira ably fulfilled his instructions. He first exerted himself to re-establish municipal government and to win the soldiers to his confidence. When he felt his power sufficiently firm, he prohibited all persons from having Indians of the villages in their service. He gradually influenced the minds of the people in favour of the Jesuits, and at length he called a meeting to take into consideration the question of their being restored. Strange to say, a large majority voted in the affirmative; upon which Sequeira gave orders to ring the bells and fire a salute; after which the Governor proclaimed a general pardon.

1662.

CHAPTER VI.

BRAZIL; ESTABLISHMENT OF THE FRENCH IN SOUTH AMERICA.

1657-1696.

ON the termination of the war which liberated *Pernambuco*, Barreto, who it will be remembered shared with Fernandes and Vidal the command of the Portuguese troops, was rewarded with the post of Governor-General of *Brazil;* and 1657. upon him fell the task of raising the proportion of the annual sum which, according to the treaty, was to be paid to the Dutch. The amount which was to be levied on *Brazil* for this purpose was 120,000 *cruzados** yearly, for sixteen years, being nearly half of the whole contribution. For this purpose Barreto convoked the Senators, who replied that they would propose the matter to the Chamber, which body readily consented to the assessment. Of the amount to be raised, the province of *Bahia* took more than one-half upon itself.

About this time *Rio de Janeiro*, together with the provinces to the south of that city, was separated, as was *Maranham*, from the general government, and was confided to Salvador Correa, who had recovered *Angola* from the Dutch. He was member of the distinguished family through whose means the French had been expelled from the city which is now the capital of *Brazil*. Correa was, from family associations, attached to the Jesuits, and thus 1660. became an object of dislike to the inhabitants of *Santos* and of *St. Paulo*, from which communities the Jesuit

* A *cruzado* = nearly five shillings.

Fathers were expelled. Having exerted himself successfully in re-establishing them, his conduct was so strongly resented by the *Paulistas* that, when he had set out on an expedition in search of mines, an insurrection was raised during his absence.

Correa received whilst at *Santos* the news of the arbitrary proceedings of his enemies; whereupon he issued a proclamation, containing offers of pardon on the one hand, and threats of punishment on the other. He then proceeded to *St. Paulo*, where in a short time he so won the good-will of the people that he had soon sufficient force at his command to enable him to regain his government.

After a term of office of six years, Barreto was succeeded by the Count of Obedos, in whose time the Carmelites of S$^{ta.}$ Teresa came to establish themselves in *Brazil*, where, in the province of *Bahia*, they ere long erected one of the most sumptuous convents in the possession of their order. The term of office of the same Governor was likewise noted for the occurrence of a dreadful outbreak of small-pox along the coast, from *Pernambuco* to *Rio de Janeiro*, which gave occasion for the display of the most heroic devotion on the part of the members of the Church of Rome, amongst whom are especially mentioned the Brethren of the *Misericordia*. So dire was the mortality that there were not sufficient hands left for agriculture; and thus the pestilence was followed by famine.

It has been mentioned that Vidal, formerly the colleague of Joam Fernandes, had been promoted from the government of *Maranham* to that of *Pernambuco*; in which post, however, he had the disadvantage of not being independent, being under the orders of the Governor-General at *Bahia*. His straightforward, impartial conduct procured him many enemies, who were not unsuccessful in prejudicing the mind of Barreto against him. He was thus placed under arrest, but was

margin: 1665.

subsequently permitted to retain his government until its expiry. The inhabitants of *Pernambuco*, however, had no reason to congratulate themselves upon the governor who was sent to replace him, and whose grasping disposition made him so intolerable that he was at length seized by stratagem and sent prisoner to Lisbon, where, on his arrival, he was condemned to perpetual imprisonment in a fortress in India.

The struggle with Spain was now terminated by a treaty which recognised the independence of Portugal; but *Brazil*, though having nothing to fear from external enemies, was troubled with foes from within its own borders, who attacked the interior settlements of *Bahia* and the islands. Whole families were cut off before succour could reach them; whilst many slaves were killed at their field-work. As a remedy, guards of troops were assigned to the outlying colonists; but, whilst the soldiers were often transfixed by arrows coming from invisible enemies, they for years never once had an opportunity of returning the injury. Such settlers as did not take refuge in the islands were compelled to convert their settlements into small forts. At length the death at the hands of the savages of Manoel Barbosa, who was in command of the garrison at *Cayru*, induced the governor of *Bahia* to complete the conquest of the country in the interior, a task which was confided to a body of *Paulistas* under Joam Amaro.

1668.

1673.

This war having been pronounced just and lawful, all prisoners taken in its course became slaves. The expedition under Amaro is said to have been composed of such a body of experienced man-hunters as, happily, no other locality in the world could supply, many of his men being trained Indians. They proceeded westward to the *San Francisco* river, turning then to the northward. The prisoners captured were sent to the capital in such numbers that their price fell to twenty *cruzados* each;* but the greater

* Under £5.

number were so short-lived that they were considered dear even at that price. Amaro did his work thoroughly, exploring the country in all parts, and so clearing it of savages that they were not again heard of for many years. He was rewarded with the lordship of a town which he founded, and which took his name.

It was at this time that the fertile province of *Piauhi* first became known. Its discovery was due to the possessor of a grazing estate to the north of the *San Francisco*, called after Domingos Affonso. As the interior of *Pernambuco* is subject to droughts, this settler sent out his people to explore more desirable grazing regions inland. In *Piauhi* he found a territory abounding in the richest pasture, and not subject to a like visitation. Whilst exploring the interior, Affonso met with a party of *Paulistas*, who engaged with him in completing the conquest of the country, which was of so inviting a nature that it was soon covered with settlers.

1776. The growing importance of *Brazil* was now shown by the elevation of *Bahia* to the rank of a Metropolitan See, which should comprise the three bishoprics of *Pernambuco*, *Rio de Janeiro*, and *Maranham*. A Franciscan convent was, in the following year, established at *Bahia*, a movement which did not fail to elicit the disapprobation of the thinking portion of the community; since it is evident that in a new country of such immense extent any institution calculated to diminish the spread of the ruling race was opposed to the first principles of political economy. An establishment of Italian Capuchin monks at *Bahia* likewise dates from this period.

1682. The city of *Bahia* was in the year 1682 thrown into a violent state of commotion by the assassination of Francisco Telles de Menezes, the *Alcaide Mar*, who had used his position in so tyrannical a manner as to incur general odium. The assassin, Brito de Castro, who had to avenge an attempt upon his own life, took refuge in the Jesuits' College. The governor, enraged at what had occurred, ordered the Secretary of State, Bernardo de Vieyra, brother to the celebrated missionary, to be thrown into prison. In vain his venerable relative pleaded for his release. The Jesuits' College was, by the governor's orders, surrounded by a *cordon* of soldiers; and so intolerable was the state of things that one of the chief inhabitants of *Bahia* was deputed to proceed to Portugal to make representations to the Crown, the result of which was that the *Marquez* Das Minas was sent out to supersede the aged governor. The Secretary of State was declared innocent, and his brother, who was now between seventy and eighty years of age, was appointed Visitor of the province.

Bahia was in this year visited by a fearful pestilence, of so virulent a nature that of two hundred persons attacked in one day only two recovered. It is remarked that the ravages of this disease were exclusively amongst the Portuguese, the natives escaping unharmed. It gave an opportunity for the display of much benevolence, one opulent widow, *Donna* Francisca de Saude, opening her house as a hospital when the *Misericordia* could no longer contain the sick, and providing for the patients at her own expense. All medicine having proved unavailing, recourse was had to the mediation of a saint, and to *Francis Xavier* is ascribed the staying of the plague.

1686.

To turn to the north:—The Jesuits had indeed been once more admitted to *Maranham*, but merely to the performance of their spiritual functions. The slave-party and the clergy who sided with them had influence enough to cause the Jesuits to be deprived of temporal authority over the Indians, whilst their spiritual management was to be divided amongst the different orders. Vieyra was expressly prohibited from residing in the province. Slave-hunting again ran riot, and was even carried on under the auspices of the governor, under the disguise of missionary expeditions. The *Paulistas* being at this time unable to pursue their attacks on the "Reductions" in *Paraguay*, in consequence of the latter being in a state of defence, turned their attention to the north, obliging the tribes upon the *Tocantins* to apply to *Belem* for protection. The officer sent for this purpose received from the *Paulista* leader a reply stating that, if any one should oppose him in his plans, he would meet with armed resistance, upon which the officer thought it better to return to *Belem*.

The proportions to which the slave-trade became developed, and the utter disregard which was paid to the restrictions on the subject, did not escape notice at Lisbon; and in the year 1680 some new edicts were promulgated on the subject. By one of these, governors were prohibited from engaging in trade, and from raising produce; nor were their servants to be permitted to do so. Another decree abolished Indian slavery, which experience had proved could not be modified or restricted by regulations, and the cruelties connected with which were so notorious. It was enacted that any person thenceforward transgressing this law should be sent home by the first vessel, thrown into prison, and proceeded against. The superintendence of the *Aldeas*, or Indian communities, should be again transferred to the Jesuits.

These laws, it is needless to say, were most unpopular. It was represented that the term of labour of the free Indians in the *Aldeas*, which was to be restricted to two months at a time, was so short as to be useless; and the Chamber of *Belem* sent a procurator to Lisbon to solicit an amendment of this law in particular, and to do his best to procure the repeal of the others. The Portuguese Ministry had granted to some merchants of Lisbon the exclusive privilege of trading with *Maranham* and *Pará* for a term of twenty years — a measure which was strongly resented by the inhabitants of *Belem*. Amongst the stipulations to which the contractors were bound was one requiring them to import five hundred negroes yearly; but during the first year no negroes were imported. Great discontent resulted both at *Belem* and at *Maranham*.

The Portuguese in *Brazil*, although they preferred to depute their labour to slaves, showed themselves eager to engage in the pursuits of trade—the governors of provinces, and even many of the clergy, embarking in such operations. It naturally followed that there was a great outcry against the monopoly which had been issued, all parties being interested in fanning the flame. The malcontents found a leader and exponent of their wrongs in one Manoel Beckman, a native of Lisbon, but of foreign extraction. The cry was against the monopoly and against the Jesuits, whose restoration had coincided with it in point of time. Beckman, inviting some kindred spirits to his *Engenho*, pointed out to them that, if they would obtain their rights, they must act in defiance of the Governor. A conspiracy was formed, of which Beckman was appointed chief, and he was aided by a friar who preached in the cathedral against the monopoly. The conspirators soon numbered sixty, and the people were summoned to a secret meeting within the premises of the Franciscan convent at *S. Luiz*. They were harangued by Beckman, who pointed out that two things were necessary for the good of the State—namely, the abolition of the monopoly and the expulsion of the Jesuits, and he added, that if those present would consult their own safety, not to mention their interests, they would carry out those measures forthwith.

1684.

One of the leading conspirators drew his sword and convinced his audience that their only safety was to proceed in their enterprise. The assembly accordingly hastened to the town, where some murders and other outrages were naturally committed, the authorities being unable to stem the torrent of violence. The *Capitam Mor* was told to consider himself a prisoner in his house; whilst the soldiers submitted themselves to the orders of Beckman, who thereupon convoked a *junta* of the three estates, namely, clergy, nobles, and people. Resolutions were passed deposing the Governor and the *Capitam Mor*, abolishing the monopoly, and expelling the Jesuits. The Chamber ratified the resolutions which had been taken. The late authorities having been confined, Beckman now notified to the Jesuits their banishment from the State, and that until means for transporting them were provided they must remain prisoners in their college. The multitude, under their self-constituted leader, next proceeded to the cathedral, where *Te Deum* was performed in honour of their exploits.

Three persons were appointed to administer the government, pending a reference to Lisbon. The next step was to despatch agents to *Belem*, to invite the people of that place to join the insurrectionary movement; but the only person who could be induced to accept this service was a friar. He was received at *Belem* in a manner which fully justified the reluctance of his colleagues to accompany him. The Chamber carried his papers to the governor, offering their service to inflict chastisement upon the rebels. Francisco de Sa was at a loss how to act, not knowing how far he might depend upon his own people, and yet feeling it incumbent upon him to take some measures for suppressing the insurrection. Meanwhile, the Chamber of *Belem* sent a reply to the insurrectionary leaders, exhorting them to submission. Beckham, however, showed no inclination to recede from the position he had taken; and Palm Sunday was distinguished by the expulsion of the Jesuits from their college; each of them, bearing the emblem of the festival, embarked under a guard in two vessels. One of the two reached *Pernambuco;* the other fell into the hands of pirates.

Antonio de Albuquerque, who was the bearer of the reply from *Belem*, was refused permission to address himself to the people. It is to be remarked that this insurrection at *St. Luiz* was kept to a certain extent within bounds; two vessels belonging to the monopolist company arrived at this time with goods and negroes, the sale of which was conducted on behalf of the Company by its agents. The governor now thought fit to offer a full pardon to all persons concerned in the insurrection, together with a large gratuity to Beckman; the latter, however, rejected the offer, whilst professing his readiness to submit to the orders of his sovereign when they should arrive; and the Governor's agents returned to *Belem* to report the fruitless result of their errand.

Beckman, however, was by no means in an enviable position. He was compelled by the wish of the people to send his brother to Lisbon as their representative; and as those who had flocked to his help gradually broke away from him to attend to their own affairs, he saw himself without the means of supporting his usurped authority. In fact he only maintained his position in virtue of the weakness of Francisco de Sa. Beckman had grievances of his own to complain of against the local authority, which, perhaps, originally urged him to make himself the mouthpiece of the legitimate public outcry against the monopoly. He may also have been stimulated by the impunity which had attended the proceedings of the people of *Maranham*, on the occasion of the expulsion of the Jesuits. It is rash, however, for any one heading a revolt against constituted authorities to found himself upon precedent. In this instance, the insurgent leader soon went beyond the limits which had been reached in the preceding case. Indeed he commenced by imprisoning the *Capitam Mor* and deposing the Governor. He may likewise not have foreseen that as the previous insurrection had been allowed to pass with impunity to its leaders and had been followed by another, the court of Lisbon would consider it the more necessary to be severe on this occasion.

The leader of the revolt took a singular course with the object of making his position more secure. This was to ally himself with Joam de Lima, a well-born Portuguese, who commanded a piratical squadron. This buccaneer now received the offer, on the part of the insurgents, of the port of *Maranham* as a harbour of refuge from which he and they might defy the Portuguese authority.

Meanwhile the news of the insurrection had been received with concern at Lisbon. In the case of the former outbreak, the Portuguese Government had perceived how difficult it would be for them to re-establish royal authority in so distant and extensive a province as *Maranham* by force of arms, and had therefore had recourse to policy. They likewise feared lest the French from *Cayenne* should renew their attempts at making a settlement on the *Amazons* and revive their claims on *Maranham*. It was of the utmost importance that a suitable man should be found for the purpose of suppressing the insurrection in *Maranham*, and the royal choice fell upon Gomes Freyre, an officer whose qualities eminently fitted him for the task before him.

After having encountered not a few difficulties in the way of making preparation for a successful discharge of his mission, Gomes Freyre set out on his voyage, the King accompanying him on board ship to take leave, and, on the 15th of May, he arrived on the coast of *Brazil*. Thomas Beckman, who had been sent to Portugal, was sent back to *Maranham* a prisoner. The new Governor was received with due submission on the part of the Senate and the people. Beckman, indeed, endeavoured to induce the people to oppose his landing; but the measures of Freyre were so decided that there was no time to carry his evil intentions into effect. Having taken possession of the government without opposition, he issued a proclamation granting pardon to all persons, excepting such as had instigated, or had taken a leading part in, the rebellion. Beckman took refuge on his estate sixty leagues distant, whilst his brother was lodged in prison. The reward offered for the former tempted a young man to effect his capture, and he was treacherously apprehended.

By the capture of the ringleader the revolt was at an end; but it was with the utmost reluctance that the Governor could bring himself to condemn him to the penalty which he had incurred. His reluctance was no doubt increased owing to the circumstances of Beckman's base betrayal by a youth whom he had befriended; and it was only upon an attempt being discovered to escape from prison that Gomes Freyre yielded to the representations which were made to him that it was his duty to the public to sign his death-warrant. In doing so, together with that of another ringleader, he at the same time took upon himself the charge of providing for his two unmarried daughters. Beckman's brother received the milder punishment of banishment for ten years; whilst the friar who had incited the people to insurrection was sentenced to be imprisoned in his convent.

The first measure of Gomes Freyre, after seizing the ringleaders of the rebellion, had been to restore all such persons as had been deprived of their offices. He likewise temporarily re-established the monopoly, whilst he recalled the exiled Jesuits. Having convened the Chambers of *Belem* and *St. Luiz*, and received their representations upon the state of the country, he came to the conclusion that the monopoly must be abolished. In his reports to Portugal he found great fault with the conduct of a portion of the clergy who had betaken themselves to trade, and were foremost in inciting discontent. The condition of the people he represented as deplorable; and he advocated, on the plea of necessity, the introduction of negroes for agricultural labour. The Indians he desired to be domesticated as far as might be possible, in order that they might afford to their countrymen an example of submission. But at the same time he pointed out that the same principle which authorized the Portuguese to purchase negroes in Africa was applicable to the savage *Tapuyas*, who granted no quarter in war.

In order to relieve the distress at *St. Luiz*, he took

from its population the materials for a new settlement between the rivers *Itacú* and *Mony*. The two streams in question approach each other so nearly at one point in the interior that it was thought that two forts might suffice for the protection of the delta thus formed against the Indians. In furtherance of this plan, an expedition was despatched against the savages of the *Meary*, who had destroyed the *engenhos* formerly existing in this district. The Governor, having accordingly erected a fort upon the *Meary*, saw the importance of establishing communication overland with *Bahia;* and an enterprising Portuguese, named Joam do Valle, boldly undertook to proceed thither by land. He succeeded in the attempt; but the fatigues which he had undergone proved fatal to his life.

Gomes Freyre found it necessary to despatch another expedition, under Sousa, against the savages of the *Amazons*. After a severe campaign, which lasted over six months, this officer effected the object entrusted to him. The lower valley of the great river was pacified; a number of dangerous chiefs, together with more than a thousand Indians, had fallen; whilst half of that number were brought back in chains.

1687. At this period the position of the French in the north of *Brazil* became a subject of disquietude to the authorities at *Pará*. Although, in virtue of the line of demarcation by Pope Alexander VI., Portugal claimed the entire Brazilian coast, from the *Plata* in the south to the *Oyapok* in the north, the maritime powers declined to admit her title. As early as the year 1608, the country between the *Amazons* and the *Orinoco* had been taken possession of by Robert Harcourt in the name of James I. for England, and that King had made him a grant of the territory lying between the former river and the *Essequibo*, which falls into the sea about the centre of what is now British *Guayana*. The scheme, however, was frustrated, as were all attempts on the part of adventurers of different nations to establish themselves about the *Cabo do Norte* and up the *Amazons*. It was during one of the expeditions of Raleigh that the harbour of *Cayenne* had first been noticed, and it subsequently attracted the attention of Harcourt. Some French adventurers settled at this locality about the year 1631. They had no commission from the Crown nor from any company ; and, being left to their own resources, such of them as survived the hostilities between the native tribes in which they took part, gradually became mixed with the savages.

A few, however, had escaped to France ; and it was on their representations that an expedition was sent out under Charles Poncet, who was appointed Lieutenant-General of the country of the *Cabo do Norte*, a district which was not too minutely defined, and which he interpreted generally to include the whole coast between the *Amazons* and the *Orinoco*. This officer took out with him some four hundred men, with whom he attempted to form settlements at *Cayenne*, *Surinam*, and *Berbice*, which three places now form settlements in French, Dutch, and British *Guayana* respectively. Owing to his cruelty, however, he himself fell a victim to the vengeance of the savages, whilst the various settlements were attacked and cut up. About forty survivors made their escape to *St. Kitts*.

The disasters, however, of *M.* Poncet *de* Bretigny did not deter the company at Rouen from pursuing the enterprise in which they had embarked ; and they continued for eight years after his death to maintain a fort at *Cayenne*. At this date a new company was formed, on the plea that the previous one had failed in fulfilling its conditions to the Crown. The chief of the next expedition, which consisted of seven hundred men, was the *Sieur de* Royville. But *De* Royville was no more fortunate than his predecessor, being murdered on the outward voyage. The twelve associates who had accompanied him lost no time upon their arrival in quarrelling amongst themselves and in beheading one of their number, whilst three others were deported to an island, where they soon fell victims to the savages. The colony was not successful; some of its members perished from disease, and others from hunger; whilst others again were brought to the *boucan*.[1] The survivors were glad to seek the protection of the English, who were by this time established at *Surinam*.

1656. A few years after this occurrence, the Dutch, finding *Cayenne* forsaken, occupied it in the name of the West India Company. This settlement promised favourably; its commander, named Guerin Spranger, fulfilled all the conditions required for forming a profitable colony; but Louis XIV., at this period, gave to a new French company the country between the two great rivers, appointing *M.* le Hevre *de la* Barre governor of *Cayenne*. Five vessels were sent out, having on board a thousand persons, and Spranger had no alternative but to submit. His country was not then at war with France, but high-handed proceedings were the order of the day. The French were so fortunate as to find themselves in possession of a ready-made colony. Two years later it was laid waste by the English; but it was immediately re-occupied by the French. In the war which succeeded the peace of Breda, *Cayenne* was again taken by the

1676. Dutch; but in 1676 it was once more captured by the French under the *Comte* d'Estrees.

Cayenne once more a French settlement, its guiding spirits lost no time in directing their attention towards the possessions of their neighbours. Their attempt to enter the *Amazons* was forbidden by the captain of *Curupá*, whilst five Frenchmen were found by the Jesuits trading for slaves in the interior.

1687. About the year 1687 the province of *Ceará* was so infested by the neighbouring savages that it was declared lawful and necessary to make war against them; and the

---

[1] The *boucan* was a wooden instrument used by Brazilian cannibals for roasting their victims. Hence the word *buccaneer*.

hostilities were prosecuted with such vigour as to free the province from their presence for the future.

In proof that the trade of *Brazil* was steadily increasing, it is stated that, in 1688, the fleet which sailed from *Bahia* was the largest which had ever left that port, and yet that it did not contain tonnage sufficient for the produce. A trade had sprung up between *Buenos Ayres* and *Brazil*, and when it was prohibited, alike by the Spanish and by the Portuguese Governments, goods to the amount of three hundred thousand *cruzados* were left on the merchants' hands at *Nova Colonia*, and of double that amount at *Rio de Janeiro*. The Government showed their appreciation of the importance of *Bahia* by putting its forts in a proper state of defence. Three additional settlements in the *Reconcave* were now large enough to be formed into towns; and the currency in *Brazil* was now put upon a proper footing by a regulation which permitted only milled pieces to pass, the practice of clipping having been hitherto prevalent. 1688.

1694.

The escaped negroes who had taken refuge in the *Palmares* or palm forests, in the interior of *Pernambuco*, have already been mentioned. In the course of threescore years they had acquired strength and daring. Not contented with being left unmolested, they infested several Portuguese settlements; one of their chief reasons being to carry off women. They were under the government of a chief who was elected, and who listened to such whose experience gave them the right to counsel him. He was obeyed implicitly. His people did not abandon the sign of the cross. They had their officers and magistrates; and the greater crimes were punished with death. As they carried on a regular intercourse with the Portuguese settlements by means of their slaves, the evil arising from them as a place of refuge became so great that it was necessary to make an effort to put an end to it.

The negro settlement in the *Palmares* was reputed to be so strong that the authorities of *Pernambuco* long hesitated to attack it; but at length Caetano de Mello determined to make a vigorous effort with the object of exterminating this formidable organization. With this end he solicited from the Governor-General the aid of the camp-master of a regiment of *Paulistas*, and that officer was accordingly directed to proceed to join him. On his way, however, at the head of a thousand men, he unwarily resolved to reconnoitre the *Palmares*, and found himself in front of a double palisade of hard wood, enclosing a circle four or five miles in extent, and within which were some twenty thousand persons. The enclosure contained a rock which served as a look-out station; and it was surrounded by a number of smaller settlements, in which were stationed selected men.

In front of this strong position the *Paulista* leader pitched his camp. On the third day the negroes sallied forth; and so fierce a conflict ensued that more than eight hundred persons were killed or wounded, with the result that the assailants were glad to retreat to *Porto Calvo*. At that point a force of six thousand men was assembled, which had been gathered from *Olinda*, *Recife*, and elsewhere. The retreat gave the negroes time to prepare for the attack which they awaited. Their fighting strength is said to have amounted to ten thousand men. The Portuguese army advanced without delay, and encamped in front of the fortifications. The negroes, not having anticipated an attack of this nature, were unprovided with sufficient powder. On the other hand, the Portuguese had neglected to bring artillery.

Under these circumstances, the struggle between the two parties became one of endurance. Any attempt to cut a way through the palisade was easily foiled; but the negroes not only felt the want of weapons, but likewise that of provisions. The Portuguese, too, were for some time on short allowance; but they were reinforced by large convoys of cattle from the *San Francisco*, and the despair which this sight occasioned to the besieged deprived them of the courage to withstand the attack which was simultaneously made. The gates were hewn down; and the chief and some of his followers, preferring death to renewed slavery, threw themselves down from the rock. The survivors of all ages were brought away as slaves.

About this time the question was formally raised as to the limits of the territory claimed by the French and by the Portuguese, respectively, *M.* de Ferrol, the Governor of *Cayenne*, claiming for France the whole to the north of the *Amazons*. He received for reply that it was the duty of the Portuguese governor to maintain possession of that which had been entrusted to his predecessors and to himself, and which included both sides of the river, together with the whole of the interior. *M.* de Ferrol, after some time, sent an expedition against the fort of *Macapá*, which had lately been erected at the *Cabo do Norte,*' and which surrendered to him. In writing to the governor of *Maranham*, *M.* de Ferrol justified this expedition on the ground that the place was within the limits of the French colony. Three hundred men were at once sent to recover the fort, which was thereupon put into a state of defence, pending a reference to Europe; but, owing to complications in European policies, it was allowed to remain in the hands of Portugal without further demur on the part of France.

Meanwhile the condition of the Indians throughout *Brazil* had gradually improved. For this they were indebted chiefly to the importation of negroes, but partly also to legislation. Throughout all the old captaincies, with the exception of *St. Paulo*, a pure Indian—that is to say one without negro blood—was declared free on demanding his freedom. This consummation must have gladdened the closing days of Vieyra's life. His memorable existence was prolonged to the age of ninety; he having been for seventy-five years a member of the Order of Jesus. His brother Gonçalo survived him by one day.

1696.

CHAPTER VII.

BRAZIL: THE SEVENTEENTH CENTURY.

1600–1700.

AT the close of the seventeenth century the Portuguese race had established themselves along the whole extent of the coasts of the vast region which now forms the Brazilian Empire,—from *Pará* in the north to *Rio Grande Do Sul* at the other extremity. Of the interior of these immense provinces, extensive spaces—equal, indeed, to the size of European kingdoms—were then, and are still, uninhabited. The clouds driven westward by the periodical winds which prevail at certain seasons on the Southern Atlantic, meeting the huge and unbroken barrier of the *Andes*, are forced to discharge their contents in continuous deluges over the entire area of Central *Brazil*, thus giving birth to the most voluminous water-systems which the world contains. But this is not the only result of the almost incessant downfall of waters which is witnessed on the eastern slopes of the *Andes*. Another result is that the superabundant moisture, falling upon a soil under the influence of a burning sun, produces an extent and luxuriance of tropical vegetation such as is nowhere else to be seen on the surface of the earth. This vegetation has hitherto, throughout all ages, baffled the efforts of man to contend with it; and ages will elapse ere the increase of the world's population will force mankind to bend themselves to the huge effort of subduing this teeming virgin forest.

To give any clear idea of the mere extent of the

BRAZIL; THE SEVENTEENTH CENTURY.

region which now forms the Empire of *Brazil* is no trifling task. It is easy to say that it extends from the fourth degree of northern latitude to about the thirty-fourth degree of southern latitude, and that at its widest extent it covers the space between the thirty-fourth and the seventy-third degrees of western longitude. But it will give a far more accurate estimate of the superficies of *Brazil* if we compare its area with something which we can realize. Its area is estimated at 8,515,848 geographical square *kilometres*, or 3,275,326 English square miles,—the area of British India being 899,341 English square miles;—that is to say, *Brazil* has an extent equaling about three and two-thirds that of British India. The area of France is 208,865 English square miles, being considerably less than one-fifteenth of that of *Brazil*. But perhaps the best way of estimating the extent of the Brazilian provinces is to spread out a map of South America and compare their united bulk with that of one of the adjoining countries even of that colossal continent. The contiguous state of *Uruguay*, for instance, covers 73,500 English square miles, being double the area of Portugal; yet Uruguay would scarcely seem to add materially to the superficies of the adjoining empire, of which in extent it forms less than a forty-fourth part. Thus the little kingdom of Portugal annexed in America alone an empire almost ninety times larger than itself.

It may be of interest to give a general idea of the progress which the Portuguese race had made in effecting the conquest and civilization of the regions lying along the immense line of coast indicated above during the seventeenth century. *Maranham* had now been in their undisputed possession for seventy years, its seat of government being placed in the island of the same name. The capital boasted three churches and four convents; the European population of the State was estimated at the middle of the century at about four hundred, a number which in ten years had increased to seven hundred, whilst in 1685 there were more than a thousand Portuguese in the city of *St. Luiz* alone. The rank and privileges of nobles were conferred upon all who had held a commission even for a few months in the local militia; indeed at one place the brotherhood of the *Misericordia*, which consisted of men of inferior rank, could find no recruits, since, with their exception, the whole population had become ennobled.

In order to reward the services of the inhabitants of *Maranham* and *Pará*, it was decreed that none of them should be put to the torture, excepting in such cases as rendered torture applicable to *Fidalgos*; they were likewise not to be imprisoned; but to be held on parole. They received the privileges of the citizens of Lisbon, and were not liable to be impressed either for land-service or for sea-service.

The revenue consisted for the most part of the tenths, which, about the middle of the century, might average five thousand *cruzados*.* There was a duty on wine; but little was imported, as the natives prepared a spirit extracted from maize and from the sugar-cane. A fifth of the slaves taken in lawful war belonged to the Crown. Some idea of the vastness of these provinces may be conceived from the fact that the voyage from *S. Luiz* to *Belem* occupied thirty days. In 1685 the latter city contained about five hundred inhabitants, with a clerical and monastic establishment out of all proportion to its numbers. The tenths of *Pará* and its subordinate captaincies amounted to about four thousand *cruzados*; whilst the saltworks produced two thousand more, and the fisheries an equal amount.

The salary of the Governor-General was three thousand *cruzados*; but on the whole the salaries to the various public officers were so small as almost to compel them to have recourse to other means of living. The priests were said to be of the very lowest order, being chiefly engaged

* £1200.

in securing gain and in exciting discontent against the Jesuits, whose mental acquirements and whose manner of life were alike a reproach to their inferior brethren. The natives of *Brazil* held in the utmost horror and detestation the lot of slavery to which so many of them fell heirs. It is even said that many captives preferred death to being ransomed for the purpose of being thrown into perpetual captivity; and instances are on record when slave-hunters in vain set fire to the dwellings of Indians with a view to inducing them to come out and be captured.

Slave-hunting in *Brazil*, independently of the miserable lot of the captured victims, was attended by an enormous waste of life. Almost all slaves were kidnapped; and great numbers perished before reaching the Portuguese settlements. On their capture they were penned like cattle until a sufficient number were collected, being shut up for months together and exposed to the varying action of the elements. Such being the case, it is not surprising that often but half their number arrived at their destination. The Indians likewise who took part in the hunt, in the service of the slave-dealers, suffered greatly in the expeditions; while the Portuguese themselves returned in a wretched condition, after having penetrated more than two thousand miles into the interior, carrying devastation before them. The object of all this inhuman exertion was, of course, gain—gain to be derived in the first instance from the sale of the slaves, who were to become the means of gain to others. The sole pretext which could be urged on behalf of the slave-hunting was that it was a necessary evil, if such an expression may be used with reference to what may be avoided, since it was impossible for Europeans to perform the work of tilling the earth in such a climate; but, as Southey very justly remarks, that men of European stock are perfectly capable of all the labour which in such climates is required for the well-being of man is abundantly proved by the prodigious fatigues which the Portuguese underwent in seeking slaves to do this "necessary" labour for them.

In *Maranham* and *Pará* the colonists occupied one of the numerous islands per family, the country being so intersected by streams of all descriptions that these became natural and convenient landmarks. Inter-communication was carried on by water; and each family relied on its own means for subsistence. Vegetation being too luxuriant to admit of land for pasturage, game became the only animal food within reach of the colonists, and this, as well as fish, was procured by means of their Indians. This, however, formed but the smallest part of the slaves' occupation, and it is stated that at this period the slaves in *Maranham* and *Pará* were, literally, worked to death,—a statement which is borne out by the fact of depopulation.

In addition to slave-hunting, there were other inducements for traders in the interior. Sarsaparilla and other drugs were found in abundance, as were cinnamon and nutmeg, the vanilla and indigo. Cacao grew in plenty. Of the cultivated produce, cotton was the most important; the cotton of *Maranham* was at this time accounted the best in America. Mandioc supplied the inhabitants with a satisfactory substitute for wheat-flour. Tobacco was one of the branches of agriculture chiefly cultivated in *Brazil* from the first. At the time in question this industry had grown into disuse in *Maranham* from want of hands. As such persons as were without a trade could only procure subsistence by means of slaves, many families in *Maranham* fell into distress owing to their not being able to procure the latter. The Portuguese had grown so accustomed to depend on slave-labour, that they allowed themselves to fall into destitution rather than work for their families; it was thought dishonourable for free men to cultivate the soil.

In strange contradistinction to the apathy of the Portuguese with respect to engaging in agriculture, was the eagerness with which they embarked in commerce. It was found necessary to restrain the civil and judicial officers by means of statute; whilst the clergy showed equal readiness to join in speculations. Still, in spite of every disadvantage, the provinces of *Pará* and *Maranham* gradually, though slowly, acquired population and importance. Such, however, could not be said of the adjoining captaincy of *Ceará*, which possesses neither river nor harbour, and is the least fertile portion of *Brazil*, being subject to fatal droughts. Owing, nevertheless, to the disadvantages which this captaincy possessed for colonization, its native inhabitants were free from the molestations which beset those of *Maranham* and *Pará*.

The settlement of the neighbouring captaincy of *Rio Grande do Norte* dates from the commencement of the seventeenth century. In this province, whilst it was under the Dutch, great efforts were made for exploring the country, civilizing the *Tapuyas*, and improving the general condition of the people. The palace of Maurice of Nassau, together with the buildings and public works erected under his auspices, are solid mementoes of his administration, which is still further commemorated in the history of *Barlœus*. During the government of this Viceroy an attempt was undertaken to discover the vestiges of some people who had possessed the country before the race of savages then existing, an attempt which has left the race in question a subject of curious speculation to the learned in such matters.[*]

Great efforts were made during the administration of Count Maurice to promote the reformed religion throughout the territories under his government. The Protestant missionaries were, it is said, regarded with much jealousy by Vieyra and his brethren. They are reputed to have succeeded to a considerable extent in imparting to the Indians the arts of civilization; but the efforts of the Dutch towards civilizing and humanizing the natives and negroes was con-

[*] *Vide Humboldt's* Researches.

fined entirely to the government and the clergy. Nothing could exceed the barbarity of these invaders, on the whole, towards both races. Their privateers freely seized such Indians as they could entrap on the rivers or on the coasts, and sold them as slaves; whilst of their imported negroes the excessive mortality was imputed by Nassau himself to unwholesome food and physical suffering. It was no unusual thing for these slaves to commit suicide after attempting in vain to kill their masters.

The Dutch conquerors introduced into their Brazilian provinces that almost excessive domestic cleanliness for which their country is remarkable; whilst they increased the pleasures of life by the attention which they, in accordance with their national habits, did not fail to bestow upon horticulture. They reared vines with great success, and from which a wine was made that was much esteemed. Being accustomed to plains and swamps, they did not take advantage of the higher lands in forming their settlements; but the malaria and damp had less evil consequences than might have been anticipated, from the fact of the men being addicted to the free use of wine and tobacco. The Dutch women, however, who were without these counteractants, suffered much from the climate. The country possessed by Holland was only cultivated to an extent of some twelve or fifteen miles inland from the shore. The native industry of the Dutch had not sufficient time to display itself; and the almost continuous hostilities prevented the development of the fisheries. Although the invaders from Holland were in *Brazil* for five-and-twenty years there was very little mixture of races between them and the Portuguese; the difference of religion was an almost insuperable barrier; and when they departed they left little or no trace behind them either in religion, language, or manners.

The population of *Bahia* and the surrounding coast is said to have numbered, in the middle of the seventeenth century, some three thousand five hundred souls, not

BRAZIL; THE SEVENTEENTH CENTURY.

including a garrison of two thousand five hundred. A few years later, however, *Bahia* is described as having fine streets, grand squares, well-built houses, and splendid churches. At the close of the century it is said to have possessed two thousand houses, built of stone. It owed its prosperity, amongst other causes, to its being a place of safety for the new-Christians, who were persecuted with such cruelty in Portugal and Spain. Superstitious as were the Brazilians, even they successfully resisted the establishment of the Inquisition amongst them. If the new Christians were, in *Brazil*, a despised race, they could at any rate count on opportunities of gaining wealth and of retaining it when gained. *Bahia* possessed abundant sources of riches; amongst others its whale fishery, which at one time was considered the most important in the world. At the close of the century it was rented by the Crown for thirty thousand dollars. The staple commodity was sugar.

In general, a scanty population was scattered along the shores and in the islands; and here and there we read of a place, such as *Porto Seguro*, possessing a population of fifty inhabitants. The numbers, on the whole, are so scanty that it seems strange that the Portuguese could have at the same time contended successfully with a foreign invader and with hostile tribes in the interior. *Espirito Santo* had five hundred Portuguese in its district; whilst the population of *Rio de Janeiro* was estimated at five times that number, exclusive of a garrison of six hundred. As a city it was inferior to *Bahia;* it was, however, advancing rapidly in wealth. It owed the eminence which it soon attained, and which it retains amongst the cities of *Brazil*, to its situation relatively to the mines which were soon to be discovered.

Ilha Grande and the island of *S. Sebastian* possessed, in the middle of the century, no more than one hundred and fifty inhabitants each; the population of *Santos* was rather greater. *S. Paulo* boasted some seven hundred inhabitants; its neighbourhood, however, must have contained a considerable number, amongst whom were enlisted the terrible bands of freebooters, who carried desolation and destruction to the frontiers of *Paraguay*, and one band of whom penetrated as far as to the province of *Quito*, where, having encountered the Spaniards, they escaped down the *Amazons* on rafts. The earliest gold found in *Brazil* was gathered at *S. Vicente* in 1655, where it was coined. *S. Vicente*, at this time, had two thousand inhabitants. To the south of this place there was a small settlement at *Cananea*, and a still smaller one at *Santa Catalina*.

It was commonly reported that Indian spices were indigenous in *Brazil*, and that their culture had been prohibited by the Government, lest it should interfere with the Indian trade. Whether this were so or not, an order was given by Joam IV. that every ship touching at *Brazil* on its way from India should bring with it spice plants. These were placed in the garden of the Jesuits at *Bahia*, and two persons were brought from *Goa* who understood the management of cinnamon and pepper plants. But, although the attempt promised success, it was not persevered in; and the subsequent discovery of mines diverted attention from this possible source of wealth. Previously to the finding of the precious metals, the production of sugar was the main object of the inhabitants of the coast.

A sugar-producing *engenho* implied the presence of various artisans, necessary for the continuous work of the machinery belonging to it. That is to say, it was a village-community in itself, more populous than many of the towns so-called then existing. It comprised in general an area of some eight square miles, the condition attached to the holding of this land being settlement and the cultivation of the necessary canes, which were to be sold at a fair price. From fifty to a hundred negroes were employed in each *engenho;* a circumstance which, owing to the great cultivation of sugar in the province, had a marked influence on the population of *Bahia*. A French traveller * estimated the proportion of negroes to the white population as twenty to one; but this is probably the highest proportion which it assumed in *Brazil*. The negroes, according to his account, were exposed to purchase, exactly like beasts at our own cattle fairs, being entirely naked, being handled, as animals are, to test their muscle, and being obliged to show their paces.

The costume of the inhabitants of *civilized Brazil* during the period of which we treat comprised every conceivable variety, from that of the almost entirely nude slave to that of the lady dressed according to the latest fashion from Lisbon. In the more flourishing settlements, such as *Olinda* and *Bahia*, nothing could exceed the luxury of the female costume, the wives of the planters being attired in silks and satins covered with the richest embroidery, with pearls, rubies, and emeralds. Black was the prevailing colour, and the use of gold and silver lace was forbidden by a sumptuary law. In describing the results of holding slaves, it is necessary for the historian to state, with whatsoever reluctance, that the ladies of *Bahia*, even those the most distinguished amongst them, and who passed for being the most virtuous, did not, according to the direct statement of the French traveller above referred to, scruple to adorn their female slaves to the utmost extent, with the object of participating with them in the profits of their prostitution. This particular form of highborn depravity is, in so far as I am aware, peculiar to *Brazil* in the annals of history. The ladies of *Bahia* were so indolent of habit that on going abroad they had to lean on their pages lest they should fall. Even the men,—if men they might be called,—were unable to descend the declivity on which *Bahia* stands, and were carried down on a contrivance called the serpentine, that is to say, a hammock suspended from a pole, a slave

* Frezier.

attending meanwhile with a parasol. Each lady on going from home was attended by two negresses.

The Portuguese in *Brazil* were exceedingly prone to jealousy, and it has been concluded that, as the punishment for convicted unfaithfulness was assured death, it is impossible to believe the often-repeated statement that connubial infidelity on the part of women was remarkably common; but the experience of many countries has shown that neither certainty of punishment nor the probability of detection can be relied upon as preventives of a breach of the marriage law; whilst it is likewise not the less certain that the risk incurred may add to the zest of the crime.

As might be anticipated from the fact that criminals were, from an early period, sent to *Brazil* to swell the ranks of the settlers, the police records of the various settlements are not gratifying reading. In the first place, the courts of justice were, in certain quarters, notoriously corrupt; robberies were committed in open day; whilst quarrels not unfrequently terminated in death. In short, the lives of the Christian settlers were certainly, as a whole, the reverse of being calculated to serve as examples to the heathen whom their missionaries were employed in converting. The very ships which brought out the Fathers too often carried out a supply of criminals whose lives serve as a practical antidote to their doctrines.

Much has been written, and probably with justice, concerning the apathy, the corruption, the extreme superstition, and the dissolute nature of the lives of the clergy in *Brazil;* but, taking them as they were, it is somewhat difficult to realize the picture of what the Portuguese transatlantic possessions would have become had they possessed no Church establishment. From the King down to the lowest peasant, the Portuguese of that age were deeply imbued with faith in the doctrines of Christianity; and, however much they might, in their practice, diverge from its precepts, they were ever ready to compound for their sins by liberal donations to the Church and to charitable establishments. The Church, on its side, however irregular might be the lives of the clergy in general, was bound to keep up a certain degree of outward discipline and of attention to the good works for which it sought donations; whilst, from time to time, a luminary, such as Nobrega and Vieyra, arose in its ranks, stimulating to good works.

We have endeavoured in the preceding pages faithfully to record in so far as our limits permitted, the devotion and extraordinary achievements of such men as Nobrega, Anchieta, and Vieyra: it is but fitting to complete the picture of the remarkable ecclesiastics of the century by taking one from an opposite category. The Father Joam de Almeida, who had sat at the feet of Anchieta, is said originally to have been called John Martin, and to have been a subject of Queen Elizabeth; but, in the seventeenth year of his age, he found himself under the care of the Jesuits in *Brazil*. We are told of an Indian captive, who not only showed no impatience under the torments inflicted upon him by his captors, but who, when offered to be relieved of them, replied that he wished they were greater, in order that his enemies might see how thoroughly he despised them. In somewhat of a similar spirit John Martin, or Almeida, seemed not only to be indifferent to pain, but almost to revel in it. Such a character is not unfamiliar to Portuguese ecclesiastical annals. Those who have visited Cintra will remember the cave of the hermit Honorius, in which he dwelt for fourteen years, and which was of such dimensions as not to admit of his standing upright.* The unfortunate person of Almeida was regarded by him, in his mental capacity, as a natural enemy, which was only to be kept in subjection by perpetual scourgings,

---

* "And lo! deep in yon cave Honorius long did dwell,
In hopes to merit heaven by making earth a hell."
—*Childe Harold.*

which were inflicted by a liberal assortment of implements; but notwithstanding which, he survived to the age of eighty-two. From this fact it must not be inferred that there was anything of evasiveness in his self-inflicted castigations. His constitution had grown accustomed to a form of suffering which his abstemious manner of living rendered possible, and which won for him the reverence of the superstitious population amongst whom he dwelt. On his demise, everything in any way connected with him became inordinately precious. The possession of portions of his autograph was almost too much good fortune to befall any one; but the porter of his convent was enabled to benefit himself and others by distributing drops of his blood and such articles as might have come in contact with the body of the dying saint. Nobrega and Vieyra, having done their work, had been allowed to sink into their rest, comparatively unobserved; but the death of the ascetic Martin created as much agitation as would have been produced by an earthquake. His funeral was attended by the whole population, from the governor downwards, and the multitude would not be persuaded to disperse until each one of them had kissed and embraced the corpse. Here it might have been thought his adoration might have been allowed to end; but it was even found necessary to set a guard over him at night, in order to protect his remains from the depredation of his pious votaries. The guard, however, would seem to have been insufficient for the purpose; since it was ascertained in the morning that one of the shoes of the anchorite was no longer to be found, whilst his pillow had likewise disappeared.

When the corpse of Martin had been committed to its coffin and confined to the grave, it might have been reasonably hoped that it would be allowed to rest in peace, or at least that the devotion of his admirers would cease to be expressed by aggressive acts. Such an idea, however, would betray ignorance of the inventiveness of superstition; since by night the grave was opened, and, the body having been removed, the precious hair was shaved off by a razor, whilst the remaining shoe and stockings were secured.

CHAPTER VIII.

PERU; PROGRESS OF THE VICEROYALTY.

1551-1774.

NOTWITHSTANDING Gasca's wise regulations, the tranquillity of *Peru* was not of long continuance. It was impossible that a country where anarchy had so long prevailed, and which contained so many discontented adventurers, should quietly settle down at once in the ways of peace. Several successive insurrections desolated the land for some years. These fierce but transient storms, however, excited by individual ambition, need not occupy attention. It is sufficient to say that in these contests a number of the early invaders perished. Indeed, as has been already said, of the men whose names are most conspicuous in this nefarious conquest, scarcely one seems to have ended his days in peace.

The Spanish authority being at length consolidated in *Peru*, it is desirable to show, in so far as may be possible, the nature of the government which succeeded to that of the *Incas*. The first visible consequence of the Spanish domination was the diminution in number of the *Peruvians*, to a degree more deplorable than astonishing. However great may have been the mortality caused among them by war, it was slight in comparison to that which resulted when tranquillity had been restored. All were now compelled to labour, their tasks bearing no proportion to their strength, but being exacted, nevertheless, with undeviating severity. Many of them were driven by despair to put an end to their own lives; whilst fatigue and famine destroyed many more. When *Peru* was divided amongst the conquerors, each of the latter was eager to obtain an instantaneous recompense for his services. Men accustomed to the carelessness of a military life had neither industry to carry on any plan of regular cultivation nor patience to wait for its slow returns. Disdaining to profit by the certain results of agriculture in the fertile valleys, they selected for their habitations the mountainous regions, which abounded in the precious mines. In order to develop these, many hands were wanted; and the natives were accordingly driven in crowds to the mountains. The sudden transition from the sultry valleys to the penetrating air of the higher altitudes combined with inordinate labour and scanty nourishment to produce an unwonted despondency, under which they rapidly melted away. In addition to this, large numbers were carried off by that scourge of the New World, the small-pox. These united causes were more than sufficient to thwart such well-meant regulations for the protection of the Indians as were promulgated by the Spanish Government, and as were invariably seconded, if not initiated, by the Church.

Nevertheless, a considerable number of the native race remained in *Peru*, more especially in the more remote regions. The fundamental maxim of Spanish jurisprudence with respect to her colonies was to consider these acquisitions as being vested in the Crown rather than in the State. By the celebrated Bull of Alexander VI., on which Spain founded its rights in the New World, the regions that had been or should be discovered were bestowed as a free gift upon Ferdinand and Isabella. Hence their successors were held to be the proprietors of the territories conquered by the arms of their subjects. All grants proceeded from them, and from them only all power issued,—with the exception, that is to say, of local municipal authority.

On the completion of the Spanish conquests in America, these were divided into two vast governments; the northern one being subject to the Viceroy of *New Spain* [*Mexico*]; the southern to the Viceroy of *Peru*. The former, with which this work has no concern, comprised all the provinces to the north of the Isthmus of *Panamá*. Under the latter were comprehended all the Spanish dominions in South America. It was so inconveniently extensive that some of its districts were separated by more than two thousand miles from *Lima*. Owing to the distance from Spain at which these respective governments lay and the difficulties of communication within them, it was inevitable that much inconvenience should arise. This inconvenience, however, became intolerable as time advanced. The population in the provinces remote from the seat of government complained with reason of their being subjected to a ruler whose residence was placed so far away as for practical purposes to be inaccessible; whilst the authority of the Viceroy over such districts was necessarily feeble and ill-directed.

As a partial remedy for these evils, a third Viceroyalty was later established, in the year 1718, at *Santa Fé de Bogotá*, the capital of *New Granada*, the jurisdiction attached to which included that over the provinces of *Quito*, *Popayan*, *Choco*, and the region called *Tierra Firma*. The Viceroys not only represented the person of the Sovereign, but likewise possessed the full regal prerogatives within the precincts of their respective governments. The external pomp with which they were surrounded was suited to their real dignity and power, their courts being formed upon the model of that of Madrid. The Viceroy had his horse-guards and his foot-guards; his household regularly established; a large number of attendants; and altogether such magnificence as hardly to retain the appearance of delegated authority.

The Viceroys were aided in the discharge of the functions appertaining to their rank by officers and tribunals similar to those in Spain, some of whom were appointed by the King, and others by the Viceroy, but all subject to the latter and amenable to his jurisdiction. The administration of justice was vested in tribunals called *Audiences*, formed on the model of the Court of Chancery in Spain. In the entire Spanish dominions of America there were eleven *Audiences*, of which seven were established in the southern division of the continent,—namely, at *Lima*, *Panamá*, *Santa Fé de Bogotá*, *La Plata* or *Charcas*, *Quito*, *St. Iago de Chili*, and *Buenos Ayres*. The number of judges in each Court of Audience varied according to circumstances. The station was no less honourable than lucrative, and was, for the most part, filled by persons whose merit and ability invested the tribunal with much respect. Both civil and criminal causes came under its cognizance; and for each peculiar judges were set apart.

The distance by which they were separated from the mother country not unfrequently tempted the Spanish Viceroys to arrogate to themselves a power to which even their Master was a stranger, namely, that of intruding themselves into the seat of justice. In order to check such usurpation, laws were repeatedly enacted prohibiting the Viceroys, in the most explicit terms, from interfering in the judicial proceedings of the Courts of Audience, or from delivering an opinion or giving a voice with respect to any point in litigation before them. In some particular cases, in which any question of civil right was involved, even the political regulations of the Viceroy might be brought under the review of the Court of Audience, which, in those instances, might be deemed an intermediate power placed between him and the people, as a constitutional barrier to circumscribe his jurisdiction. Such restraint, however, as the Court might exercise over the person of the Viceroy was limited to advice and remonstrance; in the event of a direct collision between their opinion and his will, what he determined must be carried into execution; they could but lay the matter before the King and the Council of the Indies. The mere permission, however, to remonstrate and to report upon one who represented the sovereign, gave great dignity to the persons composing the *Audience*. Further than this, upon the death of a Viceroy, without provision for a successor, the supreme power devolved upon the *Audience* residing in the capital of the Viceroyalty. The decisions of these courts, in cases affecting sums exceeding six thousand *pesos*, might be carried by appeal before the Council of the Indies.

This supreme Council was established by King Ferdinand in 1511, and perfected by Charles V., thirteen years later. Its jurisdiction extended to every department, whether ecclesiastical, civil, military, or commercial. With it originated all laws and ordinances relative to the government and police of the colonies. By it were conferred all offices, the nomination to which was reserved to the Crown; and to it was accountable every *employé* in America, from Viceroys downwards. It took cognizance of all intelligence arriving from the American colonies, and of every scheme for the improvement of their administration. It was the invariable object of the kings of Spain to maintain the authority of this great Council, whose measures and inspection were, as a rule, wise and watchful. The meetings of the Council of the Indies were held in the place of residence of the Monarch. This body, in fact, more or less corresponded with our own Secretary of State for India in Council. There was, besides, a tribunal or board for the special regulation of commercial matters. This was called *Casa de la Contratacion*, or the House of Trade, and was established in Seville, which port absorbed the commerce with the New World as early as 1501. It took cognizance of all matters appertaining to the annual fleets to and from Spanish America, and its decisions were subject alone to revision by the Council of the Indies.

The policy of Spain, with respect to her colonies in relation to other nationalities, was one of jealousy and exclusion, which augmented in proportion to their increased extent. In forming their American settlements, says the historian Robertson, the Spanish monarchs adopted a system taken partly from the colonizing principle of Greece and partly from that of Rome. The early Hellenic migrations served to enable a state to get rid of its superfluous citizens; the Roman colonies, on the other hand, were military detachments stationed as garrisons in a conquered province. The Spanish settlements in America partook of the nature of both. Whilst they soon became semi-independent, their connection with the mother country was retained by means of the rights of legislation and of the power of nominating the persons who should fill every department of the executive government.

The Spanish adventurers, who laid the foundations of the republics of South America, were much more successful in the work of destruction than in that of creation. Owing to a variety of causes, amongst them being disease, war, famine, the imposition of impossible tasks, the burden of oppressive taxes, transportation from the valleys to the mountains, labour in the mines, and being employed in the place of beasts of burden in expeditions—owing to these, the native population decreased with immense rapidity. On the other hand, owing to the jealously-restrictive policy of Spain in compelling her subjects in the New World to have recourse to the mother country for many of the necessities of life, and which could only be purchased at excessive cost, the numbers of the Spaniards did not increase in the *ratio* that might have been expected. Other reasons contributed to this, the chief one of which was the tenure of land, which was extremely unfavourable to the increase of population. Many of the conquerors obtained permission to convert their *encomiendas*, or estates with serfs attached to them, into *mayorasgos*, a species of fief, which can neither be divided nor alienated. Thus a great portion of landed property, under this rigid form of entail, was withheld from circulation, and descended from father to son unimproved, and of little value either to the proprietor or to the community. In some instances enormous tracts of country were held by one person, the reason being that only extensive districts could afford the number of labourers requisite for the working of mines with any prospect of gain. The evil effects arising from these causes were very apparent; but we must hesitate to accept the computation of Benzoni[*] that in the year 1550 the entire Spanish population in the New World did not exceed fifteen thousand.

It is estimated, likewise, that the enormously expensive ecclesiastical establishment in the Spanish colonies greatly retarded their progress. The payment of tithes was enforced to the full extent, even in the case of articles requiring artificial production. Such fertile and wealthy regions, however, as had fallen to the lot of Spain in the New World through the enterprise of her sons, could not fail in the long run successfully to emerge from the mass of trammels which had been imposed upon them by the ignorance of legislators, the force of circumstances, and the power of superstition. Gradually a new society arose, the component elements of which may be classified as follows:—

In the first place came the *Chapetones*, being the Spaniards who arrived from Europe. The Court of Spain, jealously anxious to ensure the dependence of the colonies on the mother country, made it a rule to fill all departments of the state by Spaniards born. Each *employé* was required to furnish proof of a clear descent from a family of old Christians, untainted by Hebrew or Moorish blood, and uncontaminated by having appeared in the records of the Inquisition.

[*] Hist. Novi Orbis, lib. III. c. 21.

PROGRESS OF THE VICEROYALTY.

Next in order come the *Creoles*, or the descendants of Europeans settled in America. This class very soon began to exhibit the degeneracy which has invariably resulted wherever a portion of a vigorous race inhabiting an invigorating climate has migrated to an enervating one. It resulted, for example, in a marked degree with the Portuguese in India; and if it has not the same result with the English, this is to be attributed entirely to the fact that in almost all instances Anglo-Indians send their children, at an early age, to be brought up and educated in Europe, and that they themselves are being continually recruited from the mother country. In the instance of such English as are born and brought up in India, who are fortunately too few in number to require to be classified like *Creoles*, the invariable rule of nature holds good, as it does amongst the Italians and French who, ever since the Crusades, have lived in greater or less numbers in the Levant, the word "Levantine" being a synonym for moral and physical degeneracy.

Thus the *Creoles*, though many of them were descended from the conquerors of the New World; though others could trace their pedigree to the noblest families of Spain; though some possessed the advantage of great patrimonial wealth, yet, owing to moral and physical causes, as well as to special legislation, sank naturally into a second-class position. Their mental vigour was in a marked degree lost, and such of it as remained was devoted to the indulgences of pleasure and superstition. Even the operations of commerce, in addition to the functions of government, fell to the lot of the *Chapetones* or natives of Spain.

The third class in the Spanish colonists arose from the offspring, either of Europeans with negroes, or of Europeans with original natives of America. These were called, respectively, *Mulattoes* and *Mestizas*, and they multiplied so greatly as to constitute a very considerable portion of the population throughout the transatlantic dominions of Spain. The several stages of descent in this race were distinguished by a peculiar name. In the third generation the hue of the Indian disappeared, and in the fifth the blood of the *Mulatto* became so undistinguishable that his offspring obtained all the privileges of the European. This robust and hardy race were invaluable in the Spanish settlements in practising the mechanical arts.

Amongst the inhabitants of the Spanish colonies, the fourth rank was assigned to the *negroes* pure and simple. They were in several settlements employed chiefly in domestic service. Their superior physical strength, as well as their favour with their masters, gave them an ascendancy over the natives, whom they were wont to treat with such insolence and scorn, that an implacable antipathy arose between the two races. This antipathy, which originated from accidental causes, was no sooner perceived than it was sedulously fomented, great precautions being taken to prevent anything which might form a bond of union between the two races.

Last of all, in the order of society, came the unfortunate native Indians, who had been so ruthlessly dispossessed of all their natural rights. Due regulations determined the nature and extent of the services which these were required to perform, and likewise the amount of the annual tax imposed upon all males between the ages of fifteen and fifty. When the native was an immediate vassal of the Crown, three-fourths of the tax, which may have been on an average about four shillings a head, were paid into the royal treasury. When he formed part of an *encomienda*, a like proportion belonged to the holder of the grant. As the original *encomiendas* were only granted for two lives, they then reverted to the sovereign. The benefit of the labour of the natives in like manner belonged either to the Crown or to the holder of the grant. They were compelled to assist in works of necessity, such as the culture of corn, tending cattle, forming roads, bridges, &c. ; but they could not be constrained to labour for the furtherance of objects of personal gratification or commercial profit. For the purpose of service in the mines they were called out in successive divisions, called *mitas*, in which each person took his turn. In *Peru* each *mita* could not exceed a seventh part of any inhabitants of a district, and was detained at service in the mines for six months at a time. Whilst engaged in this service, however, each labourer was duly paid, receiving from two to four shillings a day; and, after a time, a humane regulation was introduced, forbidding the deportation of the natives of the plains to the elevated regions. No Indian residing more than thirty miles from the mine might be assigned to the *mita* employed in it.

The natives living in town were subject to the Spanish laws and magistrates; but those inhabiting their own villages were left in charge of their *caciques*, by whom their affairs were regulated according to traditional usage. This dignity was in many cases permitted to continue by hereditary descent; and, for the further protection of the natives, the Spanish Court appointed, in the course of time, an officer in each district, who was styled "Protector of the Indians." It was the duty of this functionary to assert their rights and to represent them in courts of justice. Of the reserved fourth of the Indians' tribute a portion was assigned as the salaries for the protector and the *cacique*, the remainder being given for the purpose of their religious requirements, or for their own support in years of famine or other such calamity. Where so much has to be recorded of cruelty and misgovernment on the part of the Spaniards towards the natives of South America, it is gratifying to be enabled to state that hospitals were erected for the benefit of indigent and infirm in *Lima*, *Cuzco*, and elsewhere, where the natives were treated with all humanity.

On a general review of Spanish legislation with respect

to the treatment of the natives of the New World, it is admitted on all sides that, granted that Spain possessed any rights over them at all, her government, from the time of Isabella onwards, was most solicitous for their spiritual and material well-being. Several causes, however, as has been already observed, contributed to thwart the wise and humane legislation on the part of the mother country. Chief amongst these were the distance of the colonies from Spain, and the self-interest of those persons whose duty it was to see the laws and regulations enacted. In *Peru* more especially the Indians are stated to have been much oppressed, the law forbidding their employment at more than thirty miles from their homes being often broken. In several provinces, however, the natives were permitted to enjoy not only ease but affluence—possessing well-stocked farms, and being supplied with all the necessaries and many of the luxuries of life.

An important feature in the history of the Spanish colonies is the condition of the Church in the latter, and its connection with the State. Ferdinand "the Catholic" was likewise Ferdinand the politic; and in his transactions with the Holy See he had a vigilant eye for the interests of his Crown. With an early precaution against the introduction of Papal dominion in America, he solicited and obtained from the Pope, Alexander VI., a grant to his Crown of the tithes in all the newly-discovered countries, upon the condition of making provision for the religious instruction of the natives. Julius II. likewise conferred upon him and his successors the right of ecclesiastical patronage and the disposal of all benefices in the colonies. It is true that these pontiffs were entirely in the dark as to the value of that which was demanded; and when this fact became better known, their successors had occasion to lament their inconsiderate liberality. But the grants were beyond recall, and their consequence was to make the Spanish monarchs the heads of the American Church. In them the administration of its revenues was vested, and their nominations to benefices were at once confirmed by the Pope. Thus was avoided all collision between spiritual and temporal jurisdiction. This limitation of the Papal authority is the more singular when we consider the character of the nation and that of the monarch by whom it was devised.

The hierarchy of Spanish America was constituted similarly to that of Spain. The inferior clergy were divided into three classes, *Curas*, *Doctrineros*, and *Misioneros*. Of these, the first were parish priests; the second had charge of districts inhabited by subjected Indians; the third were employed in converting and instructing independent tribes. The revenues of the Church were immense; its edifices and convents were magnificent, and its display of wealth ostentatious. Nothing could be less suitable for establishments so situated as were the Spanish colonies in South America than the introduction of the monastic system; yet that system was soon to be found there to a most flourishing extent. In a new settlement, where there is room to spread, the main object should be to encourage population; but the Spaniards, with their usual blindness, began from the first to erect convents, where persons of either sex were shut up in large numbers under a vow of celibacy. The numbers who crowded into those abodes of superstition and of listless ease were utterly lost to society; and the consequence of this was the more serious, inasmuch as none but persons of Spanish extraction were admitted into the monasteries.

A considerable proportion of the secular clergy in America were natives of Spain, being for the most part such as had little prospect of advancement in their own country. They were, as a body, not remarkable for their attainments either in science or in literature. But the greater part of the ecclesiastics in Spanish America were regulars. The missionaries of the four mendicant orders had permission from the Pope to accept parochial charges in America, without being subject to the jurisdiction of the bishop of the diocese. It is to these alone amongst Spanish ecclesiastics that we are indebted for our accounts of the civil and natural history of the various provinces. Amongst them may be mentioned the history of the New World by the Jesuit Acosta, and likewise the natural and civil history of *Chili* by the Abbé Molina, from whose work I have quoted, and who, although a Chilian, is so singularly fair towards the sworn foes of his country, the Araucanians. The general purport of Catholic testimony gives but a poor report of the moral character of the South American regular clergy, many of whom are said to have been not only destitute of the virtues to the observance of which they were sworn, but even of ordinary decorum. The vow of poverty was treated with contempt, some of the ecclesiastics becoming amongst the chief oppressors of the natives whom it was their duty to protect. The vow of chastity received as little regard.

These irregularities did not escape the notice of the authorities, and one Viceroy of *Peru* took effective measures for restraining the regulars. They had recourse, however, to such influences at Madrid that their ancient practices were soon again tolerated. Being thus exempt from all restraints, they at length excited such scandal and disgust that Ferdinand VI. was constrained 1757. to issue an edict prohibiting regulars of any denomination from taking charge of parishes; and declaring that, on the demise of the present incumbents, none but secular priests, under due jurisdiction, should be presented to vacant benefices.

The early missionaries admitted natives of America into the Church with such haste that it was utterly impossible for them to comprehend the doctrines which they professed to receive; if for no other reason than that neither priests nor converts were more than superficially acquainted with the other's language. It sometimes

PROGRESS OF THE VICEROYALTY.

happened that from a desire to please their conquerors, or for some other reason altogether apart from conviction, there was a sudden rush to obtain admission into the Church. On the whole, however, it is to be feared that the Spanish ecclesiastics made but small progress in instilling into the natives the real doctrines of Christianity. Even after two centuries had passed, but few natives possessed such spiritual discernment as to be admitted to the Holy Communion. When the Inquisition was established by Philip II. in his transatlantic dominions, in 1570, the natives were exempted from the jurisdiction of that tribunal.

A fresh impulse was given to emigration to *Peru* by 1545. the accidental discovery by an Indian, as he was climbing the mountain in pursuit of a *llama*, of the silver mines of *Potosí*, which poured forth their treasures in such profusion as to astonish mankind. Some idea of the mineral wealth of the Spanish possessions in the New World may be obtained from the computation that, from the year 1492, gold and silver annually entered Spain to the value of four millions sterling. In this figure, which was regularly accounted for, is not included the treasure fraudulently imported free of duty, and which might perhaps amount to nearly as much more. These mines were not worked by the Crown, but by private adventurers, with the natural result that a spirit of gambling was very soon produced, which had a most debasing effect upon the colonial character.

But although the mines of *Peru* were the great attraction of the country, they were fortunately not the only source of wealth. To that country the world owes many products of at least as much value to it as silver and gold. It has been already mentioned that the earliest notice which we have of the potato occurs in Pizarro's first exploring expedition. That adventurer would have smiled had any one suggested to him that the root to which his starving followers had recourse in order to satisfy their hunger might be a greater boon to mankind than even the *Inca's* ransom. To *Peru* we likewise owe, exclusively, the *Quinquina*, or Jesuits' bark, which has perhaps allayed more misery than even Pizarro caused. *Cacao*, and various other products of value, quicksilver being amongst them, likewise come from the same quarter.

1568. *Don* Francisco de Toledo came out to *Peru* as Viceroy in the year 1568. He was a man well advanced in life and of much experience, but of a political morality which is not to be defended according to our ethics; although it might claim numerous precedents in Roman history. With the sole object of increasing public security, and without the least pretence of any crime on the part of the illustrious victim save that of being a living political danger, he put to death the last of the *Incas*, the young Tupac Amaru.

This Viceroy, however, was most conscientious in his desire for the well-being of the people committed to his charge. He was indefatigable as well as prudent in legislating; and he devoted five years to making a journey throughout every district of his Viceroyalty, with such success that the Peruvians admitted that their country had not been so well administered since the time of the good Tupac Yupanqui. It is to this governor that the University of St. Mark at *Lima* mainly owes its existence; and he had the advanced judgment to perceive that the two main sources of Peruvian wealth were corn and wool, rather than silver and gold. It was to the fact that *Don* Francisco de Toledo, who remained in *Peru* till 1579, was accompanied in his journeys by the Jesuit D'Acosta that we owe the valuable natural history of *Peru*, composed by that writer, the results of fifteen years of literary labour.

The commercial policy of Spain in forbidding all trade between her colonies and other nations had, in the course of time, a singularly retributive effect upon herself. Owing to various causes, amongst which was the expulsion by Philip III. of the Moors, her industrial population became so reduced that that country was at once obliged to contract her operations of war and of peace. From want of men her fleets were ruined, and from the same cause her manufactures had sunk into decay; even her agriculture was insufficient for the national consumption. The law respecting colonial trade was still enforced, and the mineral wealth of the *Andes* still flowed into Spain; but the necessities of demand and supply were above law, and her merchants had to look to other countries for the supplies which were to be sent to America in return, and thus the gold and silver merely passed through Spain on its way to England or to Holland, to France and Italy. In the name of Spanish firms those of the above nations sent their goods to America, and at length it was computed that, of the European goods supplied to the Spanish American provinces, not more than a twentieth part were of Spanish growth or fabric. The climax of this state of things was arrived at when the lord of the mines of *Potosí* was constrained to issue an edict raising copper money to a value in currency nearly equal to that of silver.

1611.

The fleets, which supplied the transatlantic colonies, were distinguished by the name of *Galleons* and *Flotas*, respectively, and were equipped annually, taking their departure from Seville and latterly from Cadiz. The galleons touched first at *Carthagena* and then at *Porto-Bello*. To the former port resorted the merchants of *Santa Martha, Caraccas, New Granada*, and other provinces; the latter port was the emporium which supplied *Peru* and *Chili*. At the right season of the year the product of these countries was transported by sea to *Panamá*; whence, as soon as the appearance of the fleet was announced, it was conveyed across the isthmus, on mules, and down the river *Chagre* to *Porto-Bello*, the noxious climate of which village gave it the unenviable distinction of being the most unhealthy spot in the world. For the greater part of the year it was the residence of negroes and mulattoes, but during the six weeks of the fair it was a *Nigni-Novgorod*, in which was transacted the richest traffic of two hemispheres. The *Flota* proceeded to *Vera-Cruz*, for the supply of *Mexico*.

The restrictive regulation of Spain, by which her enormous colonial trade was confined to a single port, had, of course, the effect of throwing the commerce into the hands of a few houses, who could regulate their own prices, with the result of checking enterprise and diminishing production. The object of the monopolists was, not to supply the colonies with as much goods as the latter could consume and could afford to purchase at prices remunerative both to producers and to merchants; but to throw upon the markets such a moderate amount of goods as might secure exorbitant prices. There were not wanting Spanish statesmen and political-economists who could discern the ruinous effects of such a state of things; and the most extravagant measures were suggested with a view to check them. It required, however, the convulsion produced by civil war, and the contact into which Spain was thus thrown with foreign nations, to rouse her into vigorous action.

The monarchs of the Bourbon line took measures to suppress a state of things which had overturned the system of Spanish trade with America. The trade with *Peru* was now thrown open to the French, whose King granted the privilege to the merchants of St. Malo, who, unlike their grasping competitors of Cadiz, furnished the Pacific Viceroyalty with European goods in liberal quantity and at a moderate price. The result was that the trade of Spain with her own chief colony was on the point of being extinguished. Peremptory instructions had accordingly once more to be issued, forbidding the admission of foreign vessels into any port of *Chili* or *Peru*.

But on her escape from this danger Spain found that she had incurred another. The treaty of Utrecht conveyed to Great Britain the *Asiento* for supplying Spanish colonies with negroes, and further granted to that country the privilege of sending annually to the Fair of *Porto-Bello* a vessel of five hundred tons with European commodities. British factories soon arose at *Carthagena* and *Panamá*; and the agents had ample means of becoming acquainted with the condition of the American provinces, with the result that contraband trade greatly flourished. Thus, by the aid of a system of wholesale bribery of the revenue officers, nearly the entire commerce of Spanish America fell into the hands of foreigners. The squadron of *galleons* was reduced from fifteen thousand to two thousand tons.

It was not to be expected that Spain should tamely submit to such a state of things. Her first measure, undertaken with the view of improving matters, was to establish along her colonial coasts a system of guard-ships, with the object of preventing smuggling. The British colonial commerce, with the Spanish settlements, was, however, so firmly established that it would not be put down; and the Spanish coasts were so extensive that no system of guardships could exercise a sufficiently vigilant watch. The consequence was, in the first place, complaints, and then, acts of violence; which brought on another war 1739. between Great Britain and Spain, the consequence being that the latter country was released from the terms of the *Asiento* granted by the treaty of Utrecht.

Left at liberty to regulate her own colonial trade, Spain now profited by experience in so far that she was induced to permit a considerable part of her commerce with America to be carried in *register* ships; which were fitted out during the intervals between the stated periods for the sailing of the *galleons* and the *flota*, by merchants at Seville and Cadiz, who obtained a license for this purpose. The advantage of thus regularly supplying the demand in the colonies was soon perceived to be so great that, in 1748, the *galleons*, which had been an institution during two centuries, were abolished; whilst the single vessels no longer proceeded to *Porto-Bello;* but, sailing round *Cape Horn*, conveyed directly the productions of Europe to the Chilian and Peruvian ports.

It may seem strange to a generation accustomed to read day by day the notice of events occurring in the most remote parts of the globe almost as soon as they happen, that a nation such as Spain, possessing as it did enormous foreign possessions, could have been contented with receiving news concerning their progress once only in the course of each year. Such, however, was nearly always the case, until about the year 1740, when register ships were permitted. Previously to that date the annual fleet of *galleons* was the sole means of postal communication between the mother country and her South American possessions. It is true that news of passing transatlantic events occasionally reached Spain through other nations, whose intercourse with her colonies it was her constant object to repress. It was not until the year

1764. 1764 that packet-boats were appointed to be despatched on the first day of each month from Coruña to *Havana* or *Porto Rico;* whence letters were conveyed in smaller vessels to *Vera Cruz* and *Porto-Bello*, to be forwarded from there to the north or to the south, as the case might be. A packet-boat sailed once in each two months for the river *Plata*, to supply the districts on the eastern side of the *Andes*. As these packet-boats were permitted to take out and to bring home a stated amount of produce, Coruña, from this time forward, shared with Cadiz the profits of the colonial trade.

1774. The year 1774 marks a further advance in Spanish liberal colonial legislation, the Viceroyalty or provinces of *New Spain*, *Guatemala*, *Peru*, and *New Granada*, respectively, being permitted the privilege of free-trade with each other. This was followed, four years later, by

PROGRESS OF THE VICEROYALTY.

the promulgation of an entirely new commercial code for the Indies, the consideration of which more naturally falls within the chapter relating to the Viceroyalty of *Buenos Ayres*. I may conclude this *resumé* of the Viceroyalty of *Peru* by a statement of the actual profit in specie, which the mother country is estimated to have derived from that possession.

The best Spanish authorities are agreed in considering that the Sovereign, owing to various causes, the chief being peculation and smuggling, was defrauded of about one half of the colonial revenue which legitimately belonged to him. But, notwithstanding corruption and illicit importation, the revenue derived by the Spanish monarch from his American possessions was still very considerable. It arose from taxes, which may be divided into three branches. The first includes what was paid to the King as Lord Superior of the New World, namely, the duty on the produce of the mines and the tribute exacted from the natives. The second branch comprehended the duties upon commerce. The third included such dues as came to the King in his capacity as temporal head of the colonial Church and as administrator of its funds. It is estimated that *Peru* yielded to the Crown a revenue of about a million sterling, one half of which may have been consumed in the expense of the provincial establishments. This amount, or whatever it may have been, it is to be remembered, accrued to the Spanish Crown from this important colony, *in addition* to the wealth derived from it by the parent state by means of its exclusive trade.

CHAPTER IX.

VICEROYALTY OF NEW GRANADA; CAPTAIN-GENERALSHIP OF VENEZUELA.

1535–1790.

FOR some time after the disastrous failure of the attempt of Las Casas to found a colony on the *Pearl Coast* of *Cumaná*, the northern portion of Spanish South America, from the *Orinoco* westwards, is almost lost to history. The powers working for good had signally failed, and the powers of evil seemed to have it almost all their own way. The regions discovered by the Spaniards were so vast, in proportion to the numbers of the discoverers, that many of them were long lost to view, and probably to memory. Such was the fate of the territory which borders the *Orinoco*, a great river flowing from the *Cordilleras*, and which throws itself and its many tributaries by forty outlets into the ocean.

It was in the year 1535 that the Spaniards first attempted to ascend this stream; but, not finding the mines they sought, they looked on it with indifference. Nevertheless, the few Europeans there sown applied themselves with such energy to the culture of tobacco that they were enabled to supply, yearly, some cargoes of this plant to the foreign vessels which came to purchase it. But this traffic was forbidden by the mother-country; whilst some enterprising corsairs twice pillaged this establishment, which could not defend itself. These disasters caused it to be forgotten.

Lying behind these extensive coasts to the westward in

the interior, is the region to which the Spaniards gave the name of the kingdom of *New Granada*, the name being applied in consequence of a resemblance which was detected between the plain around *Santa Fè de Bogotá* and the royal *Vega* which adjoins the historical Moorish capital. *New Granada* was a most extensive region, comprising as it did the entire country from sea to sea in the north, lying between 60° and 78° longitude, and from 6° to 15° of latitude.

Bogotá was attacked, from the south, by Benalcazar, 1526. the governor of *Quito*; whilst Ximenes de Quesada, who had disembarked at *Santa Marta*, marched against it from the north. They did not fail to meet resistance, which, however, was no match for Spanish discipline, arms, and valour; and the above-named leaders had the renown of adding another grand possession to the South-American dominions of their sovereigns. In the course of time the more distant provinces, of which *Bogotá* was the centre, became subject to its government. There were, however, a number of the inhabitants of this vast and varied mountainous region who either retained, throughout, their barbarous independence or who regained it from time to time.

Ximenes de Quesada came to America about the year 1535, in the suite of the Governor of *Santa Marta*, by 1535. whom he was selected to lead an expedition against the *Chibchas*, who dwelt on the plain of *Bogotá* and around the head waters of the *Magdalena*. Setting out in April 1536 with eight hundred men, he succeeded in pushing his way through the forest and across innumerable streams. He contrived to subsist for eight months, during which he traversed four hundred and fifty miles, enduring meanwhile the very utmost exertions and privations that human nature could support. It was not given to this leader to meet with an adversary sufficiently powerful or wealthy to confer upon him by his capture the splendour which has attached itself to the names of the conquerors of *Montazuma* and of *Atahualpa*; but it may be doubted whether, in so far as may be judged by reading the accounts of their several exploits, one or the other of those adventurers had more difficulties to surmount than had Ximenes de Quesada.

When he and his men had at length reached *Barranca*, they were arrested by a downpour of rain, which literally covered the country; but, in face of such discouraging circumstances, Ximenes persisted in proceeding. Sending on a party of twelve men, under Captain San Martin, he remained with the rest of his detachment, sleeping at night in the tops of trees, and subsisting on a small allowance of maize and horse-flesh daily.

On the return of San Martin with a favourable report of a cultivated country beyond, Ximenes boldly determined to pass over the mountains of *Opon*, in which attempt he lost twenty-one men in gaining a height of five thousand five hundred feet above the sea. He had recourse to ropes for pulling his horses up. On the summit a land of abundance awaited him; and as, like other Spanish conquerors of the New World, he held the convenient creed that the heathen had been given to him for his inheritance, he felt no scruple at all from the fact that the region which he and his followers meant to appropriate afforded the means of subsistence to a numerous population, which it would be necessary to dispossess.

When he had surmounted the natural difficulties in his path, his remaining force consisted of but one hundred and sixty-six men, with sixty horses. On March 2nd, 1537, he resumed his advance; and, as usually happened, the mere sight of his horsemen terrified the Indians into submission. At *Tunja*, according to the Spanish historians, he was treacherously attacked whilst resting in the palace of one of his chiefs. That he may have been so is of course possible; but the fact would commend itself the more readily to our belief had it been narrated by a *Chibcha* writer. In any case, the chief was taken, and, after much slaughter, Ximenes found himself the absolute possessor of immense riches, one golden lantern alone being valued at six thousand *ducats*.

From *Tunja* Ximenes marched upon the sacred city of *Iraca*, where two Spanish soldiers accidentally set fire to the great Temple of the Sun. The result was that, after a conflagration which lasted for several days, both the city and the temple were utterly destroyed.

But the inhabitants of this new region of the votaries of the Sun were not yet fully subdued; and, on his return towards *Tunja*, Ximenes had to encounter the force of twelve thousand desperate natives. His arms and his horses were again successful; and, after his victory at *Borja*, he received the submission of several *caciques*, and was enabled to divide among his soldiers no less a booty than forty thousand pounds in gold and eighteen hundred emeralds.

Ximenes de Quesada was neither more nor less particular than was Cortez or Pizarro in the means which he employed in order to gain his end. His object at present was to obtain information as to the retreat of a chief, whose property it was his intention to appropriate. With this view he seized upon two youths, whom he ordered to be tortured. One of them died under the operation; but by the other, who was either stronger or less courageous, Ximenes was conducted to the retreat of the chief, who was killed in the skirmish which ensued. His people fought desperately for their independence, but were overcome by the invaders, by the aid of an alliance with a pretender to the succession.

This traitor to his country's and his race's cause soon met the fate which he deserved. Imitating the Roman policy of sparing the weak and battling the powerful, the Spaniards in America were ever on the watch to take advantage of local jealousies; to which cause they owed their conquest of *Mexico* and many of their successes in the southern continent from *Peru* to *Araucania*. On this occasion the aspirant to the *Chibcha* crown swore allegiance to the King of Spain, the proof required of his sincerity being that he should deliver up the treasures of his predecessors. In the usual vaunting style of a barbarian king, he undertook to fill, within six weeks, a whole room with gold and emeralds. That he should have failed to do so was probably inevitable; but that his failure was owing to bad faith to the Spaniards was obviously an absurd imputation. He had, however, aroused their lust for plunder, and his fault was not to be forgiven. He was accordingly put to death with those refinements of cruelty of which the Spaniards were such masters.

On the 9th of August, 1538, was founded the city of *Bogotá*. Ximenes was soon here joined by Frederman, a subject of the Emperor Charles V., with one hundred and sixty soldiers, with whom he had been engaged in conquering *Venezuela*; and likewise by Benalcazar, the conqueror of *Quito*. This latter warrior had crossed the continent in triumph at the head of a hundred and fifty Spaniards, together with a multitude of native followers.

In such a wholly-unprecedented state of affairs, it is not to be wondered at that these Spanish captains, elevated severally from a humble condition to the rank of independent generals and governors, should have departed from all subordination, and should have taken for their principle that might makes right. Accordingly, it was the first idea of Benalcazar to combine with Frederman in order to expel Ximenes from his conquests. But, as he might perhaps have foreseen, the same idea had already occurred to the other, and the adventurers from *Venezuela* were, in consideration of the payment of ten thousand *dollars* to Frederman, enrolled amongst the forces of Quesada.

Benalcazar, in turn, entered into an arrangement with the two others to appoint a governor of all their territories during their absence from America, for the purpose of laying their claims before Charles V. In this representation they were not all equally successful. Benalcazar was declared independent of *Pizarro*, and was made governor of *Popayan;* Ximenes de Quesada was fined to the amount of one thousand *ducats;* was banished for one year, and was suspended for five years from office; whilst Frederman was judged to be an interloper, and obtained nothing. Shortly afterwards, however, the Emperor remitted the punishment against Ximenes, and appointed him marshal of the kingdom of *New Granada.* On his return to *Bogotá* in 1551, he, to his credit, exhibited an energy in protecting the people of the country against their invaders, equal to that which he had displayed in effecting their conquest.

Ten years later he commanded a force, organized to repel an attack from the ruler of *Venezuela;* shortly after which he was appointed *Adelantado* of the kingdom of *New Granada.* He devoted three years, and an enormous amount of toil and money, to an absurd expedition in quest of the fabled *El Dorado.* To the search of this myth were devoted three hundred Spaniards, two thousand Indians, and twelve hundred horses; of which martial array only twenty-four men and thirty-two quadrupeds returned, mutely to tell the tale of the supreme folly of their leader.

Of the life of a man who had shown himself possessed of such great qualities, in whatsoever way they had been applied, as had Ximenes de Quesada, all prominent details are interesting. It may therefore be noted that, after having founded in 1572 the city of *Santa Agueda*, this conqueror and knight-errant died of leprosy, leaving behind him debts to the amount of sixty thousand *ducats*, which circumstance would seem to have rendered it somewhat unnecessary for him to insert in his will his desire that no expensive monument should be erected over his grave. His body was transferred to *Bogotá.*

The importance of *New Granada* in the eyes of the

Spaniards lay in its being the source whence the best emeralds were procured. Many of these had found their way into *Peru;* but the rude conquerors, who were under the impression that emeralds were as hard as diamonds, having submitted them to the test of the hammer, came to the conclusion that they were valueless. In this manner many were destroyed; and the loss became the greater owing to the fact that it was impossible to discover the mine whence the *Incas* had procured them. The discovery of *New Granada* luckily supplied this important want. The provinces of *Popayan* and *Choco* had the further merit of supplying gold; which was found on the surface of the earth, and which could therefore easily be gathered by the simple means of washing.

The court of Madrid was dissatisfied that a region which had been lauded as possessing great natural advantages should furnish it with such few commodities, and those in so small quantities. It drew therefrom the conclusion that the country under the superintendence of the Viceroy of *Peru* was too vast for all parts of it to receive due attention, and that the development of the northern region would be better assured under a separate government. Accordingly, in the year 1718, the Viceroyalty of *Peru* was divided into two portions, the northern region, from the frontiers of *Mexico* as far as to the *Orinoco*, and on the Southern Sea from *Veragua* to *Tumbez*, forming the Viceroyalty of *New Granada*, of which the capital was *Bogotá*. To this region, likewise, was assigned the inland province of *Quito*. The Viceroyalty of *New Granada*, in fact, comprised what now forms the Republic of *Venezuela*, the United States of *Columbia*, and the Republic of *Equador*.

Although this was undoubtedly a step in the right direction, its good results were not at once apparent. It might have been foreseen that it would take some time as well to form capable administrators as to call order out of confusion, and to instil the habits of industry into people long used to idleness and free-living. Nevertheless, the change of things was not without effect, and the good results became by degrees apparent in Spain. Here, as elsewhere in those imperfectly-controlled regions, smuggling was the rule; and it is said that half of the gold amassed by the colony was fraudulently sent abroad, chiefly by way of the rivers *Atrato* and *Hache*. With a view to stopping this traffic, forts were erected on these streams; which, however, were ineffectual in securing the end in view.

Communication between one province and another, even between one town or village and another, was difficult or impracticable. Every traveller was more or less exposed to be robbed or to be killed by the independent Indians; but these enemies, formerly fierce and implacable, yielded by degrees to the efforts of the missionaries, and to the acts of good-will on the part of the strangers, which replaced the barbarities of a more savage age. Notwithstanding the bounties of nature in this region, many of its provinces drew their subsistence from Europe or from North America. The cost of transport from place to place forbade the culture of grain in the interior beyond the amount requisite for each individual locality.

The town of *Santa Fè de Bogotá* is situated at the foot of a height at the entrance to a vast plain. In 1774 it possessed three thousand two hundred and fifty families, or about sixteen thousand inhabitants. It was the residence of an Archbishop, holding a jurisdiction of immense extent, and who, as Metropolitan, was inspector of the dioceses of *Quito, Panamá, Caracas, Santa Marta,* and *Carthagena*. It was by way of the last-named place, although it was distant three hundred miles, and by the river *Magdalena*, that *Santa Fè de Bogotá* communicated with Europe; whilst the same route led to *Quito*.

The province of *Quito* was likewise of immense extent, but was for the most part covered with forests, or composed of marshes or deserts, inhabited here and there by wandering savages. Spaniards can only be properly said to have occupied and governed a valley of some eighty leagues in length and fifteen in breadth, formed by two branches of the *Cordilleras*.

Quito is one of the most lovely regions which the world possesses. Being in the centre of the Torrid Zone, it enjoys a perpetual spring. Nature has here gathered together all the influences which can modify the heat of the tropics, the neighbouring mountains being covered in their vast extent by snow; whilst constant breezes refresh the plains throughout the year. But, as might be expected, so elevated a region, and one having an atmosphere so charged with electricity, is often the scene of the most violent tropical thunder-storms, the terrors of which are not unfrequently added to by earthquakes. The excessive humidity at one time is often fatal to the cultivation of grain; whilst, on the other hand, contrasting seasons of heat produce dangerous maladies. Nevertheless, on the whole, the climate is a very healthy one. The air is perfectly pure, and is free from the presence of the disagreeable insects so prevalent in other parts of the continent.

The humidity of the atmosphere, and the action of the sun, succeeding each other in constant alternation, and being always sufficient for the development of plants, an almost perpetual succession of vegetation ensues; for no sooner is one plant gone than another begins to arise in its place. The trees are covered perpetually with green leaves, and adorned with sweet-smelling flowers, or laden with tropical fruits in every stage of development. This province was said to be the most populous in America. It possessed a number of towns with populations varying from ten to thirty thousand. The people of *Quito* had, fortunately for themselves, escaped the lot of labouring in the mines; since those which this district possessed were too poor to pay the expenses of working them. They must have been poor indeed, since the Spaniards consented to relinquish a mode of acquiring riches which cost them nothing but the blood of their slaves. Freed from this source of labour, the inhabitants of *Quito* were more usefully employed in manufactures, the produce of which was exchanged for wine and oil, and other commodities which were foreign to this elevated region. Notwithstanding, however, its natural advantages, *Quito*, in the latter part of last century, had sunk into an extreme degree of poverty.

This province possessed, in quinine, one production which has been ever since its discovery of the highest value to the human race, and which formed, in the colonial period, the sole article of export. The only precious portion of the *quinquina* tree is its bark, which requires no other preparation for its use than being dried. At one time the *quinquina* was supposed to be peculiar to the territory of *Loxa*, the finest quality being produced on the mountain of *Caganuma*. Later researches, however, prove that the same tree exists at *Riobamba*, at *Cuenca*, and at *Bogotá*. Europe is indebted for the introduction of this most precious article to the Jesuits, who made its invaluable qualities known at Rome in the year 1639. In the following year its use was established in Spain by Juan de Vega, physician to the Vice-Queen of *Peru*, its price being a hundred crowns a pound. The price which the invaluable article commanded and deserved, led, as a matter of course, to adulteration; and even the distant inhabitants of *Loxa*, being unable to supply the demand for genuine *quinquina*, filled up the void by a mixture of the bark of other trees. This proceeding, however, rebounded on themselves, since it deprived their special product of its unique reputation; whilst, at the same time, it led to a more diligent search for the same plant elsewhere. The natives of the region which furnished *quinquina* were in the habit of using a simple infusion of the bark in cases of fever, before they were taught by M. Joseph *de* Jussieu to produce the extract.

SOUTH AMERICA.

1728. In the year 1728 a body of merchants of *Guipuscoa* received an exclusive right to the commerce with *Caracas* and *Cumaná*, on condition of their clearing these coasts of interlopers—that is to say, of the Dutch, who, from their island of *Curaçoa*, monopolized the lucrative trade in the nuts of the cacao-tree, thus compelling the Spaniards to receive from abroad the produce of one of their own colonies. The new company, which was under the necessity of landing its cargoes at Cadiz, conducted its operations with such success that the above-mentioned reproach was soon removed; whilst the inhabitants of *Caracas* received such an impetus to their industrial life that, ere the company
1731. had been three years in existence, it was deemed expedient to detach from the Viceroyalty of *New Granada* the provinces of *Venezuela, Maracaibo, Varinas, Cumaná*, and Spanish *Guyana*, and to form them into a separate Captain-Generalship, the residence of the ruler being fixed at *Caracas* in *Venezuela*.

1771. In the year 1771 there were scattered on the banks of the *Orinoco* thirteen villages, which numbered amongst them four thousand two hundred Spaniards, half-castes or negroes, who possessed considerable property inland, besides twelve or thirteen thousand cattle, mules or horses. At the same period the Indians who had been detached from savage life were distributed in forty-nine hamlets. In all there were sixty-two centres of population, containing sixteen thousand six hundred people, three thousand one hundred and forty properties, and seventy-two thousand head of cattle.

Up to this period the Dutch from *Curaçao* monopolized the trade with this establishment. In return for the goods which they supplied, they received payment in tobacco, hides, and herds; all the affairs being concluded at *St. Thomas*. The Europeans and the negroes carried out their transactions themselves, but those affecting the Indians were conducted by the missionaries.

The province of *Venezuela* does not bear a high name

for government, even amongst the States of South
America; but, in estimating Spanish civilization in this
quarter, it is only right to consider the state of things
which it displaced. The tyranny, we are told, which
was exercised by the savages along the banks of the
Orinoco towards their women was such that infanticide
of their female children became a common practice on
the part of the latter; in order that their offspring might
be spared a repetition of their own dreadful lot, which is
thus described to a missionary by one of themselves:—

"Would that my mother had suffocated me at my
birth! I should then be dead, but I should not have
felt death, and I should have escaped the most miserable
of lots. How much have I undergone, and who knows
what sufferings are reserved for me! Figure to yourself,
Father, the miseries which an Indian woman has to undergo
amongst Indians. They accompany us to the fields
with their bows and arrows: we go there bearing one
infant which we carry in a basket and another at the
breast. They go to hunt or to fish, whilst we dig the
earth; and, after having undergone all the fatigue of
culture, we have to undertake that of the harvest. They
return in the evening unburdened: we bring back roots
for their food and maize for their drink. Once at home,
they make themselves happy with their friends; whilst
we go to gather wood and to bring water to cook their
supper. When they have eaten, they go to sleep: we
pass the greater part of the night grinding the maize and
making their *chica*. And what is our reward for our
vigils? They drink, and whilst they are in their cups
they drag us by the hair and kick us about.

"You know, Father, if our complaints are well founded.
What I tell you, you yourself see every day; but our
greatest misfortune of all is one unknown to you. It's a
sad lot for a poor Indian woman to serve her husband
like a slave, sweating with labour in the fields and deprived
of repose at home. But it is still worse to see

him, at the end of twenty years, take another wife, young, and without sense. He becomes attached to her, and she beats our children, orders us about, and treats us like servants ; and if we make the slightest murmur of complaint we are beaten with the branch of a tree. . . . What has an Indian woman better to do than to withdraw her child from a servitude a thousand times worse than death! I repeat, Father, would to God my mother had loved me enough to bury me at my birth!"

. . . .

In the year 1670 a party of buccaneers under Morgan reduced the castle of *San Lorenzo* at *Chagres*, and captured and burned the town of *Panamá;* for which reason the site of that settlement was transferred to the position it at present holds, being six miles distant from old *Panamá.* In the year 1680 the same Filibusters, under other leaders, having crossed the isthmus, took the city of *Santa Maria;* which proceeding led, five years later, to the closing of the mines of *Cana.* In the year 1698 one William Paterson undertook to establish a Scotch colony at *Puerto Escaces* on *Caledonia Bay.* Early last century several towns were established on the Atlantic Coast by Catholic missionaries, and likewise on the rivers flowing into the Gulf of *San Miguel;* but unfortunately all these were destroyed by the Indians, with whom, in 1790, a treaty of peace was concluded, in virtue of the terms of which the Spaniards abandoned all their forts in *Darien.*

NOTE.—Chapter IX. is chiefly founded on
"*Historia del descubrimiento y colonizacion de la Nueva Granada*" (Paris, 1849), by J. Acosta ; and "*Memorias para la historia de la Nueva, Granada*" (Bogota, 1850), by Antonio de Plaza.

CHAPTER X.

PROGRESS OF THE COLONY.

1604-1792.

DON GARCIA RAYMON was once more appointed to the government of *Chili*, and received one thousand soldiers from Europe and a fourth of that number from *Mexico*. He thus found himself at the head of three thousand regular troops, besides auxiliaries. With such a force at his disposal, it was natural that he should once more invade *Arauco*, in which territory he erected a fort; the existence of which, however, was of short duration, it being abandoned to the Araucanians. Raymond divided his force into two parts, both of which were successively attacked and defeated by the new *Toqui*, Huenecura, so complete being the rout that every single person was killed or taken. Such was the dread entertained of the Araucanians that, in 1608, orders were issued from Spain that a force of two thousand regular troops should constantly be maintained on the frontier. For this purpose a sum of about three hundred thousand *dollars* was to be paid annually from the treasury of *Peru*.

In the following year the Court of Royal Audience was re-established at *St. Iago*. The Captain-General, Raymon, who once more took the field, ended his days at *Conception*, greatly regretted, not only by those whom he had commanded and governed, but likewise by the Araucanians, whom, when prisoners, he invariably treated with humanity. In consequence of the representations of a Jesuit missionary, named Louis Valdivia, respecting

1604.

1610.

the injurious influence exercised by the long-continued struggle on the progress of conversion, the pious Philip III. sent orders to the government of *Chili* to discontinue the war and to establish peace, taking the *Bio-bio* as a frontier. Louis Valdivia returned to *Chili* in 1612, the bearer of a letter from the King to the Araucanian congress, with which he hastened to the frontier. In the presence of fifty chiefs he made known the object of his errand. He was thanked for his exertions, and received the promise of a favourable report to the *Toqui*.

So zealous was King Philip in the object of converting the Araucanians that, with the view the better to carry it out, he proposed not only to raise the missionary Valdivia to the episcopal dignity, but further to appoint him governor of *Chili*. But Valdivia's was not a worldly ambition. He declined the King's offers; whilst he obtained the nomination of a governor who was likely to carry out his views. This was no other than Rivera, who had been removed from *St. Iago* to *Tucuman*. Rivera now besought the *Toqui* to meet him at *Paicavi* in order to confer respecting peace. The *Toqui* brought with him to the appointed place a number of his Spanish prisoners, whom he released without ransom: his conditions were accepted by the governor, and all promised a speedy result; when the negotiations were interrupted by an unlooked-for accident.

Ancanamon was compelled, before concluding peace, to consult four of his chiefs. He was on his way to seek them, when he learned that his Spanish wife had taken the opportunity of his departure to make her escape and to take refuge with the governor with her two children. She brought with her two others, his wives, and likewise his two daughters, three out of the four having become Christians. This incident naturally changed the purpose of the *Toqui*, who at once returned to the Spanish quarters to seek the restoration of his family. This was, however, refused to him, on the ground of concern for their religious welfare, although, by the refusal, the object of the King of Spain in the negotiation with the Araucanians was imperilled. All that Ancanamon could obtain was the restoration of one of his daughters, who had not yet been baptized.

A new actor now appeared upon the scene in the person of the *arch-Ulmen, Utiflami*, who, out of gratitude to Valdivia for the release of one of his sons, undertook to manage the negotiation. He proceeded, with this object, to the quarters of the *Toqui*, taking with him three missionaries. On their appearance, however, Ancanamon was so exasperated that, without listening to their arguments, he ordered them to be put to death, together with Antiflami. Thus, out of care for the souls of the refugees, the negotiations for peace and proselytizing were brought to an end, and the war recommenced, with greater fury than ever. Ancanamon, desirous of avenging the affront he had received, never ceased to harass the Spanish provinces; and Rivera, up till his death in 1617, had no other opportunity of carrying out the special object with which he had been reappointed governor of *Chili*.

Rivera's successor, Lope de Ulloa, had to encounter a daring adversary in the *Toqui* Lientur, who was invariably successful in his encounters with the Spaniards, till, worn out by age and fatigues, he resigned his command, in 1625, to Putapichion, who pursued a like daring course. The war continued, with occasional successes on either side, for many years longer. A new governor was appointed to *Chili* in the person of *Don* Francisco Laso, who, having failed to obtain peace, carried on hostilities continuously, until at length, in 1632, Putapichion was slain in battle.

. Laso had greatly at heart the fulfilment of the promise which he had made to his King of putting an end to the war. From his talents and experience no one was more capable of doing so; but he had to do with

1618.

an invincible people. Their love of their country has probably never been exceeded, and was so strong that life had no charm for them beyond the limits of *Araucania*. All prisoners were after a time deported by Laso to *Peru*. When they came in sight of land they threw themselves overboard, in the hope of swimming ashore, and many succeeded in this manner in effecting their escape. Even from *Callao* many escaped, following, with incredible fatigue, the immense line of coast which separated them from their native country.

The court of Spain, owing to the long duration of the war and the great losses on their side, declined to retain Laso any longer in command, and appointed as his successor *Don* Francisco Zuniga, to whom was reserved the honour of concluding peace. Zuniga arrived in *Chili* in 1630, and sought a personal conference with Lincopichion, the *Toqui* of the Araucanians. On the 6th of January of the following year a solemn treaty was concluded, putting a period to a war which had lasted for ninety years. The Marquis de Baydes was attended by ten thousand persons to the village of *Quillin* in *Puren*, the place fixed for the ratification; whilst Lincopichion came at the head of four hereditary *Toquis* and a large number of *Ulmenes*. The ratification was celebrated by a three days' festival on either side, all prisoners being released.

Amongst the clauses of the treaty was one by which the Araucanians engaged not to permit the landing of any strangers upon their coast, nor to furnish such with supplies, and the prudence of this clause was not long in being made apparent. Three years previously the Dutch had made a second fruitless attempt to form an alliance with the Araucanians. Their squadron, consisting of four ships, was dispersed by a storm; and two boats' crews were put to death. In 1643 the Dutch made a last attempt to possess themselves of *Chili*. Having set out from *Brazil* with a numerous fleet, they took possession

PROGRESS OF THE COLONY.

of the deserted harbour of *Valdivia*, and began to fortify the entrance to the river. The Araucanians were invited to an alliance; but they honourably adhered to the terms of their treaty with the Spaniards, thus forcing the Dutch to retire in consequence of hunger. On their retreat a fleet under the command of the Marquis de Mancura, son of the Viceroy of *Peru*, arrived with ten ships of war, and fortified the harbour and the island which bears his family name.

From some cause which is not recorded hostilities once more broke out, after an interval of fifteen years, between the Chilians and their neighbours. They were continued with great violence for ten years, but were terminated, in 1665, by a more permanent peace; and from this time the records of this portion of South America are of a less stirring nature. In consequence of the war of the Spanish succession the French obtained, for a time, all the external commerce of *Chili*, its ports having been crowded with their vessels between the years 1707 and 1717. At this period many of this nation settled in the country, which possesses, in consequence, a portion of French blood.

A peace of upwards of fifty years' duration had naturally given room for the development of a country possessed of such abundant natural advantages as is *Chili*. Its interruption was owing to the missionaries who were sent amongst the Araucanians, and to the officers who were appointed to protect them, whose presence and pretensions the Araucanians resented; and, in 1722, it was determined to have recourse to arms. The *Toqui*, Vilumilla, even at this late date adopted so vast a project as that of the expulsion of the Spaniards from *Chili*. Having killed three or four of the missionaries' protectors, he despatched messengers to the Chilians in the Spanish provinces, inviting them to rise on the appearance of signal-fires. The native Chilians, however, declined to respond to the *Toqui's* invitation. The *Toqui*, nothing daunted, set out at the head of his troops to attack the Spanish settlements; but he was careful to give information to the missionaries, in order that, by retiring from the country, they might avoid ill-treatment. It is unnecessary to give the details of this short war, which was terminated by the peace of *Negrete*, where the treaty of *Quillin* was once more confirmed, and the title of Captain of Friends or protector of missionaries abolished.

Chili was ruled over for fifteen years with wisdom and humanity by *Don* Gabriel Cano; and his successor received instructions to gather the Spanish inhabitants into more compact societies. For this purpose he founded, in 1742, the cities of *Copiapo, Aconcagua, Melipilla, Rancagua, St. Fernando, Curico, Talca, Tutuben,* and *Angeles,* and was rewarded by the dignity of Viceroy of *Peru.* From 1753 date *Santa Rosa, Guasco-alto, Casablanca, Bella-Isla, Florida, Coulemu,* and *Quirigua;* whilst at the same time a settlement was formed on the island of *Juan Fernandez,* which till then had been the retreat of pirates.

Don Antonia Gonzaga, whilst governor of *Chili*, undertook to bring the Araucanians to live in cities, with the only result, however, of forcing that brave people to take up arms once more in defence of their liberties. An accommodation was at length arrived at, by which things reverted to their previous state, the Araucanians, in acknowledgment of their autonomy, being conceded the right of keeping a minister-resident in *St. Iago.* Thus has this brave people, although inconsiderable in point of numbers, succeeded in maintaining its independence, after having cost Spain a greater sacrifice of blood and treasure than sufficed for all her conquests in the New World.

The Spaniards in *Chili* now confined their views to consolidating their settlements in the region lying between the southern frontiers of *Peru* and the *Bio-bio,* a sufficiently extensive area, since it occupied the space

PROGRESS OF THE COLONY.

between degrees 24 and 36½ of southern latitude. This territory was divided into thirteen provinces. The Captaincy-General of *Chili* likewise included the fortress of *Valdivia*, the archipelago of *Chiloë*, and the island of *Juan Fernandez*. The Captain-General * was responsible to the King alone, unless in case of war, when he had to act in subordination to the Viceroy of *Peru*. The provinces were respectively governed by prefects, who possessed jurisdiction over both civil and military affairs. In each provincial capital there existed a municipal magistracy called the *Cabildo*. The inhabitants were divided into regiments, which were obliged to march to the frontier or to the sea-coast in case of war. In the year 1792 there were in the royal service fifteen thousand eight hundred and fifty militia troops; and besides this regular force there were likewise city bands of militia; and in addition to both there was a sufficient force of imperial troops to provide for the defence of the country.

1792.

Chili was divided into the two dioceses of *St. Iago* and *Conception*, the bishops resident in these cities, respectively, being suffragans to the Archbishop of *Lima*. The Court of Inquisition of *Lima* had a commissioner at *St. Iago*. The first ecclesiastics in *Chili* were the monks of the Order of Mercy, who were soon followed by Dominicans and Franciscans, and later by Augustins and Hospitalers of St. John of God. The Jesuits who were introduced in 1593, with the nephew of their founder, were expelled in 1767. *St. Iago* and *Conception* were the only cities which, in the colonial period, contained convents of nuns. The churches were more remarkable for the wealth which they displayed than for their architecture.

The population of *Chili* presented the usual mixture

* It is interesting to English readers to know that the high post of Captain-General of *Chili* was, in November 1787, confided to *Don* Ambrose Higgins, a native of Ireland, who was, two years later, appointed Field Marshal of the Royal Armies.

of Europeans, *Creoles*, Natives, Negroes, and *Mustees*, or half-castes. The *Creoles*, or colonial Spaniards, displayed a laudable desire for education, to complete which they, in many instances, proceeded to *Lima*. The peasantry, though for the greater part of Spanish origin, wore the Araucanian costume. Their lot was a happy one. Possessed of perfect liberty, and dwelling in a delightful climate, they lived on the produce of a fertile soil, and were robust, healthy, and lively. The language of the country was Spanish, excepting on the frontiers, when Araucanian or Chilian was likewise spoken. *Lima* was the Paris of South America, and prescribed the fashions for *Chili*. It may be added that *Chili* alone, of all the American provinces, could boast of two of its citizens being exalted to the dignity of *Grandee* of Spain.

The Chilians had the reputation of being exceedingly hospitable to strangers, and of having been such good masters to their negro slaves that the greatest punishment which could be inflicted on these latter was to lose their protection; and it is stated that in many instances they refused to avail themselves of the liberty afforded to them. The masters exercised over them an authority similar to that of the Roman *pater-familias* over his *familia*. In correcting their faults the degree of punishment was left to the master, unless in cases of capital crime. The word slavery, so repugnant to our ears, may imply widely different conditions of existence. Domestic slavery amongst the Turks, for instance, may mean that the slaves are treated merely as children—that is to say, that although a certain restriction is placed upon their movements, they receive every kindness and care, whilst as Moslem they may appeal to the laws of the *Koran*, &c. Very different, however, was the lot of the field labourer in the transatlantic colonies or of the mines in *Peru*. By all accounts the lot of the Chilian slave was of the former character, and affords a pleasing contrast to that of the natives of *Mexico* in the hands of the conquerors.

This chapter may conclude with some notice of the native tribes which have been repeatedly alluded to as taking part in the war between the Spaniards and the Araucanians. The *Pehuenches* inhabit that part of the Chilian *Andes* lying between the 34th and 37th degrees of south latitude, to the east of the Spanish provinces of *Calchagua, Maúle, Chillan,* and *Huilquilemu.* The dress is very similar to that of the Araucanians, except that instead of breeches they wear round the waist a piece of cloth after the fashion of the Japanese. Their boots, or shoes, are all of one piece, and made from the skin of an ox. These mountaineers, although having occasionally shown themselves to be valiant soldiers, are nevertheless fond of decorating themselves like women. They wear ornaments of glass beads upon their arms and amongst their hair, and suspend around their heads little bells. Although possessing herds of cattle and sheep, they prefer, like the Tartars, horseflesh to any other, but, more delicate than that people, will only eat it when cooked. They dwell in tents made of skins, disposed in a circular form, leaving in the centre a spacious field in which the cattle graze during the continuance of the herbage. When that begins to fail they remove to another situation, and in this manner they traverse the valleys of the *Cordilleras.*

Each village or encampment is governed by an *Ulmen.* In their language and religion they differ not from the Araucanians. They are fond of hunting, and often, in pursuit of game, traverse the vast plains lying between the river *Plate* and the Straits of *Magellan.* In these excursions, which sometimes extend as far as to *Buenos Ayres,* they plunder the country in that vicinity, and frequently attack the caravans of merchandise going thence to *Chili,* with such success that commerce is said to have suffered severely thereby. Their favourite weapon is the *laque* or *lasso,* which they carry fastened to their girdles. Although of a wandering and restless disposition, the *Pehu-*

enches are the most industrious and commercial of any savages. The women work cloths of various colours; the men occupy themselves in making baskets and a variety of beautiful articles of wood, feathers, or skins, which are highly prized by their neighbours. Assembling every year on the Spanish frontier, they hold a kind of fair, that usually continues for fifteen or twenty days, when, in exchange for fossil salt, gypsum, pitch, bed-coverings, *ponchos*, skins, wool, bridle-reins beautifully wrought of plaited leather, baskets, wooden vessels, feathers, ostrich eggs, horses and cattle, &c., they receive wheat, wine, and the manufactures of Europe. Being very skilful in traffic, they can with difficulty be overreached; and when indulging in the pleasures of wine, a portion of them is set apart to guard their property from plunder. They are generally humane, complacent, lovers of justice, and possess all those good qualities that are produced or perfected by commerce.

The *Chiquillanians*, whom some have erroneously supposed to be a part of the *Pehuenches*, live to the north-east of them, on the eastern border of the *Andes*, and are the most savage and least numerous of any of the Chilians. They go almost naked, merely wrapping around them the skin of the *guanaco*. It is observable that all the Chilians who inhabit the eastern valleys of the *Andes*, namely, the *Pehuenches*, the *Puelches*, the *Huilliches*, and the *Chiquillanians*, are much redder than their countrymen dwelling westward of those mountains. All the mountaineers dress themselves in skins and paint their faces; and, living in general by hunting, lead a wandering and unsettled life. They are, generally speaking, of a lofty stature and of great strength.

CHAPTER XI.

BRAZIL: DISCOVERY OF THE MINES; ATTEMPT OF THE FRENCH ON RIO DE JANEIRO.

1702-1720.

THE search for the precious metals had long shared with slave-hunting the efforts of the *Paulistas* and others. Rumours of the existence of silver and gold had long excited the hopes of the Portuguese Government, and from time to time a stray specimen was procured from some unknown spot in the interior. But up to the close of the seventeenth century nothing was actually known as to the localities where the precious minerals were concealed. With the opening of the eighteenth century, however, a new era dawned upon *Brazil*; and the discoveries which were now about to be made were destined to determine the site of her future capital.

In anticipation of the finding of gold and silver, a code of regulations had long since been issued relative to mines. Of the regulations in question, one provided that all persons in authority were bound to afford discoverers the necessary assistance; but when, about the middle of the seventeenth century, Marcos de Azevedo and a companion brought back from the *Rio Doce* samples of silver and emeralds, the only result to the discoverers was that they were thrown into prison at *Bahia* and detained there for life, because they obstinately refused to communicate the scene of their discovery to the Government. On their death renewed search was made for these mines, but in vain. A veteran, named Fernando Diaz, however, at the age of eighty, obtained permission to undertake a fresh search; and he explored the entire country now included in the captaincy of *Minas Geraes*, where he formed a number of settlements.

The court of Lisbon had so often been excited by hopes which proved delusive, and so many searching expeditions had failed, that its patience was now exhausted. The old man, during four years, underwent a series of privations and hardships such as wore out his more youthful companions; but he was at length rewarded by his being shown by a young Indian the spot where emeralds were found. The explorer, however, did not live to return to *St. Paulo*, having been overtaken by a fever, which cost him his life. The first gold known to have been produced from this district was found about the year 1691, and in the following year an expedition was formed to explore the district (now called *Villa Rica*) where it had been found. Some further specimens having been obtained, they were exhibited at *Rio de Janeiro* in 1693, in which year a commission was granted to one Carlos Silveria as *Capitam Mor* of *Taboate* and *Provedor* of the royal fifths, with orders to establish a smelting-house in that town.

Happily for the natives of *Brazil*, the discovery of the precious metals had been deferred until an age somewhat more humane than that which had witnessed the occupation of *Hayti* and the conquest of *Peru*. The preaching of humanitarians, from Las Casas down to Vieyra, had not been in vain; and when at length the day came when *Minas Geraes* was first to yield its treasures, the effect, as regarded the condition of the Brazilian Indians, was, contrary to expectation, rather beneficial than otherwise. The lust for gold superseded the lust for slaves.

The Brazilian explorers had expended unbounded energy throughout long years in searching for the mines; but the work of procuring their contents was far less toilsome. It was for the most part sand-washing taken from rivers, or surface mining; the soil containing the ore was broken up by pick-axes and exposed to the action of running water. In the natural course of things a large concourse of adventurers soon gathered from far and near; a road was opened to *Rio de Janeiro*, and at this time the foundations were laid of many considerable towns—amongst them the city of *Mariana*. At a few miles' distance stands *Villa Rica*, the capital of the captaincy. In another direction were found the mines of *Sabara;* and their discovery led to the first colonization towards the sources of the *San Francisco*. In short, the presence of gold lent its invariable allurement to the large proportion of human beings who dream that they may be amongst the exceptional persons who obtain wealth without undergoing the slow process of long labour; and thus one of the least-inviting portions of *Brazil* was rapidly colonized. The town which for so many years has so largely supplied the Bank of England with its staple owes its foundation to Thomé Cortes d'El Rei.

It was soon found necessary to alter the laws then in existence as regards mining. On the discovery of gold, persons of influence had lost no time in securing grants of land. These they were in many cases unable to work; and thus they either disposed of them to others or left them unused. It was therefore enacted that no second grant should be made to any person until he should have worked the first; and if ground were remaining after all applicants had received allotments, it should be divided amongst such as possessed more than twelve slaves. On the other hand, when there were more claimants than there were shares upon the prescribed scale, the proportions were to be lessened in order that all might be satisfied. Besides its fifths, the Crown kept for itself an allotment, to be marked out after the discoverer had taken his first grant. If within forty days an explorer had not begun to work his ground, a third of it, on information being given, was assigned to the informer, the remaining

1702.

two-thirds falling to the Crown,—unless sufficient reasons were to be pleaded for delay. The Crown allotments were let by auction; but if the biddings were not thought high enough, the superintendent was to see them worked for the Treasury by Indians. No officer of the Treasury or of justice might possess or share in a grant, either directly or indirectly.

The salary of the superintendent was fixed at three thousand five hundred *cruzados*;* that of the chief guardian at two thousand; whilst the subordinate guardians received one thousand each. The treasurer likewise received three thousand *cruzados*. There were also deputy-treasurers, receiving each five hundred *cruzados*. The above salaries were paid on taxes levied upon those who profited by the mines. Various other regulations were likewise made with a view to meeting fresh cases as they arose. The civil and military authority was vested in the superintendent. It was not permitted to bring slaves to the mines from any other locality than *Rio de Janeiro*; but it was allowed to import cattle from *Bahia*. All commodities were to be sent from *Rio*, by way either of *Taboate* or of *St. Paulo*; these restrictions being in order to prevent the clandestine exportation of gold-dust.

The passion of gambling is nowhere more consuming than in a mining district; and such did not fail to be the case in *Brazil*. Even the governor of *Rio de Janeiro* so far forgot his official character as to set out for the mining district and eagerly engage in the pursuit. It was, therefore, not without reason that in the new laws it was laid down that the governor was forbidden to visit the district unless by express orders from Lisbon, or unless in the case of some unforeseen emergency. The attraction of the mines soon told upon *Bahia*, from which captaincy many prosperous settlers betook themselves to the golden region, leaving their farms to run waste. The

* A cruzado = nearly five shillings.

cultivator who was sure of wealth by a little patience could not lose the chance of winning it by a possible piece of luck. As negroes were in great demand, the owners of sugar-plantations could not stand the competition with mining adventurers. This state of things proved most injurious to *Brazil;* for the price of sugar naturally rose in proportion to the cost of producing it, many works being abandoned and their owners ruined. Hitherto Europe had been supplied with this article almost exclusively from the Brazilian provinces; but, as exportation rapidly diminished, the French and the English, who were at this time learning to cultivate the sugar-cane in their respective islands, took advantage of the opportunity to occupy the markets. The staple commodity being thus reduced, the general trade was diminished to a corresponding extent.

The alarming consequences of the depopulation of the interior induced the Government to prohibit the passage of slaves from *Bahia* to the mines. Troops were employed to intercept them, and many seizures were made. But in spite of all efforts the illicit importation was carried on; and at length the Government revoked the prohibition and allowed enterprise to take its spontaneous course. The court of Lisbon was even converted to the opinion of the Brazilian colonists that mining was more profitable than sugar-raising. *Brazil* had become the most important portion of the Portuguese dominions. Its Church had hitherto been governed by the Constitution of that of Lisbon; but a synod was now convened at *Bahia*, and a constitution suited to the circumstances of the country was drawn up for the Colonial Church.

It was not to be expected that the motley crowd of adventurers of all classes which thronged to the mines should long continue to live together with the same harmony that might be expected from a more settled community; and *Minas Geraes* soon acquired the unenviable notoriety, which had hitherto belonged to *Maran-*

1707.

ham, of being the most turbulent settlement in *Brazil*. Its people were divided into two classes, called, respectively, *Paulistas* and *Florasteiros* or strangers. Before very long the ill-feeling between these culminated in their taking up arms. A report arose that the *Paulistas* had combined for the purpose of exterminating all strangers at the mines, and a civil war broke out, which was of so serious a nature as to call forth the presence of the governor with troops from *Rio de Janeiro*. The *Florasteiros* had, however, been fortunate in their choice of a commander, named Manoel Muñes, through whose prudence some degree of order was ere long restored; and, on the arrival of a new governor, a general amnesty was proclaimed.

The governor, having left things in a most satisfactory condition at the mines, set out to restore good government in the district of *St. Paulo*, where he found the people in a violent state of agitation. The *Paulistas* who had returned home from *Minas Geraes* were violently taunted by their wives with pusillanimity in having failed to avenge their comrades who had fallen; and the result was the formation of a strong force, which set out for the scene of struggle, and which declined to listen to the remonstrances of the governor. Albuquerque, having learned that there was an intention to seize his person, consulted his safety by escaping to *Rio*, whence he lost
1708. no time in sending messengers to the *Florasteiros* to warn them of their danger. The latter, in turn, made hasty preparations to resist an attack, which was wholly unexpected. After withstanding a siege for several days, they were relieved from danger by the news of an approaching force to their assistance, the *Paulistas* at the same time retreating in haste. Albuquerque took steps to ensure the tranquillity of the district, and was himself soon afterwards appointed governor of *St. Paulo* and of the mining country, which was now separated from the captaincy of *Rio de Janeiro*.

To turn to a more northerly region:—after the protracted war which had for so many years desolated the province of *Pernambuco*, it will readily be conceived that it was by no means an easy task to restore the order which had existed previous to the arrival of the Dutch; and it is said that much latitude was allowed to the inhabitants on account of the devoted patriotism which they had shown during the struggle, and the sacrifices to which they had so cheerfully submitted. Two generations had now passed away since the expulsion of the Dutch, and *Recife* had become an important entrepôt of trade, its influence being regarded with jealousy by the landed proprietors of *Pernambuco*. In *Olinda* and the surrounding district the descendants of the heroes of the war now constituted an aristocracy, who prided themselves, with justice, on the fact that it was to the exertions of their ancestors that Portugal owed the province. The people of *Recife*, not unreasonably, demanded that that important place should be granted the privileges of a town; but this request was long resisted by the jealousy of *Olinda*. The name of *S. Antonio do Recife*, or St. Anthony of the Reef, was, however, at length conferred upon a place which had become the third, or perhaps the second, port of greatest importance in *Brazil*.

The state of public security in the province left, certainly at this time, much to be desired. Murder was so common an occurrence that it was thought an act of oppression upon the part of the governor to arrest two persons for having murdered a gentleman in his house at night. The sympathies of the people were not with the victim, or with the law, but with the offenders; and a conspiracy was entered into to assassinate the unreasonable governor. That functionary, having ordered the people to deposit their arms in the arsenal, was shortly afterwards attacked by three armed men wearing masks, and was wounded in four places. This incident was merely the prelude to a general insurrection; and the governor consulted his own safety by taking refuge in a vessel which was ready to set out to sea. He took with him to *Bahia* those persons who were reputed to be marked for popular vengeance, they being some of the principal inhabitants of *Recife*.

Two days after his departure that town was entered by the insurgents, when its recently-acquired privileges were declared to be annulled. After having broken open the prison at *Olinda* and released the prisoners, they proceeded to deliberate as to what steps should next be taken; when it was determined to summon the bishop, who was named Provisional-Governor. His first act was to proclaim a full and general pardon in the name of the King, after which processes were made out, and depositions sent to Lisbon. It is scarcely necessary to add that meanwhile public security was not greatly increased. The streets of *Recife* became so unsafe that the inhabitants found it necessary to shut up their houses at the hour of the *Ave Maria* bell.

Vieyra de Mello, who had commanded the expedition against the negroes of the *Palmares*, at this time appeared upon the scene; and an instance which occurred in his family will show the shocking state of manners then prevailing in the province. His son, rightly or wrongly, suspected the fidelity of his wife, who resided at a sugar plantation in the interior. To this place the husband repaired with a numerous following. He lost no time in putting to death the man whom he accused. As, however, the lady was at the time *enceinte*, she was sent to be placed under the care of his mother until her child should be born, when she was to share the fate of her lover. Thus a whole family became participators in the cold-blooded affair. The younger Vieyra appeared openly in *Recife*, not only avowing the crime which he had committed, but announcing that his vengeance was not yet completed. As the matter was notorious, a worthy friar called upon the bishop-governor to beg him to prevent the intended crime; but the cautious prelate declined to interfere in the private affairs of noblemen, who ought not to live, he said, under disgrace.

The object of Vieyra's arrival at this juncture was to become the leader of the republican party, which was numerous in the province. He proposed to gain possession of the forts; and if the new governor, who was daily expected, should fail to bring out a full pardon, to refuse him admittance, and proclaim a republic. The inhabitants of *Recife*, however, were loyal subjects. Suspecting the intentions of Bernardo Vieyra, they apprised the governor of *Paraïba* of his designs, and of their readiness to help in the King's service. The governor of *Paraïba* wrote to the bishop, putting him on his guard. The prelate appears to have been not unfavourably disposed towards him; but, as his designs were notorious, he was obliged to request that he would depart from *Recife*—a request which was met by evasion.

A quarrel which arose between some soldiers of the *Recife* regiment and a party of Bernardo Vieyra's men was the means of bringing affairs to a climax. The *Recife* soldiers, sallying from the church in which they had taken sanctuary, caused the drummer to beat the rendezvous, while they raised the cry of "Down with the traitors!" The officers putting themselves at their head, the bishop retired to the Jesuits' college, and Bernardo Vieyra was speedily arrested. The forts were now secured by trustworthy men. A proclamation was issued by the troops, vindicating their own conduct and their loyalty to the King. But, meanwhile, the opposite party gathered their forces at *Olinda*; and the land-holders, who were joined by the bishop, prepared to besiege *Recife*, intercepting the supplies of food for that town. 1711. In this critical state of affairs the prudent bishop thought fit to resign the government.

A civil war thereupon commenced. The independent party hoped to reduce *Recife* by famine; but the Royalists, like the Dutch before them, had command of the port.

The insurgents had the superiority in the field; and the garrison of *Recife* had to despatch a vessel to *Bahia* to represent their danger and to request the aid of the Governor-General. After the siege had continued for three months, the Portuguese fleet fortunately made its appearance, having on board the new governor. The authorities of *Olinda* lost no time in sending on board to inform him that *Recife* was in the hands of mutineers; but the commandant of that place had been beforehand with them in going on board in person. Machado entered *Recife*, and on the following day took possession of his government at *Olinda*. He then proceeded to institute a fair inquiry into past circumstances, listening impartially to all parties. The principal offenders were then arrested and sent to Lisbon, where two of them received the sentence of banishment for life to India, the others being permitted to return to *Brazil*. The consequences of this civil war were severely felt by many of the chief families of *Pernambuco*.

Hitherto *Rio de Janeiro* had for many years escaped its share of the troubles with which the other chief centres of Brazilian colonization were visited in turn. 1710. In the year, however, preceding that which witnessed the above-mentioned events at *Recife*, the future capital of *Brazil* had been the scene of war. Five large ships were reported as being seen off Cape *Frio*. As they approached the shore the customary signals were given, but were left unanswered; and all doubts as to their nature were removed upon the capture by them of a small vessel, within sight of the forts. They indeed proved to be a French squadron under the command of *M. du Clerc*, the object of which was to plunder the city which had at one time seemed destined to belong to France, and which was now supposed to contain much of the produce of the recently-found mines.

There was at this time at *Rio de Janeiro* a force of no less than eight thousand troops, not including five thousand armed negroes and mulattoes and six hundred Indians. Yet no attempt was made to prevent the French from landing at a spot about forty miles from that city, although their force consisted of only about twelve hundred and fifty marines. They were permitted to march leisurely through the woods, the governor contenting himself with taking up an entrenched position near the hill of *S. Antonio*. His proceedings had the effect of giving the French a false confidence. They were, however, attacked by one scouting party and lost a few men. On arriving near the city, they were allowed to pass the night undisturbed at the plantation of the Jesuits. Next morning, however, they met with a resolute resistance from a detachment headed by a Friar named Menezes, who greatly distinguished himself on this occasion.

On entering the city, the French force was divided into two parties, the smaller of which was cut off, the men being quickly dispersed and yielding to panic. The governor's palace was defended by a number of students, and was vigorously attacked by the main body of the French, in the hope of capturing the governor. A sharp conflict ensued, and the French leader was glad to retire with the remainder of his men into a large warehouse on the quay. He was under the belief that his other detachment had gained the city, being deluded by the ringing of the bells on account of its defeat. In this condition he had no alternative but to surrender at discretion. The success of the Portuguese was soiled by much cruelty towards their prisoners. A number of men who asked for quarter were killed by the rabble; whilst about a hundred and fifty were massacred in the streets. In all, about four hundred of the French were killed; two hundred and fifty were wounded; and six hundred were made prisoners. Of the Portuguese, one hundred and twenty fell; many, it is said, at the hands of their own countrymen in the confusion.

The whole history of this affair reflects very little credit either on the Portuguese governor or on the inhabitants of Rio de Janeiro. With so large a force at his disposal, it should have been easy for the former to bring the invaders to account in a much shorter time and with far less loss to himself; as regards the populace, they are even charged by the French with having murdered the surgeons who were sent on shore from the French ships, by permission of the governor, to attend their wounded countrymen; whilst, some months later, M. du Clerc himself was found murdered in his house. The latter act was probably the result of private vengeance; but much blame was attached to the Portuguese authorities for having failed to institute any inquiry into the matter.

The inhumanity with which the prisoners had been treated, together with the supineness of the provincial authorities in the matter of M. du Clerc's death, roused, as might have been expected, much indignation in France. The celebrated Du Guay-Trouin proposed to undertake an expedition to Brazil, to assert the national honour. The force placed at his disposal consisted of fifteen vessels in all, the two largest carrying seventy-four guns each. The French admiral set sail from La Rochelle on the 9th of June 1711; but he did not arrive off Bahia until the 27th of the following August, and it was the 11th of September before he reached his destination.

The preparation of so extensive a naval force, although it was got ready with as much secrecy as possible, could not be unknown to the Portuguese Government; and accordingly the departure of the Brazilian fleet had been expedited, under a strong convoy. The fleet had reached Rio early in September; and thus the arrival of the French might have been looked for. Yet, after the lapse of some days, the Portuguese admiral, Da Costa, concluding that he had received a false alarm, relanded the men whom he had placed on board of the ships for the protection of the city, and relapsed into a false security. On the 10th, it was known that the enemy's fleet had passed Cape *Frio;* and on the morning of the 12th, in the midst of a thick fog, their artillery was heard at the bar of the magnificent bay. The French, who were led by an officer acquainted with the port, passed the forts with the loss of three hundred men, and by noon were off the city. The incapable admiral, who had not had sufficient patience to persevere in the measures necessary to withstand an invasion of which he had ample warning, now lost his presence of mind. The commanders of his vessels received orders to cut their cables and to set fire to their ships when they had run them on shore.

The French commander took advantage of the ensuing night to make his preparations; and on the following morning he took possession of the island of *Cobras*, which the Portuguese were preparing to abandon. On the 14th he landed his troops, three thousand three hundred in number, not including five hundred suffering from scurvy, who were soon able to resume their duties. The governor renewed his tactics of the preceding year. Although his force was double that of the French, he allowed the latter to pursue their measures without the slightest opposition. He probably looked for a similar result, should the French admiral follow the example of Du Clerc, in allowing his men to engage in a street fight; but the latter was warned by the fate of his countrymen.

Having erected one battery on shore, and another on the island of *Cobras*, Du Guay-Trouin summoned the governor to surrender at discretion, stating that he had been sent by his master to exact vengeance for the cruelties committed by the Portuguese in the preceding year. To this De Castro replied that the preceding expedition had been treated according to the laws of war, to which they had no claim, seeing that they had invaded *Brazil* as pirates, and without the King's commission. He had saved six hundred lives from the fury of the people; nor had he been wanting in any respect towards his prisoners. It had, he said, been impossible to discover the murderer of *M. du* Clerc. To the summons to surrender he made answer that he was ready to defend to the last the city which had been entrusted to him by his King.

On the day after the receipt of this reply, the French admiral bombarded the Portuguese intrenchments, and prepared to assault them on the following morning. An accidental discovery of his movements during the night, which was due to the vivid lightning, induced him to anticipate his plan; and the cannonade continued throughout the entire night. The inhabitants, notwithstanding the fury of a violent tropical thunderstorm, preferred to seek refuge in the country. The whole population fled, the troops likewise being seized with panic; and in the morning *Rio de Janeiro* fell without resistance into the hands of the French, five hundred of their lately-imprisoned countrymen being now engaged in pillaging the city, which was given up to a general sack. Notwithstanding all the efforts of the commander, three-fourths of the houses and magazines were broken open in the first twenty-four hours. So great was the confusion, that the Portuguese, had they taken advantage of the opportunity, might have a second time made a good account of their invaders; but no such effort was made on their part, and the forts were surrendered with disgraceful readiness.

The governor meanwhile intrenched himself about a league from the city, sending for assistance to the governor of *Minas*. The French commander, however, who had come for the sake of reprisals and of plunder, was only anxious to depart. Perceiving the difficulty of obtaining a store of provisions, he sent to inform the governor that unless the city were immediately ransomed he would burn it to the ground. As there was nothing to prevent the French admiral from carrying his threat into execution, De Castro offered to ransom the city for six hundred thousand *cruzados*. This proposal was at first rejected, but was ultimately accepted, with the additional condition of supplying a large number of cattle; the whole to be paid within fifteen days. De Castro had shown, as might have been expected from him, but little discretion in the matter; for on the day following the signature of the agreement, Albuquerque arrived from *Minas* with one thousand five hundred horsemen, and as many foot-soldiers carried behind them; they were followed at a day or two's distance by six thousand negroes. It is somewhat surprising that this able and independent officer, commanding a force double that of the French in number, should not have attacked them on his own account. The terms of the agreement, however, were punctually observed; and, on the 4th of November, the French re-embarked.

It may be of interest to recount the subsequent fate of this expedition, which, it should be remarked, was fitted out, not at the expense of the Crown of France, but at that of six persons who entered into it as a speculation; five of them being merchants of St. Malo, and the sixth the Comptroller of the King's Household. The expenses of the outfit had been calculated at 1,200,000 *livres*. The project had been duly approved by the Government, whose ships and troops were placed at the commander's disposal. This officer was so elated with his success at *Rio de Janeiro*, that he set sail for *Bahia*, with the intention of laying that place likewise under requisition. It was saved by the contrary winds against which Du Guay-Trouin had to struggle for six weeks, when, on account of the state of his provisions, he found it necessary to make for France. In the tempestuous weather which they encountered on the homeward voyage, two vessels of the squadron foundered, one of them being the finest ship of the fleet, and commanded by *M. de* Courserac, who had led the way into the harbour of *Rio*, and whose vessel contained a very large amount of treasure. A third vessel was driven to *Cayenne*, and there sank. There remained, however, to the partners a profit of ninety-two per cent. on their capital.

Francisco de Castro, the governor of *Rio de Janeiro*, was not at the end of his troubles with the departure of the French. The people, who had lost so much property as well as honour owing to his ill-fortune or mismanagement, declined to be any longer ruled by him, and insisted that Albuquerque should assume the authority until the King's pleasure should be known. The King's pleasure was, that De Castro should be superseded and placed upon his trial; he was degraded, and sentenced to perpetual imprisonment in a fort in India. Two other officers were likewise severely punished.

The success of the squadron under Du Guay-Trouin had been so marked that a second armament was equipped at the cost of private individuals, but with the assistance of the Government. Its objective point was *Bahia ;* but its commander was of another stamp from that in which Du Guay-Trouin was cast. *Bahia* was spared; and he contented himself with a descent upon some of the smaller sugar-islands. The Portuguese colonies were, however, 1713. about to be relieved from further alarms by the Peace of Utrecht, by which they obtained the full sovereignty over both banks of the *Amazons*, France ceding, with much reluctance, all pretensions to the country between that river and the *Oyapok*. It was likewise stipulated that the French should not trade with *Maranham*.

The people of the Mines were thanked for the promptitude with which they had brought assistance for the deliverance of *Rio ;* and *S. Paulo*, as being the capital of a captaincy, obtained the rank of a city. Some idea may

FRENCH ATTEMPT ON RIO DE JANEIRO. 185

be formed of the value of the yield of the mines at this time from the fact that, in the year 1714, the Government fifths were commuted for the equivalent of about £50,400 sterling. The commutation was, however, raised, three years later, by one-fourth. In the year 1720, the country of *Minas Geraes* was detached from *S. Paulo* and declared a separate captaincy.

1720.

NOTE.—The reader will, I fear, observe a want in this work, which has not by any means escaped the notice of the writer, but which he has found it impossible fully to supply. In almost every chapter there occur notices of large transactions in money, the coins quoted being those then current in Spain and Portugal, respectively. It would, of course, be possible to state approximately the relative value to a given standard of those various coins, respectively, at any one period ; but the value of gold and silver coins of the same name varied so constantly and so considerably that it is impossible to lay down a definite standard of value throughout the whole area of which this work treats for any considerable part of the period to which it is devoted. As an instance of the tendency to mislead in taking any fixed coin as a standard in reference to South American monetary transactions, I may mention that, in *Buenos Ayres*, in the year 1866, I found the Argentine *dollar*, a coin which most English readers would naturally estimate as the equivalent of four shillings, to be worth exactly twopence. This, of course, applies to the paper *dollar ;* but this would be the legal tender in payment of amounts stated in *dollars*, unless otherwise specified.

CHAPTER XII.

BRAZIL: DISCOVERY OF THE DIAMOND DISTRICT.

1724-1749.

1724. THE mining districts had on several occasions been the scene of serious and prolonged resistance against the constituted authorities, in consequence of the regulations respecting the mode of levying the royal share which were introduced with a view to prevent smuggling. It had been found necessary to make a severe example of the ringleaders of an insurrection; and the mining population were thenceforward amenable to law. It was established that all gold was to pass through the royal smelting-house before paying the royal fifths which were now re-established. The people of the mines had, by a timely discovery, escaped the danger of a negro insurrection; and in consequence so many negroes took to the woods that the same evil was apprehended as in the case of the *Palmares.* In order to avert such a contingency, Bush-captains were established, whose business it was to apprehend wandering negroes, for whom they received head-money from their masters. In many cases it was alleged that the Bush-captains, in order to receive the reward, made a practice of arresting negroes who were not runaways, and that this institution was only one degree less troublesome to the community than the evil which it was appointed to suppress—these individuals being likewise in the habit of detaining negroes and profiting by their labour.

The great importation of negroes into *Minas Geraes*

gave occasion to fears which were not entertained elsewhere in *Brazil*, and in consequence an order was issued forbidding the formation of free blacks into separate companies, and requiring that they should be mixed with white soldiers. No person who was a mulatto within the fourth degree might be an ordinary judge or hold any municipal office in *Minas Geraes*. The mode of mining had now undergone a considerable alteration. Instead of opening cuttings and carrying the produce in bulk to be washed, water was conveyed to the mining ground, and, washing away the mould, broke up the blocks in pits or wooden troughs, thus saving a great expenditure of labour. As water-power thus became a valuable property, those in possession of water-courses derived great advantages therefrom. Their pretensions were, however, so extravagant that it was found necessary to establish a set of laws respecting the distribution of the water.

The discovery of the mines had brought about so great an increase of wealth that the jealous restrictions against the immigration of foreigners into *Brazil* were rendered more stringent than ever. Not only were they forbidden to enter the country, but no person might embark for it unless he were appointed to an office there, or unless he were a servant of Portuguese birth accompanying his master. Even Portuguese must be provided with passports; and the clergy were likewise under restrictions.

The *Paulistas*, being greatly outnumbered by strangers in *Minas Geraes*, sought and found a new field for their energies. It was to the enterprise of one of this class of men, named Pascoal Cabral, that was due the discovery of the mines of *Cuyabá* in the centre of the Continent,— mines which should more naturally have fallen to the lot of the Spaniards from *Paraguay* or from *Santa Cruz de la Sierra*. The journey thither from *S. Paulo* was long and arduous, and was further attended with no slight risk, leading the traveller through the native country of the fierce *Puayaguas*. These people rendered the journey to

Cuyabá so dangerous that, when a colony had been established there, a strongly-armed vessel was sent thence to await the annual caravan of traders at the *Paraguay* river.

So soon as the richness of the locality became known, cattle and supplies were forwarded to *Cuyabá*, but with infinite difficulty and at proportionate cost. Mining at *Cuyabá* was attended with a danger from which *Minas Geraes* was free, namely, the presence of hostile and resolute Indians. Military discipline was found necessary for self-preservation; but the attitude of the savages was at least attended with the good result of compelling the settlers to sink their own jealousies and differences in making common cause against them. Thus the settlement of *Cuyabá* soon began to flourish as much as had those of *Minas Geraes*. As the way thither by water was so circuitous and difficult, the governor of *S. Paulo* offered a reward for the opening up of a communication by land; and this object was effected by Manoel de Lara, a house being established at the point where the *Paraná* was crossed, in order that the gold might be registered and the royal fifths collected. But such a mode of levying the dues proved ineffectual in a country where smuggling was so easy; and it was judged expedient to have recourse to a poll-tax upon the slaves.

A like measure was, after long hesitation, determined upon in respect to the taxation of *Minas Geraes*, where almost every conceivable contrivance had been resorted to in order to defraud the Crown of the royal fifths,—such measures, for instance, as corrupting the goldsmiths and employing coins. It was therefore strongly recommended to raise the royal proportion by means of taxing the produce according to the number of slaves employed; and the task of introducing this measure devolved upon the new governor, Gomes Freyre de Andrada, the son of the distinguished Gomes Freyre, who had restored order in *Maranham*.

When the edict for the capitation was posted in the

DISCOVERY OF THE DIAMOND DISTRICT.

public places throughout the captaincy, the inhabitants of two districts tore down the proclamation and prepared to resist the levying of the tax; but so conciliatory was the new governor that this threatened disturbance was quieted down; and the peace of the province was happily insured by the discovery, at this time, of several fresh mines, which promoted a general prosperity extending to the entire population.

But it was not to gold alone that *Brazil* was to owe the sudden increase of its prosperity which occurred during the early part of the eighteenth century. A rumour had long been current of the existence of diamonds; and one Bernardino da Fonseca Lobo had found specimens of these precious stones in the *Serro do Frio*, which he sent home to Portugal, and which procured him the title of *Capitam Mor of Villa do Principe* for life. Diamonds were declared to be royalties, and subject to the same duties as gold. It was difficult, however, to collect these duties in the same manner; since neither by number, weight, nor measure could any equitable plan of taking the royal fifths be devised. A capitation tax upon the slaves employed was therefore decided upon. The diamonds were to be remitted, as was gold, only in the King's ships, one per cent. on their value being charged for freight. The result of this last discovery of the produce of *Brazil* was such that, in the course of two years, the price of diamonds in Europe went down seventy-five per cent. The property of individuals was so seriously threatened that it was found necessary, without delay, to take measures for limiting the number of diamonds extracted.

In order to arrive at this end, by which the price of diamonds was to be kept up artificially, several measures were proposed, and were referred to commercial men for their opinion. The advice of Dr. Joam Mendes was to the effect that the diamond country should be reserved for the King's use; that it should be placed under special laws; and that the diamonds should be extracted for the King's account slowly. After due deliberation, the Court resolved to adopt the counsel thus given, in so far as to reserve the diamond country and to limit the extraction; but not to undertake it on its own account. An officer was therefore charged to mark out the limits of the forbidden district, and so heavy a capitation was imposed as to prevent all but a few persons from searching for the precious stones. It was thought that they could only be offered for sale at a heavy price.

Under the government of Gomes Freyre, a contract was made for employing six hundred slaves in the work of extracting diamonds, an annual poll-tax to be paid upon the slaves of two hundred and thirty *milreis*. The Crown was to have the option of purchasing stones above a certain size. When, at the end of four years, this contract expired, it had proved so profitable that the capitation was raised to two hundred and seventy *milreis;* whilst the Treasury should each year give the contractor credit for sixty thousand *milreis* of the two hundred and sixty-two thousand for which he stood engaged. This arrangement fell in with the views of all parties. The European lapidaries kept back their stock until time should have effaced the effects of the sudden glut; and whilst they gave out that the Brazilian diamonds were inferior to the Oriental, they did not fail to pass off the former as the latter. They are even asserted to have sent Brazilian stones to *Goa* to find thence their way back to Europe, until the equal value of the Brazilian diamonds with those of India was established.

The *Serro do Frio*, in which these diamonds were found, had been first explored by two Brazilians probably from the town of *Villa do Principe*, which dates from the beginning of the century. The boundaries of *Minas Geraes*, to the east, lay along the adjacent captaincies of *Rio de Janeiro, Bahia*, and *Pernambuco*. Towards the north and west there lay an undefined extent of unappropriated

DISCOVERY OF THE DIAMOND DISTRICT.

territory. To the south the province is bounded by the captaincies of *S. Paulo* and *Rio de Janeiro*. The whole captaincy is a portion of an immense mountain-range. A winter of two months' duration commences in May, when the average temperature is about 50° *Fahrenheit*; in the hot season the heat never exceeds 80°. The rainy season lasts from October till May, the rain sometimes continuing for days together. The captaincy of *Minas Geraes* was divided into four districts, of which that of *Serro do Frio*, called also the forbidden district, contained the diamond fields.

This district boasts innumerable peaks, some of enormous height, which present a scene of alpine grandeur and desolation—a grandeur which is added to by the magnificent cataracts into which the waters of the region are in many places gathered before they fall into the rivers which drain the district.

The Portuguese were now advancing in several directions into the interior of *Brazil*; more especially up the *Amazons* and the numerous tributaries of that stream. The *Paulistas* and the people of *Minas Geraes* spread themselves across the extensive region lying behind the captaincies of *Bahia* and *Piauhy*, which now forms the province of *Goyaz*; whilst from *Cuyabá* the settlers continued to advance towards the *Chiquito* and *Moxo* missions, and likewise in the direction of the western branch of the *Tocantins*. They thus secured for Portugal a country containing two hundred thousand square miles, which now forms the province of *Matto-Grosso*.

The name *Goyaz* is derived from the *Goya* tribe. The first discoverer of its mineral wealth was a *Paulista*, named Manoel Correa, who, in the seventeenth century, made his way thither at the head of a party of slave-hunters. He brought back some specimens of gold, which induced another adventurer to follow in his footsteps. He too found gold upon one of the rivers flowing into the *Amazons*. This second adventurer, called Bueno, was accompanied in another expedition by his son, then only twelve years old. They found the *Goya* women wearing pieces of gold picked up from the beds of the torrents. This was in 1670, before the age of Brazilian mining had arrived. Fifty years later Bueno's son proposed to the Governor of *S. Paulo* to go in search of the spot which he had visited in his boyhood, and which, after three years' searching, he once more found. He collected gold from five different streams, where he was appointed to establish a colony with the rank of *Capitam Mor*.

The mines of *Goyaz* soon rivalled those of *Cuyabá*, and had the advantage of a shorter and safer communication with the older settlements. Provisions came regularly from *S. Paulo*, but not in sufficient quantities to keep pace with the increasing population. The demand for food induced a portion of the community to devote themselves to rearing cattle and cultivating the ground, occupations which were soon found to be even more profitable than mining. In ten years the colony, requiring a separate jurisdiction, was made a province of *S. Paulo*; twelve years later it was declared a captaincy. Its capital, *Villa Boa*, was chartered in 1739.

1734. Mines were first discovered in *Matto-Grosso* in 1734, upon the banks of the river *Sarare*. These, too, were found by a *Paulista*. Gold was found during the first years in greater abundance than in any other quarter; but the earlier adventurers suffered the greatest hardships from want of provisions. Even the necessaries of life rose to famine prices. The gold was not enough to prevent many from starving from want of food. The settlement was at length relieved by the arrival of a supply of cattle from *Cuyabá*; but not until the original discoverer, who was at the time rolling in wealth, had fallen a victim to disease.

The undoubted riches of the region, however, did not fail to insure a due proportion of settlers; and a road was opened to *Cuyabá* from *Goyaz* by which a due supply

DISCOVERY OF THE DIAMOND DISTRICT.

of cattle was introduced. Amongst the few survivors of the first miserable year was Manoel Felix de Lima, who was destined to accomplish a remarkable geographical feat, by finding his way from the mines of *Francisco Xavier* in *Matto-Grosso* to the Spanish settlements at *Santa Maria Magdalena*. A short sketch of this journey may be given here as illustrating the enormous natural and other difficulties with which the first explorers of the interior of *Brazil* had to contend.

1742.

Manoel de Lima, who was a native of Portugal, had failed to enrich himself in the pursuit of gold; prices were very high; and, being wearied of a settled life, he induced some companions to join him in an adventure down the rivers. The party made up the number of fifty, including slaves and Indians. They were all either penniless or deeply in debt, and were glad of any excuse for escaping from their creditors. Falling down the *Sarare* in canoes, they found themselves upon the *Guapore*, when they laid in stores for the voyage before them down the river which now forms for a considerable distance the frontier between *Brazil* and *Bolivia*.

On the tenth day of the voyage the adventurers landed on the right bank, at the mouth of a stream, where they found marks of a recent encampment made by a party under one Almeida, who had set out from the settlement six months before them upon a slave-hunting expedition, and who soon joined them here. Almeida had been informed that it would be dangerous to proceed down the stream, on account of the character of the natives; he therefore proposed to ascend the smaller river, where he might pursue his object with greater safety. The intelligence discouraged the greater number of Manoel's party, but not the leader himself; he determined to pursue his course, notwithstanding the defection of fourteen of his number.

Going down the *Guapore*, they found, next day, a village, from which the Indians fled at their approach.

The course of the stream led them into a vast lake where crocodiles were numerous, and near which they captured an Indian, and had some communication, not altogether friendly, with others. Renewing their voyage, they came to a part of the stream lined with habitations, and having many canoes; but as soon as any people saw them, they set up a cry and ran away. A pilot went in front with two negroes in a small canoe, and these, on one occasion, attacked some Indians, who, however, succeeded in escaping. Next morning, as was to be expected, a number of canoes came in pursuit of the aggressors, the leader of the party being a young man attacked on the previous day. The affair, however, ended peacefully, the Indians receiving gifts. A day or two later, they shot an antelope on the river, and, landing, found a piece of cloth and a cross, which were evident signs of converted Indians, some of whom they next day encountered.

Following the side of the broad stream, Manoel was so fortunate as to meet another canoe full of converted Indians, one of whom undertook to guide his party. This native now entered a stream which joined the *Guapore* on the left, and on which they were before long accosted from a canoe in Spanish. The adventurers were now amidst a labyrinth of islands and channels, where they might have wandered indefinitely had they not had a guide. They were about, however, to lose him; but, before his departure, he assured them that they would reach *San Miguel* on the following evening. To their surprise, their guide reappeared next morning, and conducted them amidst an infinity of intricate channels.

When near *San Miguel*, the guide was sent forward with a letter to the missionary; and when the adventurers followed, their appearance excited so much curiosity that the people even clustered on the trees to behold them. At this point the companions of Manoel were seized with apprehensions of danger, from the reflection that *Paulistas* could not expect good treatment either at the hands of the Jesuits or at those of their disciples. Manoel undertook the perilous task of first presenting himself. As soon as he landed, he was met by a number of old men, who, much to his surprise, mistook him for a bishop, and, kneeling down, besought his blessing. The missionary of *San Miguel* turned out to be a German of nearly fourscore years. This "Reduction" was situated upon the river *Baures*, twenty miles from its junction with the *Guapore;* it was one of the *Moxo* missions. The missionary had charge of about four thousand Indians, who had killed some of his predecessors. .

From *San Miguel* Manoel de Lima descended the stream to the *Guapore*, and came to the second river, called the *Magdalena*, on which was situated the mission of that name. Ascending it, he and his companions arrived, on the tenth day, at cultivated fields; and they learned from an Indian that the German missionary had sent news of their coming overland. At nightfall a canoe arrived from the "Reduction," bringing the travellers a welcome present of two dozen fowls and some other provisions. Next day, Manoel, having attired himself in a startling costume, proceeded to pay his visit to the two missionaries, a Hungarian and an Italian, who received him courteously, and entertained him and his companions at a plentiful repast.

The *Magdalena* mission was a flourishing one; the church was a spacious building, having three aisles; the columns being each composed of a tall tree. Some Indian carvers astonished the Portuguese by the beauty of the work with which they were embellishing the pulpit. The golden pyx, which had been sent from *Lima*, was valued at three thousand five hundred pieces of silver; and the Jesuits showed the traveller thirty hangings of tissue and brocade which had been sent from *Lima* and *Potosi*. The settlement was enclosed by a square wall, within which was a considerable space, so as to afford room for folds and gardens. There were shops for weavers, carpenters, and carvers; an *engenho*, for the fabrication of rum and sugar; public kitchens, and likewise stocks. The plantations attached to the settlement extended for leagues along the river; and the horses and cattle were very numerous.

But, although the Portuguese received every hospitality and attention, they were not allowed to depart without receiving a hint that the "reduction" was sufficiently strong to be capable of self-defence in the case of too frequent or unwelcome visits from their countrymen. On the second morning, after breakfast, fourscore horsemen were exercised in the great square. When they had concluded their manœuvres, both sides of the square were filled with archers, who discharged their arrows in the air so that they should fall into the intervening space. They became so heated in their exercise that Manoel de Lima became somewhat alarmed, and took the precaution of firing his pistol in the air, upon which the archers thought proper to disperse. The Jesuits stated that the missionaries could bring into the field forty thousand of these Indians.

Some of the Portuguese were now of opinion that they had proceeded far enough; and they proposed to purchase from the missionaries seven hundred and fifty cattle, with which to return to the mines. The missionaries, however, not having power to dispose of any property, the Portuguese were referred to the Provincial, who was then at *Exaltacion* upon the *Mamore*, to which point the travellers now determined to proceed, partly perhaps with the object of exploring this borderland. Manoel and three Europeans determined to set out by land, whilst the others preferred their canoes.

Before Manoel had departed, an incident occurred which somewhat changed the situation. This was the arrival of a messenger with a letter from the Provincial, in which the Father was reprimanded for having entertained the Portuguese, by doing which he had incurred

DISCOVERY OF THE DIAMOND DISTRICT.

the displeasure of the governor of *Santa Cruz*, and he was commanded to dismiss them without delay. At the end of three days, therefore, Manoel de Lima and his three companions were compelled to quit the society of the Jesuits, and to proceed on their voyage in canoes. They parted with many tears on both sides. Soon after they had reached the *Guapore*, they met a canoe bearing a cross; but they received no tidings of their former companions, all hope of rejoining whom was soon at an end.

At the junction of the *Mamore* with the *Guapore* the two rivers combine to form the *Madeira*, so called from the large quantities of wood which, after the rainy seasons, it bears into the *Amazons*. The last great river received by the *Madeira* before the point at which it turns to the north-west is the *Beni*. Very soon after passing the point of their junction, Manoel and his companions came upon the falls of the *Madeira*, and rapids more formidable than any which they had yet passed. Going down the stream they were much molested by the insects; whilst they had several narrow escapes from being swamped or upset by whirlpools or rocks. On one occasion the canoe was carried by a current against a rock, with such force that the men were thrown out; whilst the canoe was borne down the stream, and was soon out of sight.

The position of the travellers was now distressing. They had advanced so far down the stream that they could not think of returning; whilst they had no means of ascertaining their distance from the nearest settlement in the direction of *Pará*, the intervening country being possessed by wild animals or savages. Fortunately their arms and ammunition were remaining, and they were thus enabled to procure the means of subsistence. They had nothing for it but to follow the course of the river by land, when to their great joy they suddenly found themselves at the end of the rapids, and discovered their canoe caught between two large stones near an island. The canoe was regained by a slave.

On leaving behind them the last rapid and the last fall, where the river leaves the mountains, they saw on their right ground which had been cleared for a settlement by the people of *Pará*, who had come up the *Madeira* so far to seek for cinnamon, sarsaparilla, cacao, and tortoises. The settlers had been cut off by the *Muras*, from which people the travellers had a narrow escape. They likewise suffered from want of food; but after some days they came upon a Jesuit mission, where they were hospitably entertained. Here, leaving their canoe, they re-embarked in a larger vessel given them by the Jesuits, and proceeded down the stream to two other establishments of the same order, below the last of which they entered the *Amazons*.

Manoel de Lima, although he had not been the first to descend the *Madeira*, had performed a remarkable journey, having been the earliest European to proceed from *Matto-Grosso* to *Pará*, and to prove that a communication by water might be established. He was, therefore, sent to Lisbon to give an account of his proceedings. He expected great rewards for his services, and was consulted by the Portuguese ministers as to the steps which should be taken in consequence of his discoveries. But his pretensions were extravagant. Not contented with the offer of the repayment of the expenses of his expedition, he insisted on being appointed governor of the countries which he had discovered; and, as this was inadmissible, since they already belonged to Spain, he passed the remaining sixteen years of his life as a disappointed suitor at the court of Portugal. Those of his companions with whom he had parted at *Magdalena* made their way back to *Matto-Grosso*.

1749. In the year 1749, a voyage was made from *Pará* to *Matto-Grosso*, inverting the route which had been followed by Manoel de Lima. It was undertaken by order of the Portuguese Government, and by a strong party, provided with instruments for laying down their course. The

DISCOVERY OF THE DIAMOND DISTRICT.

expedition had to overcome considerable difficulties, and did not reach its destination before nine months had been passed on the voyage. The voyage down the stream can be performed in one-sixth of the time. Since the above date the water communication between *Matto-Grosso* and *Pará* has been continuous; and it was by this route that the former place was supplied with European goods, this way being both cheaper and less perilous than that from *S. Paulo*.

The new provinces rapidly increased in population and prosperity, which was temporarily interrupted by a drought between the years 1744 and 1749. During this period the streams dried up, and in consequence of the severe heat the woods caught fire. A great mortality ensued; whilst the people were alarmed at mid-day by a sound as if of thunder beneath their feet, which was followed by several shocks of earthquake. This disturbance, however, was merely temporary; and in one year more than fifteen hundred persons passed from *Goyaz* to *Matto-Grosso*, bringing droves of cattle and horses. A salt lake was opportunely discovered, to remedy the distress which had been occasioned from the want of that article.

The Portuguese in *Brazil* had shown exemplary enterprise in pushing forward their settlement along the various streams which form the tributaries of the *Amazons*; and there were in consequence some disputes with Spain concerning the boundaries. They had even occasioned some fears in the minds of the Spanish authorities as to the safety of *Peru*. They had likewise, by their inland explorations by water, ascertained that there was a communication by water between the *Amazons* and the *Orinoco*, they having from the former reached the Spanish missions on the latter river.

By the middle of the eighteenth century no hostile tribes remained on the banks of the *Amazons* throughout the entire course of that stream; such as had not submitted to the missionaries had retired into the interior. Some Indians, being terrified of pursuit, did not feel themselves in safety until they had reached the French territory of *Guayana*, where they were well received and encouraged to settle.

It is stated that the Portuguese missions on the *Amazons* were in a more flourishing condition than were those of the Spaniards on the upper part of the same river or its tributaries. The reason is to be found in the fact that whereas the former depended for their communications and supplies upon the flourishing settlement of *Belem* or *Pará*, the latter were forbidden to hold any communication with their Portuguese neighbours, and had to be supplied by the long and difficult overland route from *Quito*, which place was itself a six days' mountainous journey from the sea-coast. The city of *Pará* itself is stated by a French traveller * to have presented at this period the aspect of an European town, with regular streets of well-built stone houses and with magnificent churches. During thirty years it had been gradually rebuilt; whilst by clearing the country and converting woodland into pasture the healthiness of the city had been made to undergo a corresponding improvement. It should be remarked that about the year 1730 the plague of small-pox was here stayed amongst the Indians by the introduction of inoculation at the hands of a Carmelite missionary.

The system of the Jesuits in *Maranham* and *Pará* differed considerably from that of their brethren in *Paraguay*. In the latter country they are the proprietors of the missions, and were enabled to make their own laws within their territory. In the *Chiquito* and *Moxo* missions, though they had not adopted the principle of community of goods, they were equally unrestrained. But in *Maranham* they were obliged to base their institutions on the principle of rendering their Indians serviceable to

* Condamine.

the Portuguese settlers. Registers were kept at *S. Luiz* and at *Pará* containing the names of all Indians in their villages, from the age of thirteen to fifty, who were capable of service. These registers had to be attested upon oath by the missionaries every second year; and according to them the governor allotted the Indians for terms of six months, issuing written orders to the missionary to deliver them. It was optional for the Indians to serve during the remaining six months, and many preferred to do so.

In consequence of the divided allegiance which the Indians in these missions owed to the Jesuits and to the civil authority, respectively, they did not regard the former with the same absolute devotion which the Jesuits received from the Indians in *Paraguay*. Whereas the *Guaranis* were ever ready to devote their lives in defence of their teachers, the Indians of *Brazil* would forsake their masters upon the first alarm or on the slightest displeasure. As the kings of Portugal did not allow an annual salary to the Jesuits, such as they received from Spain, the Fathers in *Maranham*, since the colleges were too poor to support them, were permitted to employ five-and-twenty Indians for the same time and at the same rate of wages as any other Portuguese. They profited by their labour in collecting cacao and other indigenous produce, which was exported in a large canoe, one of which belonged to each of the twenty-eight *Aldeas*.

By the laws of Pedro II. of Portugal, no Portuguese were permitted to dwell in the *Aldeas*, in order to avert the evil influence of the bad example which they were sure to set. But the Portuguese received free permission to visit the settlements for the purpose of hiring Indians, and they were hospitably and gratuitously entertained by the missionaries. These Fathers did much to introduce civilization amongst their charges; a task in which they persevered in the face of much calumny. It was found more practicable for themselves to learn the *Tupi* language than to instruct the natives in Portuguese. As *Tupi* was likewise used by traders, it so completely gained the ascendancy throughout *Pará* that it was used exclusively in the pulpits.

At this period a missionary net was spread over the South-American Continent, its meshes extending in every direction. From *Quito* the Spanish missionaries, as we have seen, encountered those of *Maranham* on the upper tributaries of the *Amazons*. Those on the *Rio Negro*, another tributary of that great river, met the missions on the *Orinoco;* whilst the *Moxo* and *Madeira* settlements, in Upper *Peru* and Western *Brazil*, respectively, continued the connection. The *Moxo* missions adjoined those of the *Chiquitos*, which again communicated with the "Reductions" in *Paraguay*, whence the Jesuits extended the net to the *Gran Chaco* and the *Pampas*. It seemed as if the whole of South America were on the way to become Christian and civilized; but an unexpected check occurred to the activity of the Jesuits, and South America was thrown back into a state of confusion and barbarism from which many portions of the continent have not yet emerged.

CHAPTER XIII.

FOUNDATION AND PROGRESS OF BUENOS AYRES.

1580-1800.

IN the year 1580 the foundations of a lasting city were 1580. laid at *Buenos Ayres* by De Garay on the same situation as had twice previously been chosen—namely, by Mendoza, and by Cabeza de Vaca, respectively. The same leader had before this founded the settlement of *Santa Fè* on the *Paraná*. The site selected for the future capital of the *Pampas* is probably one of the worst ever chosen for a city—a fact which is at once palpable to every one who has visited the place. That the same site should have been selected three times in succession is only to be accounted for by the tendency which exists in human nature to follow precedent, whether it be good or whether it be bad. "With a perversity of judgment," says Mr. Washburn, in a passage in which there is not a word to alter, " which seemed to characterize all his acts, Mendoza moved up the broad and noble estuary, passing by the most suitable places for a town site, until he came to a place that combined all the inconveniences that could possibly exist, on the banks of a large navigable river. The point thus selected, and where now stands the principal city of the *Plata*, has probably the worst harbour in the world for a large commercial town. Large vessels must always lie off some two or three leagues from the shore, and those of lighter draft that venture within the inner roads are liable to be left high and dry on the hard bottom, or *tosca*, when a *pampero*, or strong wind, from the west sets in. But if the wind blows strongly from the south-east, then they are liable to drag their anchors, and be carried up so high inland that, when the wind veers again, they are left many rods from the water, and can only be broken up for firewood. The cost of lightening a vessel of her cargo is much more than the freight of it from New York or Liverpool. The country in the vicinity, for as far as the eye could reach, was a dead-level plain, without bush or tree; the air in the hot, dry season being frequently so full of dust as to be almost insupportable, and the soil of that sticky, clayey character that a slight rain would render it almost impassable for man or animal. And this place was selected by Mendoza as the site of the first Spanish settlement in South America."

Notwithstanding the inconvenience of its harbour, *Buenos Ayres* soon became the chief commercial *entrepôt* of the valley of the *Plata*. The settlement was not effected without some severe fighting between De Garay's force and the *Querandis*. The latter, however, were effectually quelled; the proof of it being their submission, without further resistance, to be parcelled out amongst the conquerors in *repartimientos*. "The registers are still preserved of De Garay's followers by name, amongst sixty-five of whom he divided in lots the lands extending along the river-side from *Buenos Ayres* to *Baradero* on the *Paraná*, as well as the Indian inhabitants of the adjoining territories under their respective *caciques*." The lines of the new city were laid out about a league higher up the river than the site of Mendoza's settlement. Under De Garay's superintendence it was soon sufficiently fortified to ensure protection. It is remarkable that it was not till about three years after the foundation of this settlement that the first vessel was despatched to Spain laden with the produce of *La Plata*—namely, hides and sugar from *Paraguay*, the former being evidence of the increase of horned cattle from the original stock imported from Europe thirty years before.

The Spaniards were now nominally masters of the *Rio de La Plata*, but they had still to apprehend hostilities on the part of the natives between their few and far-distant settlements. Of this liability De Garay himself was to form a lamentable example. On his passage back to *Asuncion*, having incautiously landed to sleep near the ruins of the old fort of *San Espiritu*, he was surprised by a party of natives, and murdered with all his companions. The death of this brave Biscayan was mourned as a great loss by the entire colony. The importance of the cities founded by him was soon apparent; and in 1620 all of the settlements south of the confluence of the rivers *Paraná* and *Paraguay* were formed into a separate, independent government, under the name of *Rio de La Plata*, of which *Buenos Ayres* was declared the capital. This city likewise became the seat of a bishopric.

An English traveller, whose name is lost, has left a description of *Buenos Ayres* as it was in the year 1658. At that time only Spaniards might proceed in Spanish ships to their Indian possessions. Other nations of Europe, however, were occasionally permitted to trade with the cities on the river Plate; and at *Buenos Ayres*, in the above-mentioned year, our countryman found twenty Dutch and two English ships preparing to proceed homewards, laden with bull-hides, plate, and vigonia wool, which they had obtained in exchange for other commodities. At that time the military resources of the city of *Buenos Ayres* were not great; for we read that, on the alarm of an attack by a French squadron, they had to send for aid to the Viceroy at *Lima*, who caused to be levied, with much difficulty and by the exercise of force, a hundred men, who did not reach the eastern coast until eight or nine months after they had been sent for.

The town of *Buenos Ayres* contained four hundred

houses, and was not enclosed, either by wall or ditch. Its fortifications consisted in a bastion at the mouth of the rivulet, with two small iron guns, and in a small earthwork surrounded by a ditch, commanding the river, and on which were mounted ten iron guns. This fort contained the house of the governor of the place, who had under him a garrison of one hundred and fifty men, formed into three companies, the captains of which were appointed or removed at his will. The soldiers received pay at the rate of four *reals* a day. But the governor had further at his disposal the additional means of defence of twelve hundred horses, upon which, in case of necessity, he mounted as many citizens as could be collected together, to act as cavalry. The houses of the town were then built of sun-dried bricks. They were of one storey, and were thatched with canes and straw. They contained spacious rooms, and had large court-yards and adjoining gardens full of orange, lemon, and fig trees, of pear and of apple trees; of numerous kinds of vegetables; and of excellent melons. Wine, then as now, was almost the only article of diet which was sold at a high price; and the markets of the town were supplied abundantly with beef, mutton, venison, poultry, and game of various sorts. A partridge might be purchased for a penny. Ostriches were to be found in the neighbourhood in great numbers; and the traveller, whose description I quote from, makes a remark from general observation which indicates more subtle instinct on the part of those birds than they usually obtain credit for. "I saw one thing of these creatures very remarkable, and that is, while the hen sits upon the eggs, they have the instinct or forethought to provide for their young; so five or six days before they come out of the shell they set an egg in each of the four corners of the place where they sit; these eggs they break, and when they rot, worms and maggots breed in them in prodigious numbers; which serve to nourish the young ostriches from the time they are hatched until they are able to go farther for their sustenance."

The better houses of *Buenos Ayres* were at that time adorned with hangings, pictures, and ornaments. The wealthier inhabitants were served from plate, and their establishments contained many servants or slaves, who were employed also in the cultivation of their grounds or to take care of their horses and mules. The wealth of the inhabitants at the period referred to consisted mainly in cattle, the numbers of which increased on the vast plains with wonderful rapidity. At that time hides were to be bought in the city at the rate of seven or eight *reals* each, or at less than an English crown, and the same were sold in Europe for at least four times as much money. Cattle were used for a singular purpose in the prosecution of war, being driven to the river-side in such numbers as to defy the efforts of the enemy to penetrate through them.

The merchants of *Buenos Ayres* of the seventeenth century had the reputation of possessing considerable wealth, the fortunes of many amongst them being estimated at from two to three hundred thousand crowns. They were reputed to love their ease, and to be blessed with wives who had the credit of being as virtuous as they were lovely. For their fidelity, however, they demanded a strict return, being ready to punish by the bowl or the dagger any breach of the marriage vow on the part of the husband.

Besides the Spanish population, there were in the seventeenth century in *Buenos Ayres* a few Frenchmen, some Dutch, and some Genoese, but all these passed themselves off as being Spanish, the more surely to escape the dangers of the Inquisition.

The chief edifices and institutions of the town at that period were the cathedral, the college of the Jesuits, and the convents of the Dominicans, the Recollects, and of the Order of Mercy.

The merchants of Seville, who had obtained a monopoly of the supply of *Mexico* and *Peru*, regarded with much jealousy the prospect of a new opening for the South-American trade by way of *La Plata*, and exerted their interest successfully to obtain prohibitory enactments against all trade with *Buenos Ayres*, lest it should interfere with the sale of their periodical shipments for *Panamá*. In vain the inhabitants of the former city petitioned and remonstrated; for some years the only boon they could obtain was the permission to export yearly to *Brazil* or to the coast of *Guinea* a small quantity of wheat, jerked beef, and tallow. In 1618 this was extended to a permission to send two vessels of a hundred tons burthen each year to Spain; but a custom-house was established at *Cordova* to levy a duty of fifty per cent. on goods carried by that way. All commercial intercourse with other Spanish colonies in America was prohibited under severe penalties. Under this miserable commercial legislation *Buenos Ayres* continued to languish for the first century of its existence.

1715. In 1715, after the treaty of Utrecht, the English, as has been said, obtained the *asiento* or contract for supplying Spanish colonies in America with African slaves, in virtue of which they had permission to form an establishment at *Buenos Ayres*, and to send thither annually four ships with twelve hundred negroes, the value of which they might export in produce of the country. They were strictly forbidden to introduce other goods than those necessary for their own establishments; but under the temptation of gain on the one side and of demand on the other, the *asiento* ships naturally became the means of transacting a considerable contraband trade. One vessel is mentioned by Dean Funes, the historian, as being well known to have carried away from the *Plata* for London two millions of dollars in specie and seventy thousand dollars' worth of hides in return for European goods clandestinely introduced. This trade was carried on till 1739, when Spain attempted to stop it by means 1739. of guardships. As the English resented this measure, the two powers became involved in hostilities, with the result that the *asiento* ceased.

The English were not the only smugglers in the river Plate. By the treaty of Utrecht the Portuguese had obtained the important settlement of *Colonia* directly facing *Buenos Ayres*. It is to be remembered, however, that the majestic stream has here a breadth of about thirty miles, or more than that which separates England from France. By the same treaty the Crown of Portugal solemnly engaged to prohibit smuggling; but, notwithstanding this clause, the provinces of *Buenos Ayres, Paraguay*, and *Tucuman* were thenceforward abundantly supplied through this channel with European goods. Thus by the imbecile commercial policy of Spain, that country was not only superseded by foreign traders in the markets of her own colonies, but further lost the duties upon their produce. The yearly freight of the galleons, which a century before had been estimated at fifteen thousand tons, fell to two thousand. The Viceroy of *Peru* had even to write to the governor of *Buenos Ayres*, requiring him to punish his officers for their negligence or connivance, since it appeared that the Peruvians no longer repaired to *Lima* as a market for European goods, their wants being amply supplied from the *Plata*.

To this remonstrance Zavala was constrained to reply that he found all measures vain to repress smuggling whilst such facilities existed for carrying it on and such gains were its result. He was sufficiently advanced to perceive, and sufficiently bold and honest to express his opinion, that a trade so demoralizing to the colonists was only to be stopped in one of two ways; either by throwing open the markets to legitimate trade, whereby the Government would secure the duties, or by driving the Portuguese out of the *Banda Oriental*, or *Uruguay*. Of the two alternatives, the latter best suited the views of the Spanish Government. The Portuguese indeed, not contented with the possession of *Colonia*, had commenced a more important settlement near *Monte Video*. From this place, however, they were dislodged by Zavala, who, by order of his Government, proceeded to establish settlements at that place and at *Maldonado*.

Under the above-detailed circumstances of contention between the Crowns of Spain and Portugal, represented by their respective establishments at *Buenos Ayres* and in *Brazil*, and which were so typical of its future history, was founded the healthy and agreeable city of *Monte Video*. Some families were transported thither from the *Canaries*, whilst others removed to there from *Buenos Ayres*. Large sums of money from the mines of *Potosí* were sent by the Viceroy to carry on the works; whilst the *Guaranís* were despatched in numbers from *Paraguay* to lend their labour to the fortifications. The Portuguese, however, were not dismayed, and laboured, on the other hand, to increase their own establishments, fixing themselves permanently on the *Rio Grande*, from which they carried on the contraband trade with more impunity than ever. The value of this trade is estimated by Dean Funes at two millions of *dollars* yearly to the Portuguese, being so much loss to Spain.

The inevitable consequence of this state of things was fresh antagonism between the two countries, which it was sought to put an end to by a treaty between the two nations concluded in 1750. One of the articles stipulated that Portugal should cede to Spain all of her establishments on the eastern bank of the *Plata*; in return for which she was to receive the seven missionary towns on the *Uruguay*. But, as is told in another chapter of this work, the inhabitants of the *Misiones* naturally rebelled against the idea of being handed over to a people known to them only by their slave-dealing atrocities; and they made a gallant resistance against the united forces of the two powers, which appeared to enforce the conditions of the treaty. The result was that when two thousand natives had been slaughtered and their settlements reduced to ruins, the Portuguese repudiated the compact, as they could no longer receive their equivalent, and they still therefore retained *Colonia*.

When hostilities were renewed in 1762, the governor of *Buenos Ayres* succeeded in possessing himself of *Colonia;* but in the following year it was restored to the Portuguese, who continued in possession until 1777, when it was definitively ceded to Spain. The continual encroachments to the Portuguese in the *Rio de La Plata*, and the impunity with which the contraband trade was carried on, together with the questions to which it constantly gave rise with foreign governments, had long shown the necessity for a change in the government of that colony; for it was still under the superintendence of the Viceroy of *Peru*, residing at *Lima*, three thousand miles distant. The Spanish authorities accordingly resolved to give fresh force to their representatives in the *Rio de La Plata;* and in 1776 they took the important resolution to sever the connection between the provinces of *La Plata* and the Viceroyalty of *Peru.* The former were now erected into a new Viceroyalty, the capital of which was *Buenos Ayres.* It comprised the province of its own name, together with those of *Paraguay, Cordova, Salta, Potosí, La Plata, Santa Cruz de la Sierra,* or *Cochabamba, La Paz,* and *Puno,* besides the subordinate governments of *Monte Video, Moxos,* and *Chiquitos,* and the Missions on the Rivers *Uruguay* and *Paraná.*

To this Viceroyalty was appointed *Don* Pedro Cevallos, a former governor of *Buenos Ayres.* A formidable armament was placed under his command; twelve men-of-war escorting a numerous fleet of transports, sailed from Spain, with ten thousand men. The first act of Cevallos was to take possession of the island of *St. Katherine,* the most important Portuguese possession on the coast of *Brazil.* Proceeding thence to the *Plate,* he razed the fortifications of *Colonia* to the ground, and drove the Portuguese from the neighbourhood. In October of the following year, 1777, a treaty of peace was signed at St. Ildefonso, between Queen Maria of Portugal and Charles III. of Spain, by virtue of which *St. Katherine's* was restored to the latter country, whilst Portugal withdrew from the *Banda Oriental* or Uruguay, and relinquished all pretensions to the right of navigating the *Rio de La Plata* and its affluents beyond its own frontier line.

About the same time some important changes took place in the commercial regulations affecting the Spanish colonies. Various relaxations had from time to time been made of the old system by which the entire trade of Spain was left almost as a monopoly to the merchants of Seville and of Cadiz. Periodical packets had been established between Coruña and the principal colonial ports, with permission to export and to import Spanish and colonial goods. Direct intercourse was also permitted between *Cuba* and the other West Indian Islands; and, in 1774, the several colonies were allowed to open up a trade with each other. The above measures originated with the enlightened minister for the department of the Indies, De Galvez, who had himself passed many years in America, and who had personally witnessed to how great an extent Spain was a loser by her former system. They were followed in 1778 by the promulgation of an entirely new commercial code. The trade was still exclusively to belong to Spain and to Spanish shipping, and the tariff was based upon the principle of protection to native industry and of furthering the sale of Spanish productions. Nine ports of Spain and twenty-four in the colonies were declared ports of entry.

By these regulations it was likewise provided that for ten years Spanish manufactures of wool, cotton, linen, steel, glass, &c., should be shipped, duty free, for the colonies, which might export in return their principal articles of raw produce, such as cotton, coffee, sugar, cochineal, indigo, bark, and copper. The duty on the import of gold was reduced from 5 to 2 per cent.; that on the import of silver from 10 to 5½ per cent.; whilst vessels laden solely with natural produce were exempted from one-third of the duties. The shipment of certain articles of foreign production, such as cottons, stuffs, oil, wines, and brandies, which might interfere with those of Spain, were totally prohibited. These regulations contained, however, certain clauses framed in the old restrictive spirit. Some obsolete edicts were renewed restricting the cultivation of certain colonial productions—such as the vine and olive, hemp and flax—lest they should compete with the growth of the same articles in the mother country. The South Americans were not allowed to make their own cloth, and were debarred from the use of the wool of the *vicuña*, which was to be collected for the King's account.

Under the administration of the above-named minister the *Creoles* had to complain of the great partiality shown to Spaniards over themselves in the distribution of appointments, both civil and military, in the colonies— a mistake on the part of the Spanish Government all the greater on account of the period at which it took place, namely, whilst a struggle arising in the question of colonial rights was pending between Great Britain and her North-American possessions. It is certainly singular—indeed, it seems inexplicable—that Spain, of all countries, should have determined at this time to join with France in espousing the cause of the North Americans against England, whilst she herself was pursuing in her own colonies the very policy complained of. It was not long before the Spanish Crown was reminded by the South Americans that it had itself sanctioned the principle of the subject's right to resistance against his sovereign on the plea of wrongs unredressed.

The new commercial regulations, however, as a whole, were extremely advantageous to the colonies as well as to the mother country. *Buenos Ayres*, in particular, from being a nest of smugglers, soon rose to be one of the most important commercial cities of the New World. To take one example. Before the new regulations of 1778, the export of hides to Spain averaged about 150,000 yearly. It soon rose to between 700,000 and 800,000, whilst in one year [1783], on the conclusion of peace with England, the export attained to 1,400,000. Instead of the former two or three ships, there now sailed annually from seventy to eighty from the river *Plate* to Spain. The population of the province of *Buenos Ayres*, under these altered circumstances, was doubled in twenty years, rising from 38,000 in 1778 to 72,000 in 1800.

Until the latter part of the eighteenth century the inhabitants of the province of *Buenos Ayres*, possessing ample lands safe from incursions of the Indians, had no particular object in extending their possessions further south than the river *Salado*. The further region was left to the Indians, and was a *terra incognita* until the publication in England, in the year 1774, of an account of *Patagonia* by Father Falkner.

Falkner was an English Jesuit who had been devoted to travelling as a missionary amongst the Indians, in which duty he had passed forty years. He pointed out how vulnerable by any naval power were the Spanish possessions in that region; and, on the publication of his book, the Spanish Government lost no time in instructing the Viceroy of *Buenos Ayres* to have the coast of *Patagonia* surveyed, with a view to the formation of fresh settlements. The command of the surveying expedition was given to an officer named Piedra, who sailed from *Monte Video* at the close of 1778, and passed three months in examining the shores of the gulf of *St. Antonio*, where he left an officer and some men to build a fort, conveniently situated for exploring the rivers *Negro* and *Colorado*, and for securing the entrance of those streams against invasion. A further inducement for making a settlement here was the number of whales and seals in the neighbourhood, which likewise contained extensive salt deposits.

In April 1779 a settlement was formed on the river *Negro*, and in the following year the whole of the southern part of the coast of *Patagonia* was surveyed. The only spot which seemed to afford a promising site for a settlement was *St. Julians*, which had the advantage of a constant supply of water some three or four miles inland. The Indians in the neighbourhood were friendly and ready to offer assistance, which was of great consequence to the first Spanish settlers in the cold months of June, July, and August. This colony, however, was destined to be short-lived, as the Spanish Government, in 1783, resolved to break up the Patagonian settlements, which were the occasion of great expense to *Buenos Ayres*, and the preservation of which seemed of doubtful utility. The settlement upon the *Rio Negro* was alone preserved.

The missionary Falkner had supposed that a hostile naval power might, by ascending the *Rio Negro*, surprise the Spanish territories in the interior and even in *Chili*. In order to determine this important point, and to survey the river and its affluents, an expedition was despatched from the *Rio Negro*. Starting from the settlement of *Carmen* in 1782, it was absent for eight months. It proved the possibility of ascending the river to the foot of the *Andes*. One surprising fact was brought to light, namely, that the Indians of the *Pampas* had not to drive their stolen cattle for more than three days' journey over the *Cordillera*, from the lake of the boundary mentioned by Falkner, before reaching the fort of *Valdivia*, where they found a ready market. The party of Indians from whom the explorers learned this circumstance consisted of about three hundred people, who had left their country more than a year before for the purpose of collecting cattle for the Valdivians. They were now on their way homewards with about eight hundred head, each one of which bore the *Buenos Ayres* mark. Their return voyage down the stream was accomplished in three weeks.

In a work of this description I find considerable difficulty in giving due regard to the unities of time, &c. My object is to place before the reader, as well as I can, the general condition of South America at any one period; but the progress of events on that continent during the colonial administration was so irregular that it is scarcely possible to avoid appearing to give undue prominence to one particular region at a time, overlooking others which in these days may seem of equal or even greater importance. Thus whilst the province of *Buenos Ayres* was still a vast plain overrun by savages, *Peru*, subsequent to the Spanish invasion, had a long and interesting history. In deferring to so late a date in this volume any account of *Buenos Ayres*, which is to-day a place of the first importance in South America, I may seem to be wanting in a sense of comparative fitness. But on reflection the reader will perceive that for the first two hundred years of its existence *Buenos Ayres* possessed no history beyond that of its foundation. Its records during those years, in so far as the world in general is interested, may be comprised in a single sentence. It was on the collapse of the narrow, repressive policy of Spain, and the erection of *Buenos Ayres* into a Viceroyalty, that the history of that city and province may be said to commence. Notwithstanding its natural resources and its geographical importance, it was until that date, like *Tucuman*, merely the seat of a local government, one amongst several, dependent on the Viceroyalty of *Peru*. In the last quarter of a century, however, of its colonial existence it made colossal strides. The new prospects of commercial wealth absorbed the interests and thoughts of all; and whilst Europe was waving with the commotion caused by the French Revolution, this far-distant province of Spain, so favoured by nature and position, was steadily laying the foundations of its future importance and prosperity.

The Viceroyalty of *Buenos Ayres* was subdivided into the provinces of—

(1.) *Buenos Ayres*, the capital of which was the city of that name, and which comprised the Spanish possessions that now form the Republic of *Uruguay*, as well as the Argentine Provinces of *Buenos Ayres, Santa Fè, Entre Rios*, and *Corrientes ;*

(2.) *Paraguay*, the capital of which was *Asunsion*, and which comprised what is now the Republic of *Paraguay ;*

(3.) *Tucuman*, the capital of which was *St. Iago del Estero*, and which included what are to-day the Argentine provinces of *Cordova, Tucuman, St. Iago, Salta, Catamarca, Rioja*, and *Jujuy ;*

(4). *Las Charcas* or *Potosi*, the capital of which was *La Plata*, and which now forms the Republic of *Bolivia ;* and

(5.) *Chiquito* or *Cuyo*, the capital of which was *Mendoza*, and in which were comprehended the present Argentine provinces of *St. Luiz, Mendoza*, and *St. Juan.*

NOTE.—This chapter is founded on "Buenos Ayres and the Provinces of the *Rio de La Plata*," by Sir Woodbine Parish, 1839 ;

Falkner's "*Patagonia*" (Latin) ; England, 1774 ;

"*Rio de La Plata*," by Felix Azaro ; Paris, 1809 ;

Dean Fuñes's " History of *Paraguay*," &c. ; *Buenos Ayres*, 1816.

CHAPTER XIV.

BRAZIL; THE WAR OF THE SEVEN REDUCTIONS.

1750-1761.

1750. THE discovery of mining districts in the interior of *Brazil* caused both Spanish and Portuguese statesmen to perceive that the period had arrived when it was desirable, in the interests of both countries and of their respective colonies, to establish a boundary-line between their several possessions in South America. The famous Bull of Pope Alexander VI. had long become a dead letter. The fact of the Spanish Queen of Ferdinand VI. being a Portuguese princess, and having great influence over her husband, tended in no small degree to bringing about an amicable and equitable settlement of the territorial question existing between the two nations in South America.

All pretensions on either side founded upon the Bull of Alexander having been formally annulled, the demarcation between the two territories began on the south, at the mouth of a small stream which rises at the foot of the *Monte de Castilhaos Grande*, whence it proceeded in a straight line to the mountains, following their summits to the sources of the *Rio Negro* and continued to those of the *Ybicuy;* it then followed the course of that river to its junction with the *Uruguay*, skirting the *Uruguay* upwards until it reached the *Pepiri*, and then the latter river to its chief source; there it left the rivers and took the line of highest ground until it came to the head of the first stream which flows into the *Yguazu;*

THE WAR OF THE SEVEN REDUCTIONS. 219

the boundary then first followed this stream, and then the *Yguazu* to its junction with the *Paraná*; it went up the *Paraná* to the *Igurey*, and then up the *Igurey* to its source; there it once more took the highest ground as far as to the first stream that runs into the *Paraguay*; the water then became the line to the mouth of the *Jauru*, whence the line was to be drawn straight to the south bank of the *Guapore*, opposite to the mouth of the *Sarare*. Wherever the line reached the *Guapore* it was to follow that stream to the *Mamore*, and then the *Mamore* to the *Madeira*, and the *Madeira* to a point half-way between its mouth and the mouth of the *Mamore*; it then struck east and west until it touched the *Yavari*, when it followed that river to the *Amazons*, and went down this great stream to the western mouth of the *Japura*. It ascended this river until it reached the summits of the *Cordillera*, between the *Amazons* and the *Orinoco*, when it was to go eastward along those summits, as far as the territories of the contracting parties extended.

The commissioners were to be careful to trace the demarcation from the westerly mouth of the *Japura*, so as not to touch the Portuguese settlements on that river and on the *Rio Negro*. The Spaniards were to avoid this part, whilst the Portuguese, on their side, were to abstain from ascending the *Orinoco*, and from spreading towards the Spanish territory. The line was to be drawn, without regard to extent of territory, with the object of tracing a distinct boundary. As the limits of the vast territories which were here for the first time separated were imperfectly known to the negotiators on either side, considerable latitude was given to the commissioners at several points. They were to design a map as they traced the limits, and jointly to name all unnamed rivers and mountains; these maps were, respectively, to be signed in duplicate by both commissioners, and were to serve as authorities in case of disputes.

By this treaty Portugal expressly ceded *Colonia* to Spain, together with all the territory on the northern shore of the *Plata* as far as the point where it was now determined the line of demarcation should begin. Portugal likewise renounced all right to the navigation of the *Plata*, which thenceforward was to belong exclusively to Spain. The Spanish king, in turn, made certain concessions to Portugal on the eastern side of the *Uruguay*. It was provided that the inhabitants of *Colonia* might remain there or remove at their option; but the missionaries were to migrate from the settlements ceded by Spain, and the "Reductions" were to be delivered up to the Crown of Portugal. All trade between the two nations was forbidden; nor might the subjects of one power enter the territories of the other without previous permission from the governor of the district to which he was proceeding, unless he were going on public business and provided with passports. In case of any future war between the two contracting powers, the sovereigns desired that their respective subjects in America might continue in peace, without committing acts of hostility. Neither power should permit the use of its ports to the enemy of the other; nor should such enemy be permitted a passage through the dominions of either. Several minor stipulations followed.

This memorable treaty bears witness to the sincerity and good sense of the parties by whom it was contracted; but it is not surprising that in undertaking to decide so vast a line of demarcation, some considerations should have been overlooked on either side which were nevertheless of vast importance. In view of the distance at which the treaty was drawn up from the districts and territories to which it referred and the imperfect information possessed concerning them, it was perhaps not possible that it should have been otherwise. As it was, the treaty contained one fatal clause which not only frustrated the good intentions of the sovereigns and led to immediate war, but was productive of consequences the baneful effects of which a century has not effaced.

The territory to the east of the *Uruguay*, which had been ceded by the boundary treaty to the Portuguese, contained seven " Reductions," inhabited by about thirty thousand *Guaranís*, who had been bred up to servitude and domestic life. According to the terms of the treaty, these people, with all belonging to them, were to migrate into the Spanish territory. The Spanish King and his ministers had inserted this clause, or had agreed to it, in ignorance of the circumstances in which these Indians were placed. They were actuated, moreover, by feelings of regard to the Indians who were thereby affected. These had suffered much from the ravages of the *Paulistas*, and they had good reason to detest the Portuguese. To have left them, therefore, as subjects of the Crown of Portugal would have been ungenerous and offensive. It would likewise cut them off from the people of their own race. The negotiators were thus reduced to a choice of evils; but it had been decided that the exodus of these Indians was to take place within a year.

The commissioner sent on the part of Spain to see the treaty carried into effect was the Marquis of Valdelirios; the Portuguese commissioner was Gomes Freyre, the governor of *Rio de Janeiro* and *Minas Geraes*, who had himself experienced the inconvenience of an undefined boundary-line, and who is credited with having been the projector of the Treaty of Limits. The stipulation regarding the evacuation of the *Misiones* within a year was necessarily unaccomplished, owing to the fact that the Spanish commissioners did not reach the *Plata* until two years after the treaty had been signed. In the meantime, the Jesuits of *Paraguay* had addressed a remonstrance on the subject to the Royal Audience of *Charcas*, and had obtained from that tribunal a statement in their favour. They next applied to the Audience of *Lima*, and the Viceroy forwarded one copy of their memorial to the court of Spain and another to the governor of *Buenos Ayres*. The governor was requested to deliver it to the commissioners on their arrival.

The Jesuits, although relying on the effects of these memorials, were prepared to act in obedience to the terms of the treaty. The Provincial assembled the senior missionaries, who declared, almost unanimously, that it would not be possible to carry out the stipulations of the decree. He, nevertheless, instructed the Jesuits in the seven "Reductions" to endeavour to persuade the people to obedience; whilst at the same time he wrote to the King, pointing out the extreme difficulty of carrying the order into effect. The Superior went through the missions, making known the King's pleasure. All appeared to acquiesce, with the exception of one *cacique*, who replied, that they had inherited from their forefathers the land of which they were now to be dispossessed. In transmitting to the Provincial the promise of the *Guaranís* to obey, the Superior added, that he feared that the temper of the people would render the removal impossible.

The intention of the Government was that the dispossessed *Guaranís* should occupy the territory which had been ceded to Spain south of the *Ybicuy*. It was desirable to people the ceded territory; but the Jesuits were not anxious to be too near neighbours to the Spanish regular settlements, whose vicinity would render more difficult the task of restraining their disciples. Reconnoitering parties were sent out to search for situations suitable for the settlement of large numbers of people with their flocks and herds; but such were not readily found. It was finally agreed that the missionaries should take refuge with their brethren in the land of the "Reductions" between the *Uruguay* and the *Paraná*, and this project was accordingly carried into execution.

When affairs were in this state, the Marquis of Valdelirios arrived in the *Plata*. He was met by Father Luiz, Altamirano having full powers from the General

THE WAR OF THE SEVEN REDUCTIONS. 223

of the Jesuits over his brethren in South America. The commissioner was at once confronted by a whole load of arguments against the project of migration; and even the Jesuits in whose college he lodged urged the necessity of employing an armed force to clear the country on the *Rio Negro* from the *Charruas* before the emigrants should remove; they likewise represented that time should be given to erect places of shelter for the people when they should arrive in their new quarters; they also begged for a delay of three years in order that crops might meanwhile be raised at the new settlements to support the emigrants on their arrival. Their demands, though so far reasonable, were excessive; and all they could extort from Valdelirios was a delay of three months.

The Marquis, however, could perceive that the execution of the treaty was not altogether an easy matter; and he repaired to *Castilhos Grande*, in order to confer with Gomes Freyre, sending, at the same time, Altamirano to the "Reductions," in order that his authority might be more readily available. When that Father had reached the "Reduction" of *Yapayu*, he found that the spirit of resistance had already displayed itself. There was, it appeared, a point at which even these *Guaranís*, brought up as they had been from generation to generation in implicit obedience, could turn; and when a community is in a state of smothered discontent there is never wanting a person to urge them on to deeds. Such a person now appeared in this "Reduction" in the person of a traveller recently arrived from *Brazil*, and who pointed out to the *Guaranís* that they were being sacrificed not by the Portuguese but by the Spaniards. The discontent now assumed a more solid form, the magistrates being deposed, and persons elected in their stead who were pledged to defend the people's rights.

As might be supposed, this news occasioned alarm at 1752. *S. Miguel*, where preparations had been made for the emigration, and whence the first division of four hundred families had actually set out. The first emigrants were unfortunately met by a succession of heavy rains; and the people, declaring that if they went farther they should all perish, refused to proceed; in which resolution they were strengthened by the arrival of a messenger stating that their fellow-settlers now declined to quit their birthplace. Thereupon they returned immediately; when their insurrection assumed a more aggressive form, two of their office-bearers narrowly escaping with their lives, whilst the Indian servant of one was slain.

The inhabitants of another "Reduction" had reached their appointed place and begun to build; but, at the end of six months, wearied with labour and with the task of repelling the Indians, they returned to their former abode. With other settlements similar experiences took place. The Jesuits had in all cases shown their willingness on all occasions to obey the loyal orders; time had likewise proved the wisdom of the measures of precaution suggested to the Marquis of Valdelirios upon his arrival in the *Plata*. To that commissioner, therefore, must be ascribed the chief of the evils which arose from the precipitancy which he showed in carrying the emigration into effect. In his hasty measures, however, he was supported both by Altamirano and by the bishop of *Buenos Ayres*. The result was that the seven "Reductions" which were to be removed were now in a state of declared resistance to the treaty; whilst the other twenty-four showed that they not only sympathized with them, but were even inclined to support them. The Jesuits became the scapegoats; for whilst it was on them that the authorities depended for the measure being effected, the *Guaranís* of the "Reductions," on the other hand, publicly declared that the Jesuits had sold their towns and possessions to the Portuguese; and the magistrates forbade all persons, on pain of death, either to obey or listen to them upon any other than religious matters. A resolution was even arrived at to assassinate Alta-

THE WAR OF THE SEVEN REDUCTIONS.

mirano; but he was enabled by a timely warning to effect his escape to *Buenos Ayres.*

Fifty Portuguese and fifty Spanish troops, with a number of surveyors and other officers attached to the commission, and with a convoy of waggons and animals conveying stores, had by this time arrived at the territory of the missions, for the purpose of marking out the line of demarcation. They were to commence at *Castilhos*, on the coast, and to survey to the mouth of the *Ybicuy*. They reached an *estancia* belonging to the "Reduction" of *S. Miguel*. The men of that place, who had been in pursuit of Altamirano, turned aside on hearing of the new arrival, and the leader of the detachment informed the officer of the Spaniards that the Portuguese troops could not be permitted to enter the country. The officer, having proceeded to *Buenos Ayres*, added his testimony to that already in the possession of the authorities, to the effect that the *Guaranís* would not yield their territory excepting to force. Valdelirios had by this time returned from his conference with Gomes Freyre; and the commissioners, without referring the matter to their respective Governments, now declared war upon the people of the seven "Reductions."

When the above important decision was arrived at, Altamirano addressed an instruction to the Jesuits, requiring them to destroy all gunpowder within the disturbed districts, and to prevent the manufacture of implements of war; after which, in case they should not be able to persuade the *Guaranís* to yield obedience to the treaty, they were to quit their charges and repair to *Buenos Ayres*. The Provincial of the Jesuits now addressed, in the name of the Company, a resignation of their charges, not in the proclaimed districts alone, but in all the *Guaraní* "Reductions." But the governor and the bishop, to whom the resignation was addressed, declined to accept it; whilst Valdelirios insisted that the Jesuits should not be ordered to withdraw.

The first hostilities occurred upon the river *Pardo*, between a detachment of Portuguese and the *Guaranís* of *S. Luiz*. Of the latter, fifty were made prisoners, and they caused much prejudice against the Jesuits by stating, in reply to questions, that there were Jesuits amongst them, and that the latter had incited them to cut off the heads of the Portuguese who fell into their hands,—statements which were probably invented as being agreeable to their questioners. More serious operations soon followed. It had been arranged between the commissioners that whilst the Spaniards should advance against the *Guaranís* from *Buenos Ayres*, the Portuguese should attack them from *Rio Grande*. The Spaniards set forth in May, proceeding upon the left bank of the *Uruguay;* but they had advanced no further than the river *Iyarapuy* when want of stores and pasture compelled them to retire. They had not retreated, however, without a collision with the people of one of the "Reductions" outside of the ceded territory, and several skirmishes took place, in one of which a number of Jesuits were slain.

In the meanwhile, Gomes Freyre had advanced from the coast towards *Ybicuy*, where he determined to watch the *Guaranís* until he should receive some information respecting the proceedings of the Spaniards. He was short of provisions, and when the rainy season commenced his men were exposed to excessive hardships, being compelled to betake themselves to the trees, and the communication being carried on by means of canoes. It is said that they were quartered in this singular fashion for two months, but that they were prevented from deserting owing to the vigilance of the *Guaraní* archers. At the end of this time, Gomes Freyre thought it expedient to treat with the *Guaranís*, who permitted him to retire without molestation. They then returned to their "Reductions," thinking, like children, that the affair was at an end, and that all danger was over.

The Jesuits took advantage of the interval between hostilities to endeavour to procure a revocation of the clause in the Treaty respecting the cession of the "Reductions." But their hopes for a favourable change in the Spanish councils were doomed to disappointment. Their enemies were now numerous and powerful; and amongst the calumnies revived or invented against them was one to the effect that they desired to set up a *Guaraní* kingdom, under a king of their own, named Nicolas, such being the name of a *Guaraní* chief. Valdelirios was advised that his Government had ascertained that the Jesuits were the sole cause of the *Guaraní* rebellion; and that if the Fathers should not deliver up the "Reductions" without further resistance, they should be held guilty of high treason. Seeing that the Jesuits' Superior had resigned on their behalf their charge in the "Reductions," and that the resignation had not been accepted by Valdelirios, the treatment of the Fathers was more high-handed than logical.

1755.

The Spanish and Portuguese commissioners now prepared for a second campaign, and decided that they should form a junction at *S. Antonio ó Velho*, and enter the *Guaraní* country at *Sta. Thecla*. Accordingly Gomes Freyre set out from *Rio Grande* with fifteen hundred men, with artillery and baggage train; but before they arrived at the place of rendezvous with the Spaniards, the whole force had narrowly escaped being consumed by an accidental fire. The junction, however, was effected in the month of January, the Spaniards bringing with them a proportionate force.

1756.

S. Antonio, where the two expeditions met, was in the territory of *S. Miguel*, and about ninety leagues from the "Reductions." The forward march was under the most difficult circumstances, and occupied more than four months; as it was, they had to thank the remissness of their enemies for having accomplished it in that time. From the fact that no skill was shown by the *Guaranís*, it may safely be inferred that their defence was not directed by the Jesuits. The Indians appear to have relied entirely upon their numbers, and they were unfortunate enough to lose, at an early stage in the campaign, their only competent leader, Sepé. His death was followed by a great slaughter of his countrymen, who, however, were not thereby induced to submission. Indeed, this war, like most wars in South America, was of a protracted character, arising chiefly from the nature of the country.

So long as the *Guaranís* should keep the field, it was inevitable that the communications of the invaders should be exposed to much risk. It was therefore determined to fortify a position upon the *Jacuy*, by which stores might be received from the river *Pardo*. When the allied forces had continued their march to the plain of the *Vacacay*, they found themselves in face of a considerable number of Indians, who, however, continued to retreat so soon as the invaders prepared to attack.

The troops had now to attempt the passage of *Monte Grande*, a range of hills which forms the watershed in this direction. It was now the month of March (corresponding to October in the northern hemisphere), and the troops began to suffer from the cold, being badly provided with clothing; they also found the labour of surmounting the pass excessive. At this juncture their commander received the welcome news from the Rector of *S. Luiz* that he had at length succeeded in persuading the people of his "Reduction" to obey; they lamented their error, and besought pardon for their offence, entreating that their countrymen who had been taken prisoners might be released. The Spanish officer replied that the Father and the magistrates of the settlement should set the example of absolute submission.

At length, after three weeks of exertion, the troops succeeded in effecting the passage of *Monte Grande;* but they were still about two hundred miles' distance from the "Reductions." On the 3rd of May a considerable *Guaraní* force made its appearance; but a few cannon-shots put them to flight. On reaching the river *Chiriaby* they found the *Guaranís* skilfully entrenched, whilst they had taken measures to obstruct the passage of the stream. But the *Guaranís*, who were in an excellent position for defence, found their courage fail them at the last moment, and ran away, abandoning everything.

Two days later the army came in sight of *S. Miguel*, which place contained seven thousand inhabitants, and which struck them much by the regularity and neatness of its buildings, and the imposing appearance of its church. A considerable number of *Guaranís* appeared in front and on the flanks; but, as usual, they kept at a respectful distance. In attempting to overtake them, the general left his baggage behind him; which the enemy perceiving, they detached a large body of horsemen to cut it off. A guard, however, had been left, and they were easily beaten off. The troops then halted for two days, when they learned from a prisoner that the Jesuits, with the women and children, and many of the men, had forsaken the town, leaving orders to set it on fire.

On the following day the troops reached the plantations of *S. Miguel*, and two days later they took possession of the place. With the exception of the church, however, the place was now a ruin, every man, on sending away his family, having set fire to his own house. They had also burned the public stores and buildings, and the Jesuits' houses. Notwithstanding the heavy rains which had fallen, the place had been burning for several days. Had the dilatory Spanish general pushed forward a few horsemen on learning that it was intended to fire *S. Miguel*, he might have easily saved that settlement.

Warned by his error, Andoanegui, on the same day, despatched the governor of *Monte Video* to take possession of *S. Lorenzo*, distant two leagues. The inhabitants were surprised, and three Jesuits were arrested. On the ensuing day a letter was received from the Rector of *S. Juan* stating that he had succeeded in persuading his people to submit. The other "Reductions" followed their example;

but the greater part of the inhabitants took refuge in the woods. As so many of the people had provided for themselves, there was little difficulty in organizing the emigration of the remainder, who were admitted into the "Reductions" on the *Paraná*.

Both the Portuguese and Spanish commanders were strongly prepossessed against the Jesuits; but when they had become acquainted with the Fathers personally, and had listened to their statements of facts, the feeling against them seemed at once to disappear. Gomes Freyre, in particular, the Portuguese Commissioner, on seeing the state of things, declined to take possession of the evacuated territory, which could not be said to have been handed over to him in peace, for the former inhabitants still thronged the neighbouring woods. He likewise, meanwhile, deferred the cession of *Colonia*. Nor was the Spanish general more desirous of completing a transfer of which he disapproved. Both armies, therefore, remained in the "Reductions," whilst the Jesuits endeavoured to reclaim their scattered flocks. Both generals, at this late hour, endeavoured to procure an alteration of the treaty.

The Spanish Government, alarmed at the failure of the first campaign, had sent out some reinforcements under *Don* Pedro Zeballos, who, on arriving at *Buenos Ayres*, proceeded at once to the missions, accompanied by Valdelirios. Zeballos was requested by the Superior of the Jesuits to institute a judicial inquiry into the accusation against himself and his brethren. The result of this inquiry was to dispel all charges against these Fathers, which for the rest were utterly improbable. The Jesuits of *Paraguay* were, like those of other provinces, supplied and recruited from Europe. It is not credible that their general should have encouraged or connived at a scheme on the part of a portion of his subordinates, the success of which would have separated them from his control; nor is it any more likely that they should have engaged in such an undertaking without his sanction.

THE WAR OF THE SEVEN REDUCTIONS.

Four years had now elapsed since Valdelirios had come upon his mission, but its business was yet far from having been brought to a conclusion; and so many difficulties had attended every stage of its progress that there was now no great disposition shown on either side to obviate minor obstructions. The presence of Gomes Freyre was required in *Brazil*; and thus the commission separated without having effected anything but a very large outlay of money and an immense amount of misery to the *Guaranís*, which race had been settled for one hundred and twenty-four years in the "Reductions." 1757.

Events in Europe produced yet further delays in the settlement of this question, so important to the portion of South America which was concerned in its solution. By the death of the Spanish King and Queen, the friendly feeling which had united the two courts of Spain and Portugal was at an end, and it was succeeded by one of mistrust. Both courts, however, and both Governments, were heartily weary of the question of demarcation; and, in order to put an end to it, at any rate for the meantime, they agreed to annul the Treaty of Limits—the treaties which had been superseded by it again coming into force. The Portuguese were, on the whole, satisfied with this result, because they believed that *Colonia*, which they now retained, was of greater importance to them than the proposed increase of territory in the interior. The Spaniards were likewise pleased, because they imagined that their neighbours had stolen a march upon them in the Treaty of Limits, through the influence of their Portuguese Queen. 1761.

The actual result of the inglorious and wasteful war of the Seven Reductions was that the Jesuits, who had been falsely accused of fomenting the resistance of the *Guaranís*, had now imposed upon them the task of collecting the scattered remnants of that people, and of encourging them to repair their ruined towns and recultivate their devastated country.

CHAPTER XV.

BRAZIL; EXPULSION OF THE JESUITS FROM PORTUGAL AND BRAZIL.

1759-1767.

THE reign of Jesuitism in Europe was drawing towards its close. For two hundred years the Society had exercised unbounded influence over kings and courts. Its machinery for governing was so perfect, and its system was so subtle that it began to appear to statesmen that unless this ambitious order were speedily and effectually opposed, it must soon dominate Christendom. The alternative to its suppression was that European civilization must be assimilated to that which the Jesuits had introduced in *China* and in *Paraguay*. The doctrines of Ignatius Loyola admitted of nothing short of an absolute obedience of Papal authority. Kings were afraid to act without the approbation of an Order whose system of *espionage* was so complete as even to baffle all secret confidential intercourse between sovereigns and statesmen.

No one Catholic monarch felt himself strong enough single-handed to throw off the humiliating yoke; and, on the other hand, a combination of powers, with this object in view, was rendered doubly difficult by the fact that whatever instructions should be issued and whatever negotiations should take place, were sure to be known to the ubiquitous Order, so soon as issued or held. But the yoke was so galling that a remedy was sure to be found; and at length a man arose whose qualities fitted him for the occasion. This was *Senhor* Carvalho, afterwards the

EXPULSION OF THE JESUITS.

Marquis of Pombal, destined to hold the place in history as the most prominent statesman of his time. Pombal had represented his country in London and at Vienna, two diplomatic centres where he could not but become acquainted with the spirit then prevailing in Europe in respect to the all-powerful Order. He had altogether resided ten years in England in a diplomatic capacity.

The object of Pombal's worthy ambition was to restore his country to the former state of plenty and prosperity from which it had fallen. With this view the statesman sought to combat ignorance, superstition, and intolerance, whose main support was the clergy. He had, therefore, to count upon clerical opposition to his measures. But he took action with a full view of this fact, and availed himself of the situation of his opponents. There still existed the old jealousy between the regulars and the seculars; but on one point, if on no other, all Orders but one were agreed. That one point was envy and hatred of the Jesuits. In this feeling they had a powerful ally in Pombal. Should he succeed in crushing that one Order, he need not fear any other obstacle in the way of the realization of his views.

Pombal had himself been brought up in the school of the Jesuits, who had recognized in him great talent and force of character, and had urged for him promotion under a Government over which they ruled. In the early part of his career they had no cause to regret this course; but, unfortunately for them, their *protegé*, when in England, began to see things through his own eyes rather than through Jesuitical spectacles. Afterwards, comparing England with countries to which he was subsequently sent in the course of his diplomatic career, he made the observation that the prosperity and intelligence of the people seemed to be in inverse *ratio* to the influence exercised by the Jesuits. On his return to Portugal he found his own country, where they ruled supreme, the poorest and most backward of all. From these facts his powerful and intelligent mind drew the unavoidable inference that the way to elevate Portugal was to crush and expel the Jesuits.

The Portuguese minister was well aware that in dealing with such subtle opponents half measures would be worse than useless; he therefore awaited his opportunity when he might deal them a crushing blow with decisive effect. The opportunity now seemed to be afforded by the question of the Jesuit missions with reference to the Treaty of Limits. Pombal was at this time more than fifty years of age. Circumstances soon afforded an opportunity for the development of his extraordinary talents, and he obtained over the King an influence which enabled him to carry into effect with absolute authority his schemes for the renovation of the kingdom. Seeing the miserable condition into which Portugal had sunk, he felt the necessity of great changes; whilst his temper led him to bold and sweeping measures —measures for the justification of which must be pleaded his zeal for the service of his King and his intense love of his country.

1759. The first step taken by the statesman in declaring war against the Jesuits was a letter addressed by his master to Pope Clement XIII. in 1759, in which he informed His Holiness that his Government had determined to make over to his care all the Jesuits in Portugal. Without waiting for a reply, and before time had elapsed to admit of hurling the thunderbolts of Rome, Pombal ordered all the Jesuits to be seized and shipped for the States of the Church. His next step was to endeavour to induce other Catholic governments to follow his example; and the Jesuits were soon afterwards expelled from France through the influence of *Madame de* Pompadour.

In Spain the Jesuits had a firmer hold, but there too they had ere long to give way. A royal decree was issued banishing them from all the Spanish dominions, and forbidding them to return or to hold any intercourse with Spanish subjects. The issue of this order was followed by instant measures to put it into execution. The colleges were surrounded and the bells taken possession of; whilst the Fathers were escorted to the seacoast and placed on board of ships for Italy. But by this time the Pope had on his hands more than a sufficient number of Jesuit refugees from Portugal and from France; he determined, therefore, to refuse permission to land at Civita Vecchia to those coming from Spain. From Civita Vecchia the unhappy Jesuits proceeded in turn to Leghorn and Genoa, but at each place they were refused permission to disembark. They were, however, at last received at Corsica.

A month after the Jesuits had left Spain the King wrote to the Pope in justification of their expulsion, stating that it was the first duty of a sovereign to watch over the peace and good government of his subjects, and that the step he had taken had been one dictated by imperious necessity. The Pope, however, was greatly affected; and he addressed to the King a severe remonstrance in reply. The decision, however, of the Spanish Government had been taken and was not to be altered.

The brother of the Marquis of Pombal, who had been sent out as Captain-General of *Maranham* and *Pará*, was no less hostile to the Jesuits than was that minister himself. He either could not see their proceedings fairly, or he was determined to misconstrue their acts. The Fathers were accordingly accused of obstructing the settlement of the border-line in the north as they had been in the south. In consequence of the reports of the governor, two regiments were sent out from Portugal, and the feeling against the Order ran very high; all the old grievances against them being now revived, since it was known that they had such a powerful enemy as well at *Pará* as at Lisbon. Orders were sent to the governor to deprive all the missionaries of their temporal authority, and to form the most flourishing *Aldeas* into towns and the smaller ones into villages,

It was the desire of Pombal to emancipate the Indians and to blend them with the Portuguese of *Brazil*. With this view, a law was promulgated, abrogating all edicts whatsoever which permitted Indian slavery under any plea, and declaring all Indians in *Pará* and *Maranham* to be free, and that henceforth the price of labour should be regulated by the governor and the judicial authorities of *Pará* and *S. Luiz*. At the date of these edicts there were within the State of *Maranham* and *Pará* threescore Indian *Aldeas*, of which five were administered by the *Mercenarios*, twelve by the Carmelites, fifteen by the Capuchins, and twenty-eight by the Jesuits.

Not content with seeing the Jesuits deprived of their temporal power in Northern *Brazil*, the Captain-General played into the hands of his brother by stirring up, or listening to, a series of charges against them, to answer which a number of the most able of the Fathers were sent home as State prisoners. The whole body, as indeed were likewise the other Orders interested, were reduced almost to penury by the edict which deprived them of their means of support; and the governor of *Pará* turned a deaf ear to their reasonable application for assistance from the Treasury. Nothing therefore remained for them but to depart, their places being supplied by secular clergy. With a view the more thoroughly to blend the Indians with the Brazilians, the Captain-General was required to appoint a director for each Indian settlement, taking care that he was versed in the Indian tongue. This director was to act independently as a government agent to see that the authorities carried out the laws, and he was to report to the governor and the Minister of Justice. The King's chief desire was to Christianize and civilize the people, and to effect this must be the main object of the directors, who were especially charged to establish the use of the Portuguese language. It may be added that in this last respect they were successful, the *Tupi* language being suppressed.

The same decree in accordance with which the Jesuits had been expelled from Portugal affected in like manner their brethren in *Brazil*. The order for their expulsion is said to have been carried out with much brutality. One hundred and fifteen Jesuits were deported in one vessel from *S. Luiz*, being confined like slaves between decks; four of them died on the voyage to Lisbon. The brethren from *Ceará* and *Paraïba* were conveyed to *Recife*, and were embarked with the Pernambucan Jesuits, fifty-three in number. Of these, five died during the passage.

It should be stated, however, that while for the most part all those employed in the service of the Government made themselves too willing instruments to carry out the wishes of the all-powerful minister, and to strike the fallen when they were powerless to resist, yet there were some honourable exceptions to this rule. For instance, the Archbishop of *Bahia*, D. Jose de Mattos, in reporting his visitation of the Jesuits, sent home an attestation that he had found them blameless on the point of which they were accused, of carrying on an extensive commerce contrary to the canons, and in all other points highly useful and meritorious. This attestation was subscribed by eighty of the most respectable persons in *Bahia*. The aged archbishop had to pay the penalty of being fearless and upright. Five years before this time he had requested permission to resign the primacy, begging that half of his appointments might be continued to him. This request had not been acceded to; but, on the receipt of his report, he was relieved of the primacy, without any pension being granted to him. One hundred and sixty-eight Jesuits were deported from *Bahia*; whilst one hundred and forty-five from the southern provinces of *Brazil* were embarked at *Rio de Janeiro*, stowed in one vessel, below decks. The unfortunate Jesuits of the north on reaching

Lisbon were cast into prison for no other crime than that of belonging to their Order; and it was not until after the lapse of eighteen years that the King's death and the disgrace of Pombal restored to them their liberty. Those from the south were not permitted to set foot in Portugal, but were conveyed to the Papal States.

Amongst the measures inaugurated by the Marquis of Pombal was the establishment of an exclusive company for the trade of *Maranham* and *Pará*, and of another for that of *Pernambuco* and *Paraíba*. The *Brazil* company, which had been promoted by Vieyra, and which had rendered such essential service in the Dutch war, had been abolished after an existence of seventy years. The establishment of a new company was now protested against by the Board of Public Good; but in forwarding this protest to the King, that body unsuspectingly signed its own death-warrant, for it was immediately thereafter abolished, and its members were banished for different terms of years.

These new institutions materially affected the British Factory at Lisbon. At that period *Brazil* was supplied, almost exclusively, with English manufactures through the Portuguese merchants of the capital, who obtained long credit from the Factory in consequence of the length of time which they took to obtain returns, there being but one fleet sent to *Brazil* each year. Thus the Brazilian trade was carried on by means of English capital, the sudden stagnation of which would be seriously felt. Great Britain had at the time the right by treaty of trading directly with *Brazil;* but her ambassador at Lisbon was of opinion that it would be inexpedient to assert the right in question, as he considered that the newly-established monopoly, being erroneous in principle, would shortly be abandoned.

Pombal was too despotic in his views to be much concerned as to the degree in which his measures might affect individual interests; and it is but right to add that his grant of a monopoly to companies for the trade with *Maranham* and *Pernambuco* were productive of considerable good to those provinces, since the employment of so large a capital gave an impulse both to agriculture and to commerce. In particular, many negroes were imported into *Maranham*, and their labour made it more easy to carry out the laws in respect to the Indians, one species of slavery being exchanged for another. It is stated, however, that the impulse now given to industry and trade in *Maranham* soon produced a most civilizing effect upon the people of that province. Another measure of the same minister was the establishment of a company with the exclusive right to the whale-fishing, and which likewise obtained a contract for supplying the greater part of *Brazil* with salt—a monopoly which was attended with disastrous results to the country.

But it was not by such measures as the grants of monopolies, whether their results were good or the reverse, that Pombal obtained his reputation as a statesman. He did not scruple to attack prejudices, however rooted; whilst he made the law respected amongst populations who, before his time, had been notoriously lawless. In short, his system was that of a benevolent despotism; for no one denies his enlarged views and good intentions. At a period long gone by, when *Brazil* was a wide and unexplored world, it had been found convenient to make vast grants to such persons as should undertake the settlement of different captaincies. As, however, colonization advanced, the claims of the representatives of the donatories were found to be not unfrequently antagonistic with the public good, and the Government had, from time to time, purchased them in exchange for the grant of honours and wealth. It being represented to the Minister at Lisbon that the existing system was productive of much evil in *Brazil*, he, by one somewhat arbitrary but beneficial act, extinguished the remaining donatories, and purchased their rights for the Crown.

Pombal, too, made his absolute power felt where a display of it was most needed, namely, in the lawless captaincy of *Goyaz.* As usual in all newly-formed settlements, more especially where there are mines, there were there in large numbers the dregs of other populations. And it was the same recurrence of crime which had previously existed in *S. Paulo, Minas Geraes,* and *Cuyabá.* In some instances the inhabitants even thought it advisable to go armed to mass; and it is said that the priests were in no way behind the rest of the people in profligacy and contempt of authority. By the orders of the Minister a Board of Justice was now created, from whose authority there was no appeal. Examples were from this time regularly made of criminals, with the result that there was a speedy amendment in public manners.

1762.

The Portuguese Minister had, however, now to provide for more important interests than the police of a province; he had to take measures for the protection of the whole colonial empire of Portugal from foreign aggression. France and Spain were at this time engaged in an alliance against England; and as Portugal sided with her ancient ally, it was agreed between her two powerful neighbours that the nearest should annex the mother country, whilst France should possess herself of *Brazil.* Pombal, however, relying upon England, was not alarmed for the safety of Portugal; nor, indeed, did he much fear the execution of the wholesale project as regarded *Brazil.* The result of the Pernambucan war was still sufficiently recent to prevent alarm on this account. He thought, however, that there might probably be an attempt on the provinces north of the *Amazons* from the direction of *Cayenne.* He was not prepared for the blow which actually fell from a wholly unexpected quarter.

The Governor of *Buenos Ayres,* who had foreseen the rupture between Spain and Portugal, was prepared to take advantage of it so soon as it occurred. Zeballos, having raised a force of militia, and brought *Guaranís* from the "Reductions," declared war before *Colonia*, and immediately laid siege to that settlement. On the second day a breach was made; but it was not until after a siege of four weeks that the garrison capitulated. The Spanish commander was ere long roused by the arrival of an English squadron of eleven sail, bent upon recovering *Colonia*. But the waters of the Plate have not been fortunate for English arms. After a close fight of four hours, the "Lord Clive" took fire, and was quickly enveloped in flames; the other ships were obliged to get off with all haste, and many men were drowned in endeavouring to reach the shore. Some eighty prisoners were sent to *Cordova*, where they settled, and where they are said to have introduced improvements in agriculture and in arts. The remains of the squadron, having partially refitted, effected their passage to *Rio de Janeiro*.

Cheered by this event, Zeballos lost no time in pursuing his success, and marched with a thousand men against Fort *Sta. Teresa*, which place capitulated; whereupon the Spanish general pushed forward his troops to *Rio Grande*, the short passage by which the waters of the *Lagoa dos Patos*—the largest lake in *Brazil*—discharge themselves into the sea. It may be of interest to observe that the great lake in question, which is one hundred and eighty miles in length, owes its name of "lake of ducks" to the fact of some Spanish vessels being driven into the *Rio Grande* by stress of weather in 1554, and leaving there some ducks, which spread in enormous numbers. Zeballos directed his arms against the town of *S. Pedro*, the inhabitants and garrison of which place fled with precipitation.

When the news of these proceedings reached Portugal, the far-seeing Pombal became alarmed for the safety of *Minas Geraes*. As his imagination was filled, day and night, with the thought of the Jesuits, he conjured up the notion that by their aid the enterprising Zeballos might obtain a powerful army from the "Reductions."

Had time permitted, there is no doubt that such a force would have been brought into the field. Indeed the Jesuits on the *Moxo* frontier were now in arms, and the Spaniards and Portuguese were in conflict in the very centre of the continent. As, however, the operations which they undertook resulted in the *status quo ante* being reverted to by the Peace of Paris, it is unnecessary to recount them in detail. By this treaty, however, the question of demarcation was left in the same condition. Zeballos was required to restore *Colonia*, but he did not think it necessary to give up *Rio Grande*.

At this period the important step was taken of transferring the capital of *Brazil* to *Rio de Janeiro*, the chief reasons of this decision being its vicinity to the mines and likewise to the *Plata*, the importance of which latter region was daily becoming more manifest. *Rio de Janeiro* likewise presented greater facilities for being fortified than did *Bahia*. The vigour which Pombal had infused into the administration at Lisbon was extended to the colonies; and *Brazil* felt the benefit of his enlarged views. One of his prudent measures in regard to this country was to put a stop to the highly unsuitable institution of nunneries. It had not been possible for ministers entirely to put down silly prejudices which were the growth of centuries; and we are told of a wealthy inhabitant of *Bahia* who, there being no more nunneries in *Brazil*, thought fit to send over his six daughters, each with a portion of six thousand *cruzados*, to be incarcerated for life in the convent of *Esperanza*, where none but persons of the first condition were admitted. Under Pombal the Brazilians were prohibited from sending their children to Portugal for such a purpose without the special permission of the King,—a measure so evidently beneficial that it won for the minister the approbation even of his enemies.

Another measure of the same statesman was even more to be commended. Happily for *Brazil*, that country

EXPULSION OF THE JESUITS.

never boasted an establishment of the Inquisition. Nevertheless, some of the agents of the Holy Office had found a field for their energies on the other side of the Atlantic. These agents had arrested and sent to Lisbon a large number of new Christians,—persons fulfilling every duty of citizenship, but whose crime it was to be wealthy. These unfortunate people, having confessed to being Jews, escaped with their lives at the expense of all their property,. which of course went to the informers. In consequence of this profitable practice many *engenhos* had to be stopped, and widespread ruin ensued. Even Pombal did not venture to proclaim toleration for the Jewish faith, but he made it penal for any person to reproach another for his Jewish origin, whilst he removed all disabilities attaching to Jewish blood, even if their ancestors had suffered at the hands of the Inquisition. He likewise published an edict decreeing severe chastisement against such persons as should retain lists of persons of Jewish origin.

At this period Portugal was deprived by the Moors of 1765. the last remnant of her possessions on the Mediterranean. The inhabitants of *Mazagam*, who had defended their city in a manner not unworthy of their race, were transported to the province of *Pará*, where, in honour of their gallant defence, the name of *Mazagam* was given to the place where they settled, on the western bank of the *Matuaca*, a tributary of the *Amazons*. These eighteen hundred colonists, though adding to the military strength of the empire, were but ill-fitted for purposes of colonizing. The situation chosen for their settlement was unfavourable, and many of them perished from the climate. Near this position a strong fort was erected at *Macapá*. In his desire to strengthen *Brazil*, the minister despatched many families from the Western Islands to be settled at *Macapá* and *Mazagam*. He likewise did something to foment the trade of *Brazil* by withdrawing the prohibition which had hitherto prevailed against single trading ships, apart from the annual fleet.

As the Portuguese islands could not afford colonists in sufficient number to satisfy the aspirations of the minister, their complement was made up from the dregs of the mother country. But this measure was not followed by the good results for which no doubt its originator looked. Crime became so frequent in *Matto-Grosso, Minas Geraes*, and elsewhere, that orders had to be sent out from Portugal, compelling all persons without any settled abode to live in civilized communities, and to divide amongst them the surrounding lands. All persons who should evade this regulation, with the exception of three classes, were to be proceeded against as robbers,—the classes exempted from this rule being agriculturists with their slaves and servants on isolated farms; *rancheros*, or persons established on the public roads to facilitate communication or to entertain travellers; and *bandeiras*, that is to say, bands of respectable persons employed in making discoveries. The above three classes of citizens were empowered to arrest and imprison vagrants.

It is now necessary to review what had been going on during the last few years in the mining districts. The experience of fifteen years having according to general opinion proved the injurious nature of the capitation tax, the offer was accepted of the people of *Minas Geraes* to make up the annual assessment to one hundred *arrobas*, should the royal fifths be less than that amount. In the year 1753, the fleet from *Rio de Janeiro* was believed to bring home gold, silver, and goods to the amount of three millions sterling. In that year the fifths from *Minas Geraes* amounted to nearly £400,000. The bullion and jewels which were sent to Lisbon in the following year were estimated at a million *moidores*. On an average of sixteen years the royal fifths exceeded one hundred *arrobas*; but when the trade had been opened to single ships, the average production of gold was found to decrease,—probably from the conviction or experience that trade was on the whole more profitable than mining.

The temptation to evade the payment of the royal proportion was so strong that not even the severe laws in force were sufficient to overcome it. Gold might circulate within the captaincy before it had been stamped and before the royal fifth had been taken; but it was unlawful to carry it beyond the border until it should have paid the duty and passed through the mint. Gold-dust, which was the only circulating medium in *Minas Geraes*, was found to be so debased by the traders before it reached the mint that there was usually a loss upon it of 10 or 12 *per cent.* in addition to the 20 *per cent.* duty, a desire to avoid which loss, even more than to avoid the duty, led to the frequent practice of endeavouring to smuggle it across the frontier. When it had once reached the cities, goldsmiths were readily found either to convert it into bars or to work it into jewellery. The knowledge of these practices naturally led to a law against jewellers, whose presence had long been forbidden in *Minas Geraes*, and was now no longer tolerated in the sea-ports.

The less productive province of *Goyaz* yielded in some years a capitation tax of forty *arrobas*. This advanced province had to bear the burden of a war with a brave tribe, called the *Cayapos*. The province of *Minas Geraes* was likewise exposed to incursions from other native tribes; but, notwithstanding occasional disturbances, the interior of *Brazil* continued on the whole to make steady progress towards civilization.

The government, however, was still disturbed by the retention by Spain of her conquests in the province of *Rio Grande*. Portugal appealed to Great Britain to procure the execution of the Treaty of Paris in accordance with the intentions of the contracting parties, of which

England had been one. It had certainly not been her intention that the Spaniards should retain their conquests in *Brazil*. It was to the Brazilians themselves, however, that they were to owe the recovery of the Spanish posts in *Rio Grande*. Aware that the Spaniards of the *Plata* 1767. were sufficiently occupied elsewhere, they secretly collected a force of eight hundred men, with which they took their enemies by surprise, thus regaining by arms that which Great Britain was engaged in endeavouring to obtain for them by diplomatic means.

CHAPTER XVI.

PARAGUAY; EXPULSION OF THE JESUITS FROM BUENOS AYRES AND PARAGUAY.

1649-1805.

FROM the date of the removal of Bishop Gardenas as governor of *Paraguay* [1648], that province had enjoyed freedom from internal dissensions; until, in 1717, *Don* Diego Balmaceda was named governor by the Viceroy of *Peru*. His nomination was unpopular, and, after two years, serious charges were preferred against him before the Audience of *Charcas*, which that body were occupied during the three succeeding years in investigating. Meanwhile *Don* Jose de Antiquera had obtained the provisional succession to the post of governor; and he hastened to *Paraguay* to assume power. Balmaceda was, however, reinstated in authority, and he ordered the usurper to resign his pretensions. But meanwhile Antiquera had organized a considerable force, and he refused to submit to the orders of the Viceroy, and sent a party to *Corrientes*, who brought Balmaceda a prisoner to *Asuncion*.

On learning this rebellion against the Crown, the Viceroy sent instructions to the military commander of *La Plata* to dispossess Antiquera of his authority, and to reinstate Balmaceda. On reaching the river *Tebicuari*, General Garcia de Ros found Antiquera too strong to be opposed. On his retiring, Antiquera, with a view to conciliating Zavala, the governor of *Buenos Ayres*, sent six hundred troops to assist him in the defence of *Monte Video* against the Portuguese. This manœuvre, however, did not avail him, and Ros was sent a second time to assert the royal authority, with two hundred Spanish troops, backed by the forces of the Jesuit missions. The Jesuits had been expelled by Antiquera from *Asuncion*. On reaching the *Tebicuari*, Ros was encountered by Antiquera, with a force of three thousand men, and, being defeated, was compelled to return to *Buenos Ayres*.

1724.   The rebellion had now assumed such proportions that it could no longer be trifled with, and Zavala received peremptory orders from the Viceroy to hasten to *Paraguay* in person, and to send Antiquera to *Lima* for trial. The latter, now aware of his desperate situation, prepared to defend himself. His followers, however, began to desert him, and in March 1725 he fled from *Paraguay*, and took refuge in a convent at *Cordova*. Thence he proceeded to *Bolivia*, intending to throw himself on the protection of the Audience of *Charcas*. But he was looked upon as a public enemy, and was arrested at *Chaquisaca*, and sent to be tried at *Lima*. He was brought before the Audience, but, although his guilt was patent from the first, it was not until the trial had lasted for several years that he was condemned to be executed. The 5th of July 1731 was the day fixed for his execution. By this time the public feeling had completely veered round in his favour, and, as it was feared a rescue would be attempted, the Viceroy gave orders to fire upon the prisoner. The order was answered by a volley of musketry, and the condemned man and two friars near him fell dead from their horses.

After the flight of Antiquera from *Paraguay*, the Jesuits had been permitted to return to *Asuncion*. They were met at the distance of twelve miles from the capital by a procession headed by the governor, the bishop, and the chief civil and military functionaries. But the return of the Jesuits was displeasing to many, more especially to those who had been the partisans of Antiquera. When the governor resigned, the people claimed the right

EXPULSION OF THE JESUITS.

of choosing his successor—a right which in certain emergencies had been granted them by Charles V. When the news of Antiquera's execution reached *Asuncion*, the indignation of the people manifested itself by their falling on the Jesuits, and expelling them from the city.

There were now two declared parties in *Paraguay*. That which was against longer submission to royal authority took the name of *Comuneros;* whilst those who were for the King were called *Contrabandistas*. On the resignation of Governor Barua, the *Comuneros* improvised a government composed of a *junta*, with a president as the executive head. A hostile collision was now to be feared between the dominant party at *Asuncion* and the nearest Jesuit "Reductions." It was averted by the arrival of a new governor, *Don* Manoel de Ruiloba. Reaching the missions, he sent forward overtures to the insurgents, which so far satisfied them that he was permitted to take possession of the government. One of his first acts was to attempt to disband the *Comuneros;* but this was vehemently resisted; and he found himself in open opposition to the most numerous party in the state. The rebels defied him, and civil war was commenced. In the first action the governor fell. 1733.

The Bishop of *Buenos Ayres*, who happened to be at that time at *Asuncion*, was now elected governor; but he was a mere instrument in the hands of the *junta*, and was compelled to sign sweeping acts of confiscation against the Jesuits and the Royalists. Realizing his false position, he thought fit to embark for *Buenos Ayres* to résume his episcopal duties. The rebels in *Paraguay* had again to deal with Zavala, who had recently been appointed President of the Audience of *Charcas*, and who now blockaded *Paraguay* on all sides. Taking with him six thousand trained troops from the missions, he advanced to the *Tebicuri*, and, meeting with no opposition, proceeded to *Asuncion*, where he was received with acclamations.

As Zavala's rapid success had been gained by means of the Jesuits' troops, it was but natural that the Fathers should follow in their wake. They were now more powerful and arrogant than ever, and it became pretty clear that it was their intention to reduce *Asuncion* and all *Paraguay* to the same state of blind obedience to their sway in which they held their missions. To contend against them so long as they retained the ear of the King was hopeless; and the Spanish colonists now undertook to enlighten their sovereign by exposing the false pretensions of the Fathers. The Jesuits were accused of a design of founding an empire, and they were shown to have created in South America a more absolute despotism than Europe had ever known.

The reign of the Jesuits, however, was then drawing to its close. Their expulsion from the Portuguese dominions has already been recorded, and it was not long before the Jesuits of Spain shared the fate which had befallen their brethren of Portugal and of France. We have here to review the circumstances of their expulsion from South America. Zeballas had been recalled from his high post on account of his sympathies with the devoted order.

1767. However strong may have been the reasons for the expulsion of the Jesuits from Spain, their suppression in South America, although it may have been a necessary sequence of the first measure, had certainly an air of gross ingratitude, and seemed likely considerably to diminish the Spanish power in its colonies. The Jesuits had been the means of greatly extending the Spanish territories in the interior, and had thereby prevented the Portuguese from securing to themselves a still larger portion of the centre of the continent. They had raised many thousands of native troops who had often done good service in *Paraguay*, and who had fought successfully against the Portuguese both on the *Guaypore* and at *Colonia*. They had likewise delivered the Spaniards of *La Plata*,

Paraguay, and *Tucuman* from their formidable native enemies, whom they had been able to conciliate. The very latest Spanish successes in *Rio Grande* had been due in a great measure to their assistance.

But the expulsion of the Jesuits from their headquarters of *Paraguay* had been included in the plan of the King of Spain and his counsellors, and four days after the issue of the royal decree banishing the order from the mother country, a ship of war was despatched to the *Plata*, with orders to the Viceroy to take immediate measures for the simultaneous seizure of all the Jesuits within his jurisdiction. The Viceroy, Bucareli, who received his orders on the 7th of June 1767, lost no time in carrying them into execution. Without delay he despatched sealed instructions to the governors and local authorities within his Viceroyalty, which were not to be opened until the 21st of July. On the following day all Jesuits were to be seized in the name of the King and sent to *Buenos Ayres*.

It may here be of interest to give a short account of the condition in which the royal order found the "Reductions." They were now beginning to recover from the evils which had fallen upon them owing to the Treaty of Limits. But on account of that blind measure, together with illness and a subsequent war, their numbers were now reduced from one hundred and forty-four thousand to one hundred thousand. The Fathers possessed large estates and many negro slaves, who are said to have been treated with every consideration. Whatever civilization penetrated into the interior of the country was through the Jesuits. For example, one Father Schmid instructed the *Chiquitos* not only in the common arts of life, but in working metals and making clocks. It is said that the *Moxo* and *Paure* missions displayed more civilization than did the important Spanish city of *Santa Cruz de la Sierra*; whilst to the Jesuits *Cordova* owes its press. The Jesuits of the *Guaranis* printed books in one of the "Reductions" before there was any printing press either in *Cordova* or in *Buenos Ayres*.

The news of the expulsion of the Jesuits from Spain became public in *Buenos Ayres* on the 3rd of July, being eighteen days before the time fixed upon for their arrest. Orders were therefore sent to the provinces to anticipate this measure; whilst the Fathers in the college at *Buenos* were made prisoners on the same night. Those nearest to that city soon shared the same fate; and in the following month the college at *Cordova* was likewise taken possession of, and its inmates sent to the capital, whilst their invaluable library was destroyed. Nowhere did the Viceroy's troops meet with any resistance; and the captured Jesuits were transmitted to Spain in groups of some forty individuals, being thence sent on to the Papal States.

The Fathers of the Paraguayan missions, however, had still to be dealt with. Their first move was to cause an address to be signed by their *Guaraní* foremen, and to present it to the governor, praying that the Jesuits might continue to live with them. That this petition came from the Jesuits themselves, and not from the Indians, was apparent. Bucareli, accordingly, taking it as an indication that they did not mean to surrender without a struggle, took energetic measures to compel them to submit. Occupying the pass of *Tebicuari*, and sending a force to *S. Miguel*, he ascended the *Uruguay* at the head of a further force. By way of proving the worthlessness of the *Guaraní* petition on behalf of the Jesuits, he caused another document to be prepared and signed by the Indian judges and *caciques* of some thirty towns, expressing thankfulness to the King for having relieved them from their former arduous life. Whatever else these respective petitions may show, they certainly prove how thoroughly the *Guaranís* had learnt the lesson of implicit obedience to whatsoever instructions they might receive, irrespective of their convictions, if they had sufficient individuality left to possess any.

But by this time it was evident that resistance was hopeless. Many of the missions had fallen into the hands of the governor, and the Fathers did not venture to bring their disciples into the field. They were sent to *Buenos Ayres*, and shared the fate of their brethren who had preceded them. There was indeed no discretion left to the authorities in executing the measures for the expulsion of the Jesuits from the Spanish dominions. One of the most able and conscientious of the number, the aged Father Chomé, being confined to his bed by illness, was carried from the *Chiquito* missions in a hammock to *Oruro*, where he died from the effects of the journey. Another missionary, Father Mesner, an old and infirm man, who had laboured for thirty years in the *Chiquito* "Reductions," was sent on a journey of four hundred and fifty miles to *Santa Cruz*. After remaining there for five months, until the season for crossing the *Andes* had come, he was placed upon a mule, whilst riding upon which he died. It is right to add that the Spanish Minister, on learning these facts and others of a similar nature, indignantly reproved the South-American authorities for their inhumanity. In all one hundred and fifty-five Jesuits were expelled from *La Plata, Tucuman*, and *Paraguay*.

The suffering in the "Reductions" did not fall alone or chiefly on the Jesuits. Their system of government had been so absolute, and their disciples had been reduced to such a condition of being merely thoughtless animals or machines, that, when the guidance of the Fathers was withdrawn, the whole system established by them suddenly and absolutely collapsed. No plan of government suitable to the altered condition of affairs was devised by the Spanish authorities. Priests of the mendicant orders replaced the missionaries, but without their temporal authority. The missions were formed provisionally into two governments, and an administrator was appointed to superintend each "Reduction," with which last measure the prosperity of these communities ceased. The administrators, ignorant of the *Guaraní* tongue, made their commands obeyed by the lash; and before a year had elapsed the Viceroy had the mortification to learn that the *Guaranís*, in order to escape from the intolerable oppression of their new masters, were making their escape in numbers to seek the protection of their old enemies, the Portuguese.

On learning this unexpected occurrence, Bucareli displaced the administrators and appointed others in their stead, but with no better result as regarded the *Guaranís*. As the governor and the priests disputed regarding their respective powers, the Viceroy decreed that the former was to reside at *Candelaria*, where he was to be assisted by a staff of administrators, under whom the *Guaranís* were to labour as of old for the benefit of the community. The end was that cruel and compulsory work made the Indians miserable or drove them into the woods. The arts introduced by the Jesuits were neglected; their gardens and fields lay uncultivated, and their once flourishing villages, which had contained the evidences of a civilization of a century and a half, were almost deserted.

From the date of the rebellion of the *Comuneros* in 1735 until the close of last century, *Paraguay* enjoyed uninterrupted peace and quiet. In the year 1796, Ribera Espinosa was appointed governor, who, by the aid of his agents, constituted himself a general exporter, monopolizing the whole trade of the country; so that the producers realized for their goods about a tenth of what these were worth in the markets of *Buenos Ayres*. This state of things naturally produced such grave complaints against Ribera's government as to provoke the intervention of the Crown. He was recalled, and was replaced by a man of a very different character, *Don* Bernardo Velasco, who was destined to be the last Spanish governor of Paraguay. 1803.

In the year 1803 the King of Spain issued a decree constituting the country lying between the *Paraná* and the *Uruguay*, which included all the missions, a separate province, which was called *Misiones*, of which Velasco was appointed governor. In 1805, the same officer was appointed governor of *Paraguay*, another of the same name being instructed by him as his lieutenant in *Misiones*.

CHAPTER XVII.

BRAZIL IN THE EIGHTEENTH CENTURY; ARRIVAL OF THE BRAGANZAS.

1776-1806.

1776. IN tracing the course of the progress of *Brazil* it should be mentioned that in the year 1776 the fort of *Nova Coïmbra* was founded on the Upper *Paraguay*, in the province of *Matto - Grosso*, as a protection against the formidable tribe of the *Guaycurús*, which people, it is estimated, inflicted upon the Portuguese the loss of four thousand lives and three millions of *cruzados*. It should also be mentioned that about the same time the Academy of Sciences and Natural History was founded at *Rio de Janeiro*. One of the first meetings of this body was made remarkable by the statement of an army surgeon who had served in the war of the Seven Reductions, that a Spaniard who had been in *Mexico* had pointed out to him the *cochineal* upon several varieties of the cactus in *Rio Grande*. It was found soon afterwards in the island of *S. Catherine*, and plants with the insects were brought to the botanic garden of the Academy.

The attention of the Brazilian Government was, however, soon turned from this discovery to cares of a different description. Don Joseph Moniño, subsequently Count Florida Blanca, had recently been appointed Minister of Spain; and he sought the opportunity of distinguishing his administration in the pending disputes with Portugal concerning the limits of *Brazil*. He was urged on by Zeballos, now appointed the first Viceroy

ARRIVAL OF THE BRAGANZAS.

of *La Plata* and sent thither with a force of nine thousand men, with twelve ships of war and a transport. The first object of the expedition, which reached the coast of *Brazil* in February 1777, was the possession of *Sta. Catherina*, an island about thirty-six miles in length and from four to ten in breadth. The Portuguese had several times endeavoured to establish themselves on this island, but in vain. They, however, considered it as belonging to *Brazil;* and at length some families were transported thither from the *Azores.* At the date of the expedition it was defended by a fort and garrison, represented by the Spaniards as strong and numerous.

The enemy landed about nine miles from the capital of the island; but no resistance was made, and every fort and battery was deserted without firing, or even spiking, a gun. The governor fled to the mainland, his timorous example being followed by the garrison; and although he was now safe he, for unexplicable reasons, thought fit to capitulate and surrender to the King of Spain not the island of *St. Catherine* alone, but likewise all its dependencies upon the mainland. After this capitulation, Zeballos despatched orders to the governor of *Buenos Ayres* to march against *Rio Grande* with all the force he could collect. Don Juan de Vertiz accordingly set out for *Sta. Teresa* with two thousand troops and some cavalry; but the Viceroy, owing to contrary winds, was unable to enter *Rio Grande*, and therefore made for *Monte Video*, whence he proceeded without delay against *Colonia*.

The commandant of the latter place had long been aware of his risk, and had applied to *Rio de Janeiro* for reinforcements and provisions; but these had not reached him, having fallen into the hands of the enemy's cruisers. Nor was this the only misfortune which befell him, for one of his despatches had likewise been captured, in which it was stated that his garrison could not hold out longer than the 20th of May. Zeballos reached *Colonia* two days after this date, when the Portuguese had only five days' supply of food left them. Resistance seemed useless; and, at the recommendation of a council of war, an officer was sent to propose terms of capitulation. He was detained the entire day, and at nightfall sent back by Zeballos with the reply that when his works were finished he would communicate the orders of his sovereign. When his batteries were in order, he informed the Portuguese that he had been sent to punish the insult which they had committed by invading *Rio Grande* in time of peace; and they were required to surrender at discretion. They had no choice but to submit, and were treated with much inhumanity.

After this second success Zeballos was preparing to advance on *Rio Grande* when he received official information that a preliminary treaty of limits had been signed at Madrid. By it Portugal ceded *Colonia* with all its claims upon the northern bank of the *Plata*, and acknowledged the exclusive right of the Spaniards to the navigation of that stream and likewise of the *Uruguay* as far as to the mouth of the *Pepiri Guazú*. The Spanish line of frontier was to begin at the mouth of the *Chui*, where fort *S. Miguel* stood. Thence it went to the sources of the *Rio Negro*, which, with all other rivers flowing into the *Plata* or into the *Uruguay* below the mouth of the *Pepiri Guazú*, now belonged to Spain. The *Rio Grande* was assigned to Portugal. The *Uruguay* missions were to remain as they were, and a line was drawn fixing the frontier so as to protect them, the commissioners being instructed to follow the line of the tops of the mountains and so to arrange the boundary that the rivers from their source should flow always within the same demarcation. The lakes *Mirim* and *Manqueira* and the land between them, and the narrow strip between the latter and the sea, became neutral territory, which was not to be occupied by either people. The Portuguese were not to go further south than the river

Tahim, nor the Spaniards further north than the *Chui*. The artillery taken at *Rio Grande* was to be restored, as was *Sta. Catherina*.

This treaty was looked upon with much pride by Florida Blanca as having settled a dispute which had lasted for two centuries and a half. The demarcation between the two territories from the mouth of the *Pepiri* northwards was in every respect the same as in the former Treaty of Limits which had been cancelled. It should be stated that by this time Pombal had fallen into disgrace, on the death of King Jozé. Many of the measures of that minister were now annulled, amongst them the companies of *Maranham* and *Pernambuco*. These had, however, done their work by the increased impulse which they had given to commerce, more especially to the growth of cotton, which they had promoted at *Maranham*, and which was extended to *Pernambuco*.

It is scarcely necessary to refer to the hostilities which, simultaneously with those of *Colonia*, had broken out between the Portuguese and the Spaniards on the *Matto-Grosso* frontier, and in which the *Guaycurús* were involved. This powerful tribe, however, soon made peace with the Spaniards, and at a later period this peace was extended to the Portuguese.

In another quarter of *Brazil* we find the first dawn of rebellion in the province of *Minas Geraes*, where in the year 1789 a conspiracy broke out with the view of declaring that captaincy a separate commonwealth. Fortunately, however, this plot was nipped in the bud, the chief conspirators, including the prime mover, being condemned to be hanged. The latter, however, was the only one upon whom the capital sentence was executed. 1789.

When the governor of *Rio Grande* had received advice of the war which had broken out in Europe, he did not wait for instructions from the Viceroy, but issued a declaration against the Spaniards, who were attacked 1801.

both on the western frontier and towards the south. The fort of *Chui* was surprised and sacked, as were the Spanish forts upon the *Gaguaron* and their establishments towards the *Jacuy*, whilst at the same time a movement was made upon the seven "Reductions." The Portuguese, who were formerly the objects of hatred, were received as liberators by the *Guaranis*, so effectually had the Jesuits' successors done their work of estranging them from Spain. The commander was permitted by the Portuguese leader to retire with his men, but he and they were made prisoners by another band whom they met on their march.

But these colonial hostilities were of short duration, peace having been concluded between Portugal and Spain before they were effected. The Portuguese, however, insisted on retaining the seven "Reductions," on the ground that they were not specified in the Treaty of Badajoz; and they accordingly remained a portion of *Brazil*. At the time of these last-mentioned hostilities, the Spaniards and Portuguese likewise appeared in arms against each other on the upper waters of the *Paraguay*, where *Nova Coïmbra* was besieged by the former and the fort of *S. José* destroyed by the latter.

By the Treaty of Madrid, which followed that of Badajoz, France obtained from Portugal a cession of territory on the side of *Guyana*. As the limits of this cession were subsequently annulled, the frontier reverting to the *Oyapok*, no advantage would be gained by detailing them. Brazil fortunately remained at peace when the revolutionary war was renewed: but that war was to have a momentous influence on the destinies of the great Lusitanian colony, bringing about as it did the removal of the Braganzas from Portugal to *Rio de Janeiro*. By this event the last-named city became the seat of government of the Portuguese dominions; and there can be no doubt that it was owing mainly to the presence of the royal family that, whilst the Spanish dominions in South

America, on their separation from the mother-country, became divided into as many as nine separate states, the empire of *Brazil* has remained one and undivided to the present day.

That vast empire had continued to make marked progress during the eighteenth century. Amongst the old captaincies none, it is said, had undergone greater change than had *Pará*, where the people had been reclaimed from their former chronic state of turbulence and insubordination. The slavery of the Indians was at an end, which was one great step in advance, although it was reserved for another century to witness, as it may be hoped, the extinction of negro slavery. As regards the Indians, however, the regulations decreed by Pombal for their protection had been disregarded. That statesman had wished that the aborigines should be placed on a position of equality with the Brazilians of Portuguese race—a measure which might possibly have been carried out by the aid of the Jesuits, but which with their expulsion became impossible. As it was, the Indians were governed with a high hand by the directors, who had been appointed with the view simply of guiding them.

The *aldeas* or settlements established by the Jesuits had undergone great depopulation, owing to the marking out of the limits as laid down in the treaty. In so vast a country, and with such imperfect means of transport, it was inevitable that the work of marking out the borders should be a tedious one, and many natives, who were required for the service of the commissioners, sank in the course of years from the labours imposed upon them or from the fevers to which they were exposed. On the departure of the Jesuits the Indians found themselves emancipated from all moral restraint. The directors did not care to exercise any, nor did they show them an example, whilst the new priests were without power. The bishop of *Pará*, who between the years 1784 and 1788 went over his extensive diocese, laments the decay of the *aldeas* and the degraded condition of the Indians.

There were twelve towns at the close of last century on the left bank of the *Amazons* under the government of *Pará*, amongst them being *Faro* to the far west, *Obidos, Alemquer, Montalegre, Outeiro, Almerin, Mazagam, Villa Vistoza,* and *Macapa*. The settlements on the southern side of the great river were more numerous and more important. They included *Samtarem*, which in 1788 contained 1300 inhabitants, and *Villa Franca*, which contained a similar number; also *Mundrucus*, so called from the tribe of that name who had begun to cultivate the arts of civilization. Towns and settlements were likewise increasing upon the river *Zingu*. *Vieiros, Souzel,* and *Pombal* contained in 1788 about 800 inhabitants each; whilst *Gurupa*, which was considered the key of the *Amazons*, contained 400 of European blood. *Melgaço, Oeyras,* and *Portel* were likewise considerable settlements inhabited by Indians in the same captaincy. Cameta was, with the exception of *Pará*, the largest town in the State, containing about 6000 white inhabitants. The communication between this place and *Pará* was carried on by one of those natural canals which are so narrow as only to afford a passage for canoes.

The province of *Rio Negro*, after the edict by which the Jesuits were removed, seems to have suffered no detriment from that measure. Its most remote establishment was distant from *Pará* four hundred and eighty-five leagues, which, in ascending the river, was accounted a journey of nearly three months.

Pará itself had become a populous and flourishing city, the cathedral and the palace being built on a grand scale. The Jesuits' College had been converted into an episcopal palace and a seminary, which boasted professors of Latin rhetoric and philosophy. The city possessed a judicial establishment, a theatre, a hospital, a convent

ARRIVAL OF THE BRAGANZAS.

of Capuchins and likewise one of Carmelites. Ships for the navy were constructed at *Pará*, and timber was exported to Lisbon for the use of the arsenals. Amongst its exports were Oriental and other spices, cacao, coffee, rice, cotton, sarsaparilla, copaiba, tapioca, gum, India-rubber, chestnuts, hides, and molasses.

It unfortunately happened that the Portuguese sent to this magnificent province were of the lowest description, and who, on finding themselves in so luxuriant a locality, gave way forthwith to incurable indolence. Bishop Brandam draws a dark picture of their mode of life, and a still darker one of that of their slaves. There was a brighter side, however, to the picture of society as it existed at this time at *Pará*. The establishment of a wealthy colonist was so extensive as often to exceed in number the population of a town. For instance, that of Joam de Mores included more than three hundred persons, thirty sons or daughters, with their children, sitting down every day at the family dinner-table. The estate contained a pottery, a sugar-plantation, and several nurseries of cacao. The negroes were treated like children, and were well looked after. Such treatment of slaves, however, in this province, was the exception.

Passing to the adjoining captaincy of *Maranham*, *S. Luiz* was accounted the fourth city of *Brazil* in commercial importance, the number of ships leaving it annually towards the close of the century being nearly thirty, the result of the cultivation of rice and cotton. The population of the city was estimated at twelve thousand. The Carmelites, the Mercenarios, and the Franciscans had each a convent here. The opulent merchants possessed large estates and numerous slaves, some of them having as many as a thousand or fifteen hundred. *Alcantara*, on the opposite side of the bay, was a large and prosperous town, as was *Guimaraens*, ten leagues to the north. The interior of the province was ill peopled.

Many rivers enter the sea in this captaincy, some of

which are navigable for a considerable way, and the banks of all of which are more or less peopled. The most important of these is the *Itapacura*, the territory between which and the *Paraïba* was in great part peopled by a population of European blood or by domesticated Indians, by means of whom large quantities of rice and cotton were raised.

Although the course of the *Tocantins* was well known in *Goyaz* and *Pará*, it was not until the year 1798 that an attempt was made to trace its connection to *Maranham*, for the purpose of opening up a communication by water between the two provinces in which it respectively rises and ends. But although the effort of the Government failed, the communication was established by means of a runaway Indian, who had made his way in a canoe bound for *Goyaz*. A settler named Barros, into whose territory the Indian penetrated, then built a canoe on which he embarked with the Indian and three slaves upon the river *Manoel Alves Grande*; this stream in a day and a half carried them into the *Tocantins*, on which in due time they met a vessel from *Pará*. After this successful expedition, Barros was employed in opening up a communication along this important route. Throughout *Maranham* the cultivation of cotton had, for the most part, superseded that of the sugar-cane. The captaincy produces an abundance of fruit of the finest quality. The navigation of the coast of *Brazil* is so difficult, on account of both wind and current setting in at certain seasons from the south, that it was easier for *Pará* and *Maranham* to communicate with Portugal than with *Bahia* or *Rio de Janeiro*; for which reason the bishops of *Pará* and *S. Luiz* were suffragans of the Patriarch of Lisbon.

Maranham, Pernambuco, Bahia, and *Minas Geraes* all looked chiefly to *Piauhy* for their cattle. That country was explored and conquered, not for the sake of its mines and slaves, but on account of its pastures, on which cattle increased to an enormous extent, the mode of life being

ARRIVAL OF THE BRAGANZAS.

similar to that on the *Pampas* of the *Plata*. The difficulty of utilizing these herds lay in transporting them to the market over the waterless tracts that intervened. By means, however, of tanks this difficulty was overcome.

It is unnecessary to go over the whole extent of *Brazil*, but one or two instances may be given, showing the progress which it had already made at the beginning of this century. When the Dutch possessed *Paraïba*, that captaincy contained seven hundred families and twenty *engenhos*; in the year 1775 its population was estimated at fifty-two thousand—a population which was more than doubled in the course of another quarter of a century.

Pernambuco was, in the early part of this century, one of the most flourishing parts of this great colonial empire; and its chief port, *Recife*, was only inferior in importance to *Bahia* and *Rio de Janeiro*. It contained about twenty-five thousand inhabitants. No other city had derived such benefit from the growth of the cotton trade. It seems to have been a favourite place of resort with the religious Orders; the Fathers of the Oratory, the Franciscans, and the Carmelites had each a convent; whilst the Italian Capuchins and the Almoners of the Holy Land had each a *hospice*. There was likewise a *Recolimento* and a hospital for lepers. The Governor resided in what had been the Jesuits' College. Although people of Portuguese race are perhaps the most temperate in the world, excepting Mahommedans and some other Asiatics, the water-drinkers of *Recife* were dependent for that element on canoes, by which it was conveyed from the *Capivaribe* or the *Beberibe*—there being no aqueduct. The neighbouring city of *Olinda* well maintained the reputation from which it takes its name.

In the agricultural or cattle-breeding districts in the interior of *Brazil* the mode of life was primitive; but, owing to the influence of commerce at the ports, it was somewhat more civilized than in *La Plata* or *Paraguay* at the same period. Water was served in houses of all classes for ablution before and after meals. It was the general custom to sit on the ground. Knives and forks were superfluities, as were beds, which were replaced by hammocks. The dress of the drover when away from home was somewhat elaborate, as is that of the *Pampas gaucho*. The home dress of the women was exceedingly simple; nor was their costume luxurious abroad. The cattle were so numerous that the population ate animal food three times a day, taking with it a cake made of mandioc or of rice. Wild fruits were so abundant that none were cultivated save water-melons. It is stated that the scattered population, in these thinly-peopled districts, were indebted for their civilization to a considerable extent to pedlars. These itinerant dealers supplied the farmers and their families with almost every imaginable commodity, including calico, earthenware, rum, tobacco, horsegear, and Irish butter. They usually received payment in the shape of some other commodity.

In the thinly-peopled districts parishes were of enormous extent. Sometimes one could not find a church within eighty or one hundred miles; and this state of things gave rise to a class of itinerant priests, who travelled about carrying a portable altar and its appurtenances in a pack-saddle. These travelling ecclesiastics were furnished with licenses from a bishop, and were assisted at mass by the boy who drove the pack-horse. As laws were but indifferently observed in the *Sertam*, and murders were frequent, the services of the priest were often required for absolution. Wherever a customer willing to pay could be found, the altar was erected, and the service took place. These priests could likewise perform the ceremonies of marriage and of baptism.

Although rural crime was still frequent, it had decreased towards the end of last century. There had existed a set of *bravos* who used to frequent fairs for the purpose of provoking quarrels, and who were a constant source of very real danger; but so many of these gentry had come to their deserved end that bucolic life was now much more secure. There was at one time, likewise, a custom to parade certain towns at night, the strollers being cloaked and masked, and in this guise committing any pranks which occurred to them. This habit, too, was put down.

The large number of ports in *Pernambuco* gave that province the inestimable advantage of a ready means of export for the produce of the interior. Its richest and most influential inhabitants, whether agricultural or commercial, were those most interested in the preservation of order. They were the great promoters of civilization, exercising a liberal hospitality. The long-continued Dutch war had left the Pernambucans proud memories. Many of the chief inhabitants looked upon themselves not only as being the landed aristocracy, but also as being the descendants of the military aristocracy of *Brazil*. They had indeed about them many of the distinguishing characteristics of a nobility. Their estates went from father to son, and none of their slaves were ever sold. The latter thus enjoyed the comforts and advantages of a permanent residence, and they were, like the adherents of an old Scottish chieftain, permitted to adopt the family name, of which they were not a little proud.

The estates belonging to the monastic orders might boast of a similar stability. Their slaves, likewise, were never parted with; and the treatment of these was so paternal that corporal punishment was neither needed nor thought of. Amongst the smaller proprietors, most of which class were of mixed blood, the condition of slavery was alleviated by the fact that master and slave were employed in the same work, and partook of the same food. That food consisted in the last century, as it does to-day, of jerked beef, salt fish, and mandioc flour. It was further alleviated by the nature of the religious services in which the half-coloured masters and their slaves took part, both worshipping at the shrine of the same Virgin Mary, who was depicted as a negress.

In *Pernambuco* there were two regiments of pure blacks, entitled, respectively, the Old and New Henriques, in honour of Henrique Diaz, whose services will be remembered in the Pernambucan War; there were likewise mulatto regiments. It is remarkable that the gipsies should have found their way into this province, where they preserve themselves intact from other parts of the population. The wild Indians of this province were, at the close of the century, well-nigh extinct.

The population of *Bahia* was estimated, at the close of last century, at one hundred thousand souls, two-thirds of whom were mulattoes or negroes. It abounded in convents, nunneries, and other religious establishments; but it likewise possessed public tribunals, and professors of the liberal languages and sciences, as well as a theatre and a mint. It is singular that this city should have been without a single inn; but this circumstance becomes the less remarkable when it is considered that its communication lay wholly with Portugal and with Portuguese, who must have come to it provided with letters of introduction. There were empty lodgings to be hired, as well as eating-houses and coffee-shops.

The chief port of this magnificent bay presented a constant scene of animation, eight hundred launches and boats of different sizes arriving daily. Most of these, it is said, were laden with fruits and flowers. But the port was the centre of trades of various descriptions. There was in the neighbourhood a whale-fishery; there was a sugar-plantation in the interior, which, in the *Reconcave*, contained the richest and most populous portion of *Brazil*. This term included the whole sweep of this bay, varying in breadth from twelve to forty miles. One of its largest towns contained, at the beginning of this century, one thousand and eighty-eight families. Its neighbourhood produced copper, and likewise a plant that supplied the place of hemp or flax.

At the time of the capital of *Brazil* being removed to *Rio de Janeiro*, that city was estimated to contain a population of one hundred thousand souls. At a time when the communication between Europe and India was round the Cape of Good Hope, the position of this city gave it great commercial advantages. Its harbour, beyond question the most beautiful, was likewise one of the most capacious and commodious in the world. The translation of the court from Lisbon to *Brazil* gave it freedom of trade and increase of capital. It must always occupy an important position; but a full description of this incomparable place must be deferred for the present.

The lately established captaincy of *Minas Geraes* had made very considerable strides. In the year 1776 the province contained about three hundred and twenty thousand inhabitants. The whole sum of gold extracted was estimated at forty-five millions sterling, which was probably rather under than over the amount. If it effected no other good, it certainly encouraged the spirit of discovery, and led to the population of vast territories which would otherwise have remained unexplored; whilst by its means Portugal was enabled to pay the balance of trade against her. It is needless to observe that in *Minas Geraes*, as in all other mining districts throughout the world, whether in California, Australia, or Africa, the proportion of crime was enormous.

The captaincy of *S. Paulo* is one of the greatest provinces of all those of *Brazil*. The elevation of the capital makes it in point of climate more desirable than that of any other city in the empire. It contained at the time of the removal of the royal family about twenty-four thousand inhabitants, one-half of them being European. Like all other places in this country, it possessed almost a superabundance of religious establishments; but it was likewise well provided with places of education.

The name of *Paulista*, which is synonymous with that of an inveterate slave-stealer, has given a reputation to the inhabitants of this province in general which certainly many of them did not deserve.

It has been remarked as singular that so immense a country as *Brazil*, formed as it was by an invading European race, should have maintained its cohesion as it has done; but when the circumstances of the country are considered, the wonder ceases; for in such a vast extent the scanty population were so scattered that combination on any formidable scale became almost impossible. As has been already said, the connecting tie between the various units which form *Brazil* became doubly knit by the arrival of the family of Braganza, there to make their home.

Note.—This and the preceding Chapters of Vol. II. relating to Brazil are founded on

" History of *Brazil;* " by Robert Southey;

" *Barlœi* (Casp.) *Rerum per octennium in Brazilia*," 1680;

" History of *Brazil;* " J. Henderson, 1821;

" *Reise nach Brazilien, durch die Provinzen von Rio de Janeiro und Minas Geraes;* " Burmeister, Berlin, 1853;

" Purchas," iv. ;

" Travels in *Brazil*," Koster (H.); 1817;

Conder (Josiah), " *Brazil* and *Buenos Ayres*," 1830;

" *Relation d'un Voyage dans l'Interieur de l'Amérique Meridionale aux cotes du Brazil;* " Maest, 1778; and

" Duguay-Trouin, *Mémoires de;* " Petitot, 2nde ser., lxxv.

CHAPTER XVIII.

REPULSE OF GENERAL WHITELOCKE AT BUENOS AYRES.

1806-1807.

SPAIN having taken part with Napoleon against the English, by granting the former a monthly subsidy, gave the latter power to make reprisals on the Spanish colonies. The first act of war was the seizure of four transports coming from *La Plata*—an act which decided Charles IV. to declare himself openly the ally of Napoleon in the war, which declaration was followed by the destruction of the Spanish fleet by Nelson at Trafalgar. 1805. To this disaster may in a great measure be traced the facility with which the Spanish possessions in South America were subsequently enabled to throw off the yoke of Spain.

At the time when Nelson and the waves were accomplishing their work of destruction the English Government despatched to the Southern Atlantic a force of six thousand six hundred and fifty men, under the orders of Sir David Baird. The destination of this expedition was kept a secret, but it took the direction of *Brazil*, then in alliance with England.

Sobremonte, the ninth Viceroy of *La Plata*, when he heard of the arrival of this force at *Rio de Janeiro*, became alarmed for the safety of the provinces under his charge, and judged it probable that the English would in the first instance attack *Monte Video*. He therefore transported thither all his available troops, abandoning *Buenos Ayres* to the care of the local militia of that place; but scarcely had he completed his preparations for the defence of the Uruguayan capital, when he learnt that the English had turned their prows in the direction of the Cape of Good Hope, which important position they wrested from Holland. The Viceroy breathed again, and returned to *Buenos Ayres*.

It was at that time the prevailing opinion in England that the Spanish colonies in the southern continent of America were as anxious to throw off the yoke of the mother country as had been her own colonies on the northern continent to free themselves from their connection with Great Britain; and this opinion was confirmed by General Miranda, a native of *New Granada*, who had been long resident in England. This officer, who had been banished from France, succeeded in persuading the English Government that they had only to show themselves on the Southern Atlantic and Pacific to be hailed as liberators. The assurance was the more welcome in that the spoil was tempting, for South America was still the land of gold and silver.

From the Cape of Good Hope it seemed feasible enough to make a dash on *La Plata*. Even should it not be successful, it would at any rate create alarm in Spain, and compel that country to weaken its strength at home by sending out reinforcements to its transatlantic dominions. Accordingly Sir David Baird and Admiral Popham, who commanded the fleet, resolved to send a limited force to *Buenos Ayres*, which place they were assured by an American officer recently arrived from there was not in a condition to offer resistance, since Sobremonte had removed the garrison to *Monte Video*. Sir Home Popham took the command of the flotilla, on which were embarked one thousand six hundred and thirty-five men under the orders of General Beresford.

1806.   On the 6th of June 1806, the squadron arrived at

the mouth of the *Plata*, which stream the vessels had some difficulty in ascending; and it was only on the 25th that they were able to come to anchor near the village of *Quilmes*, at a distance of fifteen miles to the south of *Buenos Ayres*. The Viceroy had, on the 17th of the month, learned of the presence of the fleet in the river, and he had forthwith commenced his preparations for defence; but, owing to the impossibility of communicating with *Monte Video*,—since the English were masters of the river,—he could do no more than muster the militia and transport the contents of the treasury to *Lujan*, a small town at some miles' distance in the interior.

On the 25th, the English disembarked without resistance, and throughout that night the alarm-bell at *Buenos Ayres* sounded unceasingly. The Viceroy, realizing the uselessness of resistance, now thought only of preparing to depart; but at daybreak a body of seven hundred horsemen with six pieces of artillery, hastily gathered together and badly armed, advanced towards the hostile force. This demonstration, however, did not survive the first fire of the English skirmishers; the seven hundred horsemen dispersed, leaving half of their artillery behind them, and Beresford met with no further resistance on his march to the suburb of *Barracas*, where he encamped on the evening of the 26th.

On the same night the Viceroy abandoned the city and set out with his family for the interior; when the remaining Spanish authorities thought only of capitulating. General Quintana, who commanded the militia, drew up some conditions which he sent to Beresford, whose troops were already in movement, and who, without halting, replied verbally that he would grant what was required of him after he had taken possession of the town. At three o'clock in the afternoon his force occupied the principal square and the fort, on which the English flag now replaced that of Spain.

Next day the municipality received orders to hand over to the English the public treasury as well as the money which the Viceroy had sent to *Lujan*, the commander giving it to be understood that this treasure was the price exacted for exempting *Buenos Ayres* from pillage. With this possibility before them, the municipality hastened to beg Sobremonte not to prolong a useless resistance and to accept the terms offered. The terms were accepted, and an English officer was sent with an escort to *Lujan*, whence, on the 5th of July, he returned with four cars, bearing half a million of silver pieces, which treasure was forthwith transported on board the "Narcissus," the flag-ship of Sir Home Popham. This ransom money, together with all that found in the public offices, was sent to London, and deposited with great ceremony in the Bank of England.

The English general now announced the conditions to be granted to the conquered, who were required, in the first instance, to swear allegiance to George III. The Catholic religion might be freely professed; private property would be respected; all merchant-ships taken in the port would be restored; commerce would be free as in English colonies; and civil and judicial authorities who should swear allegiance to England should be permitted to retain their functions.

But, notwithstanding the seemingly complete submission, the great majority of the people of *Buenos Ayres* were not the mere passive spectators which they appeared. The greater proportion of the public *employés* took the required oath of allegiance; the colonial society opened its *salons* to the English officers, and the *Porteña* beauties were not displeased to number them amongst their admirers; but the townspeople in general could not tamely reconcile themselves to see their city, with its seventy-two thousand inhabitants, at the mercy of a paltry force of sixteen hundred men.

The Viceroy, Sobremonte, having tried in vain to

assemble the militia, set out for *Cordova*, to which place he announced he had transferred the capital. General Beresford, on his part, was so sensible of the weakness of his position that he lost no time in begging Sir David Baird to send a reinforcement to enable him to retain his conquest. He likewise thought of seizing *Monte Video*; but, as this place was garrisoned by regular troops, he did not flatter himself with the idea that it would fall into his hands as easily as had *Buenos Ayres*, the malcontents of which latter place had a round-about means of communication with the royal troops by way of *S. Fernando*, the islands and the *Uruguay*.

The Spanish colonies of South America had been so treated throughout by the mother country as mere political children, that the people of *Buenos Ayres*, although they saw the disgrace of the position in which they were placed, were almost incapable of the political vigour necessary for the effort to escape from it. What they wanted above all was a leader; and had they depended solely on colonial genius at this juncture it is very unlikely that General Beresford would have been disturbed in his possession, or at least that any local leader would have been found with the necessary qualities to effect a successful revolt. But the needful leading spirit was found in the person of a Frenchman.

Jacques Liniers had been thirty years in the service of Spain. He had for some time occupied the post of governor of *Misiones*, and at the time of the English invasion was captain of the small port of *Ensenada*. He was brave, active, and enterprising, but somewhat apt to be carried away, and without much solidity of character. On learning the triumph of the English, he had asked and had obtained permission to visit his family at *Buenos Ayres*, but had declined to take the oath of allegiance. It was easy for him to perceive that the common people did not accept the foreign domination with the same resignation which was displayed by the wealthier colonists, who had much to lose in the case of a continuance of military operations; he likewise realized the fact that the *gauchos* of the surrounding *pampas* might materially aid a movement which should take the shape of partisan warfare in which they might fight after their own loose fashion. By good luck and a little daring he might easily get the better of an enemy so inconsiderable in number.

Having arranged his plan of action, and acting in accord with *Señor* Puirredon and other *Creole* patriots, Liniers quietly quitted *Buenos Ayres* and made the journey to *Monte Video*, where he communicated his project to General Huïdobro, who commanded there, and from whom he asked some troops, by whose aid he assured him he would compel the English to re-embark. Huïdobro was willing to aid these patriots with all the resources in his power; and Puirredon and two others were sent into the country in different directions to arrange for a rising. At the same time a small force of regular soldiers, placed under the orders of Liniers, marched for *Colonia*, opposite to *Buenos Ayres*, where it was awaited by a flotilla of light boats such as might easily evade the English vessels in the shallow waters of the *Plata*. Under a thick fog the flotilla crossed to the right bank, and the men disembarked at twenty-one miles to the north of the capital.

Meanwhile Puirredon with some raw forces had encountered the English. A small column of five hundred men and three guns had been sent by Beresford to drive the insurgents from *Moron* and other small villages where they had assembled. At the first fire the untrained levies were scattered; but the practised horsemen merely continued to circle round the enemy, and in this manner accidentally arrived near one of the field-pieces, of which by a sudden charge they were able to obtain possession. The English column returned to *Buenos Ayres* much chagrined at this misfortune at the hands of an enemy which they had no means of overtaking.

When Liniers arrived at *San Fernando* he found the *gauchos* all excitement at the piece of luck which had befallen them, and which revealed to them their own value in partisan warfare against the English. His small force was composed of sixty-six grenadiers, two hundred and twenty-seven dragoons, a hundred and fifty-eight volunteers, a hundred and forty Catalonians, a hundred artillerymen, three hundred Spanish seamen, sixty seamen from the islands, and seventy-three men belonging to a French privateer, who wished to take part in the affair; in all, of eleven hundred and twenty-four men, with two large guns and four small pieces. After the *gaucho* success, however, he had good reason to believe that he would be joined by numerous recruits, and he therefore boldly marched on *Buenos Ayres*.

On the afternoon of the 10th of August he reached the northern suburb, and with such despatch had his operations been conducted that up till now the English had had no notice of his proceedings. His prognostication had been correct as to his receiving recruits, for his little army was already nearly tripled in number; but unfortunately most of the new arrivals were without arms. Such volunteers, however, besides giving his force the appearance of being more formidable than it really was, were of use in the way of contributing to the transport.

On the morning of the 11th, Liniers sent a flag of truce to Beresford, requiring him to surrender. On receiving his reply in the negative, the colonists resolutely entered the town, and took possession of an edifice in which they established their headquarters; and the English, beset on all sides, were obliged to concentrate their defence in the central square and the neighbouring streets. On the morning of the 12th the Catalonian sharp-shooters, together with the men of the French privateer, penetrated as far as the cathedral, the front of which looked on the square. Then commenced a general street-fight, in which regular troops are under many disadvantages. From the balconies and the flat-roofs of the houses there rained on the English a shower of missiles of all sorts. They were driven back into the square and were forced to abandon the neighbouring streets.

Having thus cleared his way, Liniers was enabled to bring up his artillery and to pour small shot into the English as they were packed round the fort. It was then that Captain Kennet of the Engineers, General Beresford's secretary, fell at the side of his chief. The noise of the firing and the cries of some fifteen thousand men who took part in the struggle were so deafening as to prevent the orders of the officers from being heard; and Beresford perceived that it was necessary to retreat within the fort, which he was the last of his force to enter.

A well-sustained fusilade proved fatal to all such as showed themselves above the ramparts, which in addition were commanded by the flat roofs of the houses, whose inmates might fire in perfect safety on the devoted English. Thus, seeing resistance useless, Beresford ordered a flag of truce to be hoisted; but this signal not being understood or regarded by the assailants, and the fire continuing, the Spanish flag was raised and the future victor of Albuera, showing himself upon the rampart, flung his sword into the ditch, whereupon the firing ceased.

Liniers readily granted his brave adversary all the honours of war. An hour later the English general and his staff, together with the 71st regiment, whose colours bore the names of various actions in the United States and also of *Saint Jean d'Acre*, had to lay down their arms and standards before the raw forces of the Gascon, by which they were marched in line, and whose prisoners of war they remained. The English occupation of *Buenos Ayres* had lasted forty-seven days. Its abrupt termination was chiefly due to the utter absence of any intelligence-department in the occupying force. It is difficult to attach blame to General Beresford in this or indeed in any other respect. He had, in obedience to superior orders, undertaken an enterprise for which the force at his disposal was utterly inadequate, and so rapid were the movements of Liniers that he could not possibly anticipate his coming at the head of an expedition capable of opposing him. Even had he anticipated his arrival it is not easy to see what he could have done, quartered as he was in a little fort commanded on three sides by the houses of a hostile town, which had so well disguised its hostility as to afford him no pretext for treating it in an unfriendly manner. Had he adopted the alternative course of destroying all the houses whose vicinity to the fort endangered his position, he would have, doubtless, raised the population against him, and would have found it impossible to obtain provisions for his troops. As it was, he saw the insecurity of his position and had demanded succours from the Cape of Good Hope; but the intelligence and activity of Liniers anticipated their arrival.

This victory on the part of the inhabitants of a province, unaided by Spain, had immense results, since it showed the colonists at the same time their own strength and the inability of the mother country to defend them. Liniers had in fact, to use the words of Mr. Canning, called a new world into existence.

. . . .

After the surrender of Beresford the city of *Buenos Ayres* assumed control of its own destinies. The fugitive Viceroy, Sobremonte, who, had he acted from the first with decision, would have placed himself at the head of the armed forces at *Monte Video*, and there raised the national standard, had at length succeeded in assembling a militia force with which he advanced to the capital. But his evident incapacity had made him odious to the people of *Buenos Ayres;* and these, elated by their triumph, resolved no longer to submit to his authority. The municipality summoned the principal inhabitants for the purpose of choosing a new government. On the 14th of August, two days after the surrender of Beresford, the meeting took place. But the citizens had scarcely assembled when the hall was crowded by the people, who with one voice demanded the election of Liniers. This selection made, a commission was appointed to notify to Sobremonte that he was no longer chief of the provinces of *La Plata.*

Sobremonte, on receiving this information, had nothing better to do than to betake himself to *Monte Video,* where his militia forces might be of use in defending that place, which was still menaced by the fleet of Admiral Popham. The representatives of *Buenos Ayres,* foreseeing the probability of a future visit from the English, now decided that their town should be put in a state of defence forthwith. The people had already grasped the idea that they could govern themselves better than could Spain, and likewise that they were better qualified to select a suitable governor than was the court of Madrid. Nevertheless, as yet no one thought of raising his voice in favour of a separation from the mother country.

But Liniers was not long in realizing the fact that, although he had been elected Viceroy, the people who had elected him were nevertheless his masters; and he was compelled to withdraw the concessions which in a spirit of soldier-like generosity he had granted to Beresford and his men. When things had calmed down a little, the municipality had leisure to reflect that it might be well to send some explanation to Spain regarding the events which had occurred; and the envoy chosen for this purpose was Puirredon, who could claim the honour of having captured the first English piece of artillery taken. There were indeed already two parties in *Buenos Ayres;* the one that of Liniers, who as Viceroy represented the Spanish Government, and the other that of Puirredon, who represented the colonial democracy; and this rivalry was sedulously taken advantage of by those who aimed at the independence of the colony, and whose spokesman was Moreno. These men suggested that the new battalions to be enrolled for the defence of *Buenos Ayres* should be pledged to that province as a nationality. Four battalions of infantry were formed, and amongst the local militia was a corps of mulattoes and negroes, whilst there were six squadrons of *gaucho* cavalry.

Whilst thus in the lower Platine provinces all was preparation for the struggle which every one foresaw, in England bright hopes were built on the capture of the South-American city whose loss was not yet known. Sir David Baird, who was still at the Cape of Good Hope, received orders to reinforce Beresford with fourteen hundred men; and on the 11th of October, 1806, a squadron, commanded by Admiral Sterling, and carrying four thousand three hundred and fifty soldiers, under the orders of Sir Samuel Auchmuty, set sail for the *Plata*. On the 12th of November, another expedition of four thousand three hundred and ninety-one men, under the command of General Crawford, set out for *Chili*. The fourteen hundred men from the Cape of Good Hope reached the River *Plate* after the surrender of Beresford, and when Admiral Popham had realized that it was of no use to think of retaking that town. Even *Monte Video* was by this time so well prepared that it was impossible for him to reduce that place with the insufficient forces at his disposal. He therefore thought fit to land at *Maldonado*, a small harbour on the left side of the river, where he disembarked his men, and awaited an addition to his strength.

No sooner was the defeat of Beresford known in England than the ministry despatched a fast vessel from Portsmouth with orders to General Crawford to join Sir Samuel Auchmuty; whilst, shortly afterwards, a third body, consisting of sixteen hundred and thirty picked troops, set out under the orders of Lieutenant-General John Whitelocke, who was to assume the command-in-chief of the united English forces in *La Plata*, whose number would amount to twelve thousand men, supported by a fleet of eighteen men-of-war, together with eighty transports.

General Auchmuty was the first to arrive. Taking with him the fourteen hundred men whom Popham had landed at *Maldonado*, and likewise three hundred men from the fleet, he invested *Monte Video* on the 28th of January. He was attacked by Sobremonte, with some mounted militia, but who were quickly dispersed, and who retired to *Colonia*. Auchmuty then established his batteries, and commenced to bombard *Monte Video* from the south. On the 2d of February the breach was declared practicable, and at daylight on the 3d the general ordered an assault.

An English writer, who as a youth was present at the assault on *Monte Video*, gives a vivid picture of the scene. Arriving with high hopes in the river *Plata*, in December 1806, the author of "Letters on *Paraguay*," and his fellow-travellers, learned to their dismay that *Buenos Ayres* had been retaken by the Spaniards, and that General Beresford and his army were prisoners. Sir Samuel Auchmuty was now investing *Monte Video*, and, with the exception of the country immediately around that town, there was no footing for Englishmen in Spanish America. The "Enterprise" was ordered to proceed to the roadstead, there, together with hundreds of other ships similarly situated, to be under the orders of the English admiral.

Monte Video was strongly and regularly fortified. Its

harbour presented a scene of the greatest animation; brigs-of-war were running close under the walls, and bombarding the citadel from the sea, whilst thousands of spectators on board ship were tracing, in breathless suspense, the impression made by every shell upon the town, and by every ball upon the breach. The frequent *sorties* made by the Spanish troops, and the repulses which they sustained, were watched with painful interest.

At length, one morning before dawn, the breach was enveloped in one mighty spread of conflagration. The roar of cannon was incessant, and the atmosphere was one dense mass of smoke, impregnated with the smell of gunpowder. By the aid of the night-glass, and by the flashes from the guns, it might be seen that a deadly struggle was going forward on the walls. It was succeeded by an awful pause; and presently the dawn of day revealed the British ensign floating from the battlements. The sight was received by a shout of triumph from the fleet.

That day the travellers might land, and might view the scene of the terrible carnage which had ensued. The grenadier company of the 40th regiment, missing the breach, had been annihilated. Colonel Vassall, of the 38th regiment, had been the first to mount, and whilst waving his sword had fallen, shot through the heart. The breach had been barricaded again and again with piles of tallow in skins, and with bullocks' hides, which as they gave way carried the assailants with them on to the points of the enemy's bayonets. The carnage on both sides was dreadful and was long uninterrupted; and piles of wounded, or of dead and dying, were to be seen on every side, whilst sufferers were being conveyed on litters to the hospitals and churches.

This writer bears the highest testimony to the discipline of the British troops as well as to the energy and philanthropy of their general, owing to which a speedy stop was put to the scenes of pillage which invariably accompany the capture of a fortified city. But to those who have witnessed the terrible effects produced by a bombardment, it is astonishing how quickly its results may be made to disappear, and such was now the case at *Monte Video*. In a week or two, says Mr. Robertson, the more prominent ravages of war disappeared, and in a month after the capture the inhabitants were getting as much confidence in their invaders as could possibly be expected. This early confidence was mainly attributable to the mild and equitable government of the commander-in-chief, Sir Samuel Auchmuty, who permitted the civil institutions of the country to remain unchanged, and who showed the greatest affability to all classes. The hundreds of vessels in the harbour now discharged their human freight, who were able somehow to procure accommodation on shore; and *Monte Video* soon began to have the appearance of being an English town, since to its mixed population of Spaniards, *Creoles*, and Mulattoes were added some four thousand English soldiers, together with two thousand merchants, traders, and adventurers of the same nation.

The loss of the Spaniards in the assault had been seven hundred men. The garrison, together with its commander General Huïdobro, became prisoners, six hundred of whom were despatched to England. The news of the capture of *Monte Video* produced such commotion in *Buenos Ayres*, that the people who could not yet readily believe that they were not invincible, chose to impute the blame to Sobremonte. He was accordingly solemnly deposed by a popular vote, the chief authority being vested in the High Court of Justice, pending the receipt of orders from Spain, whither Sobremonte was sent. Thus the province of *Buenos Ayres* was in full course of revolution. It was the people who had taken the lead in every movement which had followed the attack on Beresford; but as they were acting against the enemies of the King of Spain, everything was done in the name of that monarch, even to the degradation and dismissal of his Viceroy. The High Court of Justice, to which was temporarily confided the executive power, was composed exclusively of Spaniards. The magistrates, though they did not fail to perceive the revolutionary tendency of events, were yet aware that the *Creoles* alone were in a position to withstand the English; they therefore yielded to the current. The leaders of the revolutionary party took advantage of the complaisance of the Spanish authorities; and the municipality, who were greatly influenced by popular meetings, assumed every day greater importance.

On the capture of *Monte Video* the English established themselves in that most desirable place in a manner which showed that they had every intention of retaining possession of it. Whilst General Auchmuty occupied the chief city and likewise *Maldonado*, Colonel Pack had driven the Spaniards from *Colonia*, and the side of the river *Plata*, which to-day belongs to the Republic of *Uruguay*, was then in full English possession. Already the merchant ships thronged the river-side, carrying more goods than the people could afford to buy. In *Monte Video* goods were sold at a hundred per cent. less than the prices which, owing to Custom-House exactions, they had hitherto commanded. Even a half-English, half-Spanish journal, called the "The Southern Star," was set on foot under English auspices, with a view of proclaiming the downfall of Spain.

General Whitelocke did not reach the *Plata* until three months after the capture of *Monte Video*. He was promptly joined by General Crawford, who had been overtaken on the Atlantic by the despatch-boat sent after him. With the united force at his disposal the reconquest of *Buenos Ayres* and its territory seemed to the commander-in-chief, as to everybody else, a very simple affair, as indeed it was. It was impossible to conceive that where a force of sixteen hundred men had in the first instance succeeded, one of ten thousand of the same army should fail. The reason, however, is not far to seek. It lay in the difference between Beresford and Whitelocke.

The English force was divided into four brigades. The first, composed of a battalion of rifles and one of infantry of the line, was commanded by General Crawford; the second, composed of three battalions, was led by Sir Samuel Auchmuty; the third, of two battalions and a regiment of dismounted dragoons, was under General Lumley; the fourth, likewise of two battalions and a regiment of dismounted dragoons, was under Colonel Mahon. The mounted batteries were kept in reserve, under the immediate orders of the commander-in-chief. The entire effective force amounted to nearly ten thousand men, some two thousand having been left for the defence of Monte Video, together with a small body of militia composed of all the English residents.

The expedition set out amidst the cheers of the fleet, and on Sunday, the 28th of June, the troops disembarked at the small port of *Ensenada*, forty-eight miles south of *Buenos Ayres*. Why a spot so distant from the city should have been selected it is not easy to imagine; but this was in accordance with all the subsequent proceedings of the general. Their landing was unopposed by the Spaniards, who, of course, anticipated that it would be effected nearer the town, probably at *Quilmes*, where Beresford had set foot. Without loss of time the advanced guard, under General Levison Gower, the second in command, was *en route*, and it was followed by the main body of the army, which marched without opposition to *Quilmes*. So far, notwithstanding the low marshy ground and the immense bogs and lakes which intervene between *Ensenada* and *Buenos Ayres*, all went well, and it seemed scarcely possible to anticipate any but a favourable result of the enterprise. As no communication could be kept between the naval and land forces, the army had to encumber itself with the immense load of provisions necessary for the subsistence of ten thousand men during one week. For hours together the men were up to there middle in water, their artillery being often swamped in the marshes. Their provisions were scanty and wet; nor was there any shelter from the intense cold, even the supply of wine and spirits running short. The troops marched through a desert, the inhabitants having vanished, together with their horses and cattle.

Buenos Ayres was no longer the timid colonial city which Beresford had found it. The president of the municipality was *Señor* Alzaga, an energetic partisan of the King, and who carried great authority in the city, where his fortune placed him in the front rank. The people were armed. The national battalions were animated by the best spirit. Liniers, always brave, had now to sustain his high reputation and to win from the Crown the confirmation of the title which he had received from the people. Their past success gave both chief and soldiers confidence. They had seen what street-fighting was, and Whitelocke and his men would have to run the gauntlet of armed streets before reaching the fort.

Such was the spirit by which the colonial forces were animated, when, on the 1st of July, General Whitelocke reached the village of *Quilmes*, fifteen miles to the south of the town. A force of six thousand eight hundred and fifty men, with fifty-three guns, marched out of the town to defend the passage of the *Riochuelo*. On the succeeding night the two armies were encamped, respectively, on either bank of the stream which separated them. Next morning at daybreak the Spaniards were drawn up in battle order, anticipating an attack from the enemy; but General Gower, after having exchanged some shots, moved his troops to the left, with the intention of passing the *Riochuelo*, three miles higher up. Liniers followed his movement, but he did not arrive in time to interfere with his effecting the passage. He, however, succeeded in placing himself between the enemy and the town, near the *Miserere*, on the south-west of the city.

A combat now took place between the *Creole* militia and the brigade of General Crawford; but the discipline of the English troops and their great superiority in artillery quickly decided the day in their favour. The *Creoles* abandoned the field, leaving the whole of their artillery behind. The colonial force then became divided into two bodies. The cavalry, passing the English left, gained the plains. Liniers, who now gave up the town for lost, following the horsemen, gave them orders to rendezvous at *Chacharita*, a well-known farm three miles to the English rear. This was a wise measure on the part of the general; for had these fugitives entered the town they would doubtless have added to the dismay of the citizens, whilst from this position he could still annoy the English. The infantry took refuge in *Buenos Ayres*, where the general feeling had now undergone considerable revulsion. The night was cold and wet; the fugitives, worn out by the fatigues of the preceding day, were exhausted and beaten; the general was absent, no one knew where.

And here was renewed the series of infatuated mistakes committed by General Whitelocke. Instead of pursuing the broken enemy and taking advantage of their panic, he allowed them a night of repose, during which the energy of Alzaga was able in a great measure to repair the disastrous effects of the rout of *Miserere*. The chief of the municipality had not allowed himself to be carried away by the despair of the troops in the absence of the governor; he rather felt stimulated to increased energy. By his orders the soldiers were carefully tended in the municipality and in the barracks, and were cheered with the hope of better fortune in the future. Alzaga likewise caused ditches to be dug in the streets round the principal parade, facing the fort. He also sent messengers to Liniers, who, making a long detour, suc-

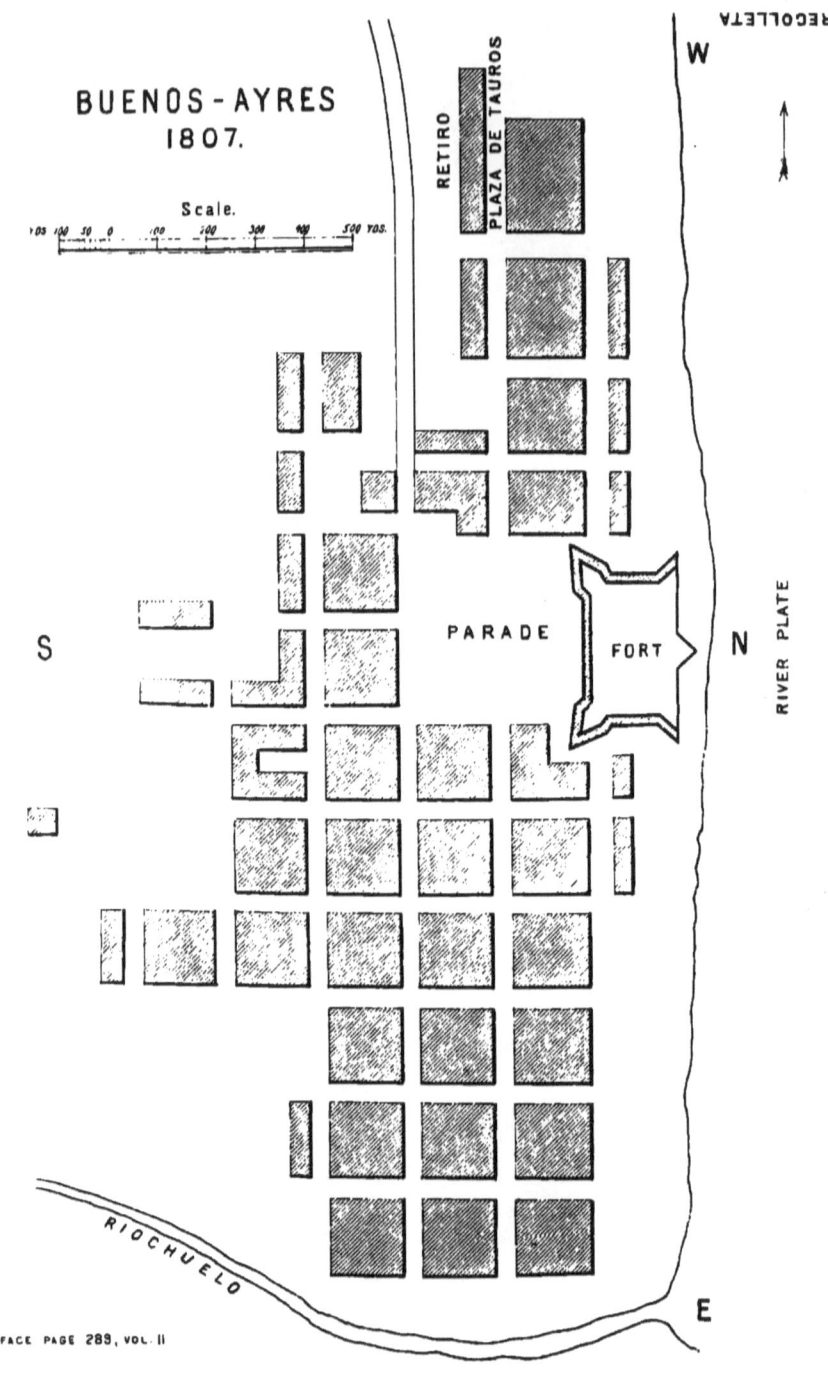

REPULSE OF GENERAL WHITELOCKE. 289

ceeded in throwing himself into the town together with his horsemen.

On the morning of the 2nd of July, *Buenos Ayres* was already in a state of defence. The troops were distributed on the roofs of the churches, on the terraces of the houses, and on the balconies; whilst some pieces of artillery were put in position behind the ditches and behind the barricades which had been erected round the parade and round an open space called the *Retiro*. Thus when General Gower, who led the advanced guard, summoned the town to surrender, the aspect of affairs was entirely changed from that of the preceding evening; confidence had succeeded discouragement, and good hopes were entertained of yet saving the town. Alzaga replied, that he would not listen to any proposition for the surrender of the garrison.

Under these circumstances the English had to consider their mode of attack, and they employed the following day in making their preparations. On the 4th, the garrison made a *sortie*, and compelled their assailants to abandon some houses in the suburbs where they had taken shelter. There was also a slight encounter between the 88th regiment and one of mulattoes. The result of these two slight affairs did not fail to encourage the Spaniards.

Buenos Ayres, according to a plan before me, at that time consisted of twenty-four square blocks of buildings of a hundred and fifty yards on every side, to the east of the centre parade facing the fort, and of six complete blocks of the same dimensions, together with a number of incomplete ones, lying in the opposite direction. The back of the fort faced the river, having six square blocks to the east and four to the west. The city being laid out on a perfectly regular plan, was divided by parallel streets cutting each other in prolonged lines between the various square blocks of buildings. The central space in front of the fort would have held four blocks; that is to say, it was about three hundred and fifteen yards square. The city was entirely blockaded from the side of the river, and General Whitelocke had the means at his disposal of blockading it in like manner on the other three sides, and thus of very quickly starving it into submission without striking a blow. Since he had failed to take it by a *coup de main* after the fight of *Miserere*, this would have been his simplest plan, more especially in view of Beresford's disastrous experience of street-fighting. It would likewise have had the advantage of being unattended by any appreciable loss of life. He might, on the other hand, have bombarded the town, since its garrison refused to surrender; or, he might have advanced by degrees, clearing out each square block of houses as he proceeded, and making each a ground from which to operate on the next.

But General Whitelocke seemed infatuated, and left no one thing undone to play into the enemy's hands. Having given orders that his troops should not load their pieces, lest they might be tempted to delay for the purpose of returning the enemy's fire, he divided his entire force into eight bodies, who should penetrate simultaneously into the town, and, disregarding the street-fire which was sure to be poured upon them from the tops of the flat-roofed houses, should make straight for the river, whence, turning to the right and to the left, respectively, they should make for the central parade and occupy the highest buildings.

In accordance with the above plan, the 45th regiment, which was on the right, penetrated without difficulty to the *Residencia*, of which it took possession. The light division, composed of rifles and light infantry, notwithstanding a hail of balls which fell on it from the balconies, windows and roofs, was able to arrive in front of the Dominicans' convent; and, breaking open the gates, the men penetrated into the church, where they found the flags which had been taken from the 71st in the previous year. Ascending the turrets, the rifles there hoisted the same flags, and from this commanding position they directed a very effective fire on the citizens who occupied the terraces of the neighbouring houses. But the fort, perceiving the English flag on the towers of the convent, directed towards it such a cannonade that the English who were there shut up and who had been meanwhile cut off there by the militia, were forced to surrender at discretion. One of the prisoners was Colonel Pack, who had already been made prisoner with Beresford, and who, having escaped, had joined in the attack on the convent of *San Domingo*.

Another English column, under the orders of Colonel Cadogan, after having lost a fourth of its number, was obliged to lay down its arms, being enclosed in a circle of fire near the Jesuits' college. A like fate befell the 88th regiment under Duff, after it had penetrated by the central streets to the parade. The 36th regiment, which had entered by the streets of *Corrientes* and of *Tucuman*, was compelled to fall back on the *Retiro*, in spite of the heroic efforts of General Lumley. The 5th regiment, having suffered less, arrived at the convent of *St. Catherine*, where it took up its quarters, to the scandal and terror of the nuns.

The 87th regiment, under the orders of Auchmuty, had attacked the *Retiro* and had been cut up by the fire of the troops shut up in the *Plaza de Tauros;* but Colonel Nugent, having seized a battery which defended the approaches on this side, turned the guns against the edifice occupied by the Spaniards, and the six hundred men who had resisted the attack of Auchmuty, being crushed by the fire of Nugent, were obliged to surrender.

Night put an end to the dismal combat. The 5th regiment remained in the convent. Auchmuty and Whitelocke were besieged in the *Retiro*. The greater part of the 45th occupied the *Residencia* together with a German battalion which had been left as a reserve. This fatal day had cost the English 1130 men killed and wounded, amongst whom were seventy officers. There were likewise made prisoners and shut up in the convents and barracks, a hundred and twenty officers and fifteen hundred soldiers, after having surrendered their arms and ammunition to the local militia or the citizens.

On the morning of the 6th General Whitelocke had still at his disposal some five thousand effective men. He placed himself in communication with the fleet, from which he could receive provisions and reinforcements, as well as big guns to use against the town.

Liniers seeing that it was still possible for either side to fight, and wishing to avoid an unnecessary effusion of blood, took the bold step of sending a flag of truce to the English general, with the proposal to surrender all his prisoners, including those taken with Beresford, providing he should consent to at once embark with all his forces, and depart.

And now occurred an incident which, but for its grave consequences, would border on the ludicrous. In drawing up his communication to the English general, Liniers had merely stipulated that in return for his prisoners, the latter should evacuate the territory of *Buenos Ayres*. Being a brave officer himself, it never occurred to him that General Whitelocke, who was still in possession of *Monte Video*, and at the head of an army of seven thousand effective men, not to speak of the fleet, could be asked to surrender his hold on *Uruguay*. But Alzaga thought otherwise. He insisted that the terms of convention should include the surrender of *Monte Video*. Liniers remonstrated that they had not taken *Monte Video*, and that they might be quite satisfied by obtaining the relief of *Buenos Ayres*. To this Alzaga replied that there could be no harm in inserting a clause demanding the restoration of *Monte Video*, since, at the worst, it could only be objected to. The clause was accordingly inserted —and complied with without remonstrance.

When Whitelocke received the above proposals he at

first rejected them; but he nevertheless demanded an armistice of twenty-four hours to carry away the wounded. Liniers, whose wounded were safely housed, replied by reopening a fire on the *Retiro*. The English made a *sortie*, in which they are said to have suffered even more than on the day preceding. The Buenos Ayrian writers admit that the English troops, officers and soldiers alike, penetrated through the deadly streets with the utmost intrepidity; but their confidence was entirely broken, as well it might be, when they saw themselves the victims of such a general. They fought as it was their duty to fight, but not with the least hope of conquering. The colonists, on the other hand, were full of confidence; and Alzaga was more than ever determined that the terms of capitulation should include *Monte Video*.

In the course of the afternoon General Gower presented himself at the fort under a flag of truce. He was the bearer of propositions from General Whitelocke almost identical with those that had been drawn up by Liniers under the advice of Alzaga. The English plenipotentiary was received by Liniers, by Generals Balbiana and Velasco, and by the Mayor Alzaga. The proposals of General Whitelocke were accepted; forty-eight hours were accorded to the English in which to evacuate *Buenos Ayres*, and the term of two months for embarking from *Monte Video*, and quitting every part of the *Plata*. The capitulation was ratified next day (the 7th of July) by the English general, and the city of *Buenos Ayres* not unnaturally gave itself over to triumph when, on the following day, it saw the English ships weigh anchor previous to their departure.

In reviewing the series of events which sprang from the same cause that produced the victory of Trafalgar, and which ended so ignominiously for England, the result is to be traced wholly to the personal character of three individuals—Liniers, Whitelocke, and Alzaga. But for the sparkling Frenchman, who was in effect the father of the South-American republics, it is probable that General Beresford would not have been disturbed in his possession of *Buenos Ayres* until he had been placed in a position of security by the arrival of reinforcements from the Cape of Good Hope, and that, therefore, the expedition of Whitelocke would never have had its part to play. Next, but for the pitiable character of that officer,* to which, rather than either to Liniers or to Alzaga, was due the repulse of the English, it seemed scarcely possible that so mighty a force should have failed to reduce a city defended only by a single fort, and by troops that had been already vanquished. Lastly, but for the pertinacity of Alzaga, *Monte Video* and its charming territories would in all probability have, like the Cape of Good Hope, belonged to England at the present day. The latter result is especially to be deplored; since *Uruguay*, which under English administration might have proved an earthly paradise, and a pattern to other States on the same continent, has been foremost amongst the South-American republics as a standing piece of irony on the famous phrase of Canning.

As the further fate of General Whitelocke and his luckless command, although interesting to Englishmen, does not properly belong to South-American history, I reserve it for an appendix.

NOTE.—Chapter XVIII. is founded on "*La Plata*," *par* Santiago Arcos; Paris: Michel Lévy Frères, 1865;
"Letters on *Paraguay*," by J. P. and W. P. Robertson. John Murray, London, 1839;
"Trial of General Whitelocke;" London, 1808;
"Whitelocke's Expedition." By an Officer. London, 1808.

* The following was told me by a lady now in her eighty-first year, as having been current in her youth:—

"My first is an emblem of purity,
"My second's a thing of security;
"My whole is a name, which if yours were the same,
"You would blush to hand down to futurity."

APPENDIX.

I.

A GENERAL court-martial was held at Chelsea Hospital, on Lieutenant-General Whitelocke, on January 28, 1808. Its members included the conqueror of Agra and Lasswarree, and the future hero of Coruña. They were General the Right Hon. Sir W. Medows, General the Hon. Chapel Norton, General Viscount Lake, General Hulse, General Ogilvie, General Cuyler, Lieutenant-General the Right Hon. H. E. Fox, Lieutenant-General Sir James Duff, Knight; Lieutenant-General Harris, Lieutenant-General Viscount Cathcart, Lieutenant-General Dundas, Lieutenant-General Ross, Lieutenant-General Pigot, Lieutenant-General Sir George Nugent, Bart.; Lieutenant-General Loftus, Lieutenant-General Wilford, Lieutenant-General Garth, Lieutenant General Lloyd, Lieutenant-General Stavely, Lieutenant-General Sir John Moore, K.B.

First Charge.—That Lieutenant-General Whitelocke, having received instructions from his Majesty's Principal Secretary of State to proceed for the reduction of the province of *Buenos Ayres*, pursued measures ill calculated to facilitate that conquest; that when the Spanish Commander had shown such symptoms of a disposition to treat, as to express a desire to communicate with Major-General Gower, the second in command, upon the subject of terms, the said Lieutenant-General Whitelocke did return a message, in which he demanded, amongst other articles, the surrender of all persons holding civil offices in the government of *Buenos Ayres*, as prisoners of war: that the said Lieutenant-General Whitelocke, in making such an offensive and unusual demand, tending to exasperate the inhabitants of *Buenos Ayres*, to produce and encourage a spirit of resistance to his Majesty's arms, to exclude the hope of amicable accommodation, and to increase the difficulties of the service with which he was intrusted, acted in a manner unbecoming his duty as an officer, prejudicial to military discipline, and contrary to the articles of war.

Second Charge.—That the said Lieutenant-General Whitelocke, after the landing of the troops at *Enseñada*, and during the march from thence to the town of *Buenos Ayres*, did not make the military arrangements best calculated to ensure the success of his operations against the town, and that having known, previously to his attack upon the town of *Buenos Ayres* upon the 5th July 1807, as appears from his public despatch of the 10th of July, that the enemy meant to occupy the flat roofs of the houses, he did nevertheless, in the said attack, divide his forces into several brigades and parts, and ordered the whole to be unloaded, and no firing to be permitted on any account; and, under this order, to march into the principal streets of the town unprovided with proper and sufficient means for forcing the barricadoes, whereby the troops were unnecessarily exposed to destruction, without the possibility of making effectual opposition; such conduct betraying great professional incapacity on the part of the said Lieutenant-General Whitelocke, tending to lessen the confidence of the troops in the judgment of their officers, being derogatory to the honour of His Majesty's arms, contrary to his duty as an officer, prejudicial to good order and military discipline, and contrary to the articles of war.

Third Charge.—That the said Lieutenant-General did not make, although it was in his power, any effectual attempt by his own personal exertion or otherwise, to co-operate with, or support, the different divisions of the army under his command, when engaged with the enemy in the streets of *Buenos Ayres* on the 5th of July 1807; whereby those troops, after having encountered and surmounted a constant and well-directed fire, and having effected the purport of their orders, were left without aid and support, or further orders, and considerable detachments under Lieutenant-Colonel Duff and Brigadier-General Craufurd were thereby compelled to surrender; such conduct on the part of the said Lieutenant-General Whitelocke tending to the defeat and dishonour of his Majesty's arms, to lessen the confidence of the troops in the skill and courage of their

APPENDIX.

officers, being unbecoming and disgraceful to his character as an officer, prejudicial to good order and military discipline, and contrary to the articles of war.

Fourth Charge.—That the said Lieutenant-General Whitelocke, subsequent to the attack upon the town of *Buenos Ayres*, and at a time when the troops under his command were in possession of posts on each flank of the town, and of the principal arsenal, with a communication open to the fleet, and having an effective force of upwards of 5000 men, did enter into, and finally conclude a treaty with the enemy, whereby he acknowledges in the public despatch of the 10th of July 1807—" That he resolved to forego the advantages which the bravery of his troops had obtained, and which advantages had cost him about 2500 men in killed, wounded, and prisoners ; " and by such treaty he unnecessarily and shamefully surrendered all such advantages, totally evacuated the town of *Buenos Ayres*, and consented to deliver, and did shamefully abandon and deliver up to the enemy the strong fortress of *Monte Video*, which had been committed to his charge, and which, at the period of the treaty and abandonment, was well and sufficiently garrisoned and provided against attack, and which was not, at such period, in a state of blockade or siege ; such conduct on the part of the said Lieutenant-General Whitelocke tending to the dishonour of his Majesty's arms, and being contrary to his duty as an officer, prejudicial to good order and military discipline, and contrary to the articles of war.

The proceedings of the court-martial on Lieutenant-General Whitelocke fill a volume of 671 pages, from which I give the following extracts :—

In opening the case the Judge-Advocate described it as being "the most important occasion, in the military history of the country, that ever called for inquiry of a nature like the present." The expedition, he said, had not only totally failed, with the lamentable loss of a great proportion of the gallant army engaged in it, but it ended in the absolute surrender of those valuable advantages which the valour of British troops under another commander had previously acquired in the important post of *Monte Video*. "By this most unfortunate event," he said, "all the hopes have been defeated which had been justly and generally entertained, of discovering new markets for our manufactures, of giving a wider scope to the spirit and enterprise of our merchants, of opening new sources of treasure, and new fields for exertion in supplying either the rude wants of countries emerging from barbarism, or the artificial and increasing demands of luxury and refinement, in those remote quarters of the globe. Important as these objects must be at all times to this country, the state of Europe, and the attempts that have been daily making to exclude us from our accustomed intercourse with the Continent, have added to the importance of these objects, and to the disappointment of these hopes.

"The disappointment has been cruelly embittered by the disgrace which such a failure, under all the circumstances, has attached to the British arms. The diminution of our military fame must be felt at all times as a great national calamity, but at no period so severely as in this crisis of the world, when our military character has become more essential than ever, not merely for our honour or our glory, but for the independence, the liberties, the existence of Great Britain. It is, however, a great consolation, that whatever may have been the stain which our military renown has received, the conduct of the troops has had no share in producing it. I believe, the more this attack of the 5th of July is examined, the more clearly it will be found that no troops ever showed more courage; that no officers (with the exception of whatever may turn out to be connected with the subject of these charges, and I hope the result of this inquiry may prove the exception to be undeserved), but, with that exception, that no officers ever displayed more zeal, more conduct, more devotion of themselves to the common cause in the course of the most triumphant engagement, than was displayed by the British officers through the whole of that destructive day. . . . But it is not upon reports that these charges are founded; they rest upon better evidence. They are taken, not from idle talk or vain rumour, but the orders and despatches of General Whitelocke himself. There is not a fact alleged against him which is not derived from his authority. The character assigned to these facts does, indeed, invoke imputations of the most grave and serious nature; but

APPENDIX.

the facts themselves are founded upon his own account of his own conduct; so much so, that I might be well warranted in contenting myself, on the part of the public, with laying the orders and the despatches of General Whitelocke before you as documents, of themselves, and without any other evidence, abundantly sufficient to call upon him for his defence. He is his own accuser: he has furnished the strongest testimony against himself."

Copy of a letter from Lieutenant-General Whitelocke, to the Right Honourable William Windham, dated Buenos Ayres, July 10th, 1807.

BUENOS AYRES, *July* 10*th*, 1807.

SIR,—I have the honour to acquaint you, for the information of his Majesty, that upon being joined at Mount Video, on the 15th of June, by the corps under Brigadier-General Craufurd, not one moment was lost by Rear-Admiral Murray and myself, in making every necessary arrangement for the attack of *Buenos Ayres*. After many delays, occasioned by foul winds, a landing was effected, without opposition, on the 28th of the same month, at the *Ensenada de Barragon*, a small bay about 30 miles to the eastward of the town. The corps employed on this expedition were—three brigades of light artillery, under Captain Fraser; the 5th, 38th, and 87th regiments of foot, under Brigadier-General Sir Samuel Achmuty; the 17th light dragoons, 36th and 38th regiments, under Brigadier-General the Honourable William Lumley; eight companies of the 95th regiment, and nine light infantry companies, under Brigadier-General Craufurd; four troops of the 6th dragoon guards; the 9th light dragoons; 40th and 45th regiments of foot, under Colonel the Honourable T. Mahon; all the dragoons being dismounted, except four troops of the 17th, under Lieutenant-Colonel Lloyd.

After some fatiguing marches through a country much intersected by swamps and deep muddy rivulets, the army reached *Reduction*, a village about nine miles distant from the bridge over the *Rio Chuello*, on the opposite bank of which the enemy had constructed batteries, and established a formidable line of defence. I resolved, therefore, to turn the position, by marching in two columns from my left, and crossing the river higher up, where it was represented fordable, to unite my force in the suburbs of *Buenos Ayres*. I sent directions at the same time to Colonel Mahon, who was bringing up the greater part of the artillery, under the protection of the 17th light dragoons and 40th regiment, to wait for further orders at *Reduction*. Major-General Levison Gower having the command of the right column, crossed the river at a pass called the *Passo Chico*, and falling in with a corps of the enemy, gallantly attacked and defeated it; for the particulars of which action I beg to refer you to the annexed report. Owing to the ignorance of my guide, it was not until next day that I joined with the main body of the army, when I formed my line by placing Brigadier-General Sir Samuel Achmuty's brigade upon the left, extending it towards the convent of the *Recolleta*, from which it was distant two miles, the 36th and 88th regiments being on its right, Brigadier-General Craufurd's brigade, occupying the central and principal avenues of the town, being distant about three miles from the great square and fort; and the 6th dragoon guards, 9th light dragoons, and 45th regiment being upon his right, and extending towards the *Residencia*. The town was thus nearly invested; and this disposition of the army, and the circumstances of the town and suburbs being divided into squares of 140 yards each side, together with the knowledge that the enemy meant to occupy the flat roofs of the houses, gave rise to the following plan of attack :—Brigadier-General Sir Samuel Achmuty was directed to detach the 38th regiment to possess itself of the *Plaza de Tauros* and the adjacent strong ground, and there take post. The 87th, 5th, 36th, and 88th regiments were each divided into wings, and each wing ordered to penetrate into the street directly in its front. The light battalion divided into wings, and each followed by a wing of the 95th regiment and a 3-pounder, was ordered to proceed down the two streets on the right of the central one, and the 45th regiment down the two adjoining, and after clearing the streets of the enemy, this latter regiment was to take post at the *Residencia*. Two 6-pounders were ordered along the central street, covered by the carabineers and three troops of the 9th light dragoons, the remainder of which was posted as a reserve in the centre. Each division was ordered to proceed along the street directly in its front, till it arrived at the last square of

APPENDIX.

houses next the river *Plata*, of which it was to possess itself, forming on the flat roofs, and there wait for further orders. The 95th regiment was to occupy two of the most commanding situations, from which it could annoy the enemy. Two corporals, with tools, were ordered to march at the head of each column, for the purpose of breaking open the doors. The whole were unloaded, and no firing was to be permitted until the columns had reached their final points, and formed. A cannonade in the central streets was the signal for the whole to move forward.

In conformity to this arrangement, at half-past six o'clock of the morning of the 5th instant, the 38th regiment moving towards its left, and the 87th straight to its front, approached the strong post of the *Retiro* and *Plaza de Tauros;* and, after a most vigorous and spirited attack, in which these regiments suffered much from grape-shot and musketry, their gallant commander, Brigadier-General Sir Samuel Achmuty, possessed himself of the post, taking 32 pieces of cannon, an immense quantity of ammunition, and 600 prisoners. The 5th regiment, meeting with but little opposition, proceeded to the river, and took possession of the church and convent of Saint *Catalina.* The 36th and 88th regiments, under Brigadier-General Lumley, moving in the appointed order, were soon opposed by a heavy and continued fire of musketry from the tops and windows of the houses, the doors of which were barricaded in so strong a manner as to render them almost impossible to force: the streets were intersected by deep ditches, on the inside of which were planted cannon, pouring showers of grape on the advancing columns. In defiance, however, of this opposition, the 36th regiment, headed by the gallant general, reached its final destination; but the 88th, being nearer to the fort and principal defences of the enemy, were so weakened by his fire as to be totally overpowered and taken. The flank of the 36th being thus exposed, this regiment, together with the 5th, retired upon Sir Samuel Achmuty's post, at the *Plaza de Tauros*, not, however, before Lieutenant-Colonel Burne, and the grenadier company of the 36th regiment, had an opportunity of distinguishing themselves, by charging about 500 of the enemy, and taking and spiking two guns. The two 6-pounders moving up the central streets, meeting with a very superior fire, the four troops of the carabineers, led on by Lieutenant-Colonel

APPENDIX.

Kington, advanced to take the battery opposed to them; but this gallant officer being unfortunately wounded, as well as Captain Burrell, next in command, and the fire, both from the battery and houses, proving very destructive, they retreated to a short distance, but continued to occupy a position in the front of the enemy's principal defences, and considerably in advance of that which they had taken in the morning.

The left division of Brigadier-General Craufurd's brigade, under Lieutenant-Colonel Pack, passed on nearly to the river, and, turning to the left, approached the great square, with the intention of possessing itself of the Jesuits' college, a situation which commanded the enemy's principal line of defence; but, from the very destructive nature of his fire, this was found impracticable; and after sustaining a heavy loss, one part of the division throwing itself into a house, which was afterwards not found tenable, was shortly obliged to surrender, whilst the remaining part, after enduring a dreadful fire with the greatest intrepidity, Lieutenant-Colonel Pack, its commander, being wounded, retired upon the right division, commanded by Brigadier-General Craufurd himself. This division having passed quite through to the river *Plata*, turned also to the left, to approach the great square and fort, from the north-east bastion of which it was distant about 400 yards, when Brigadier-General Craufurd, learning the fate of his left division, thought it most advisable to take possession of the convent of *Saint Domingo*, near which he then was, intending to proceed onwards to the Franciscan church, which lay still nearer the fort, if the attack or success of any other of our columns should free him, in some measure, from the host of enemies which surrounded him. The 45th regiment, being further from the enemy's centre, had gained the *Residencia* without much opposition; and Lieutenant-Colonel Guard, leaving it in possession of his battalion companies, moved down with the grenadier company towards the centre of the town, and joined Brigadier-General Craufurd. The enemy, who now surrounded the convent on all sides, attempting to take a 3-pounder which lay in the street, the Lieutenant-Colonel with his company, and a few light infantry under Major Trotter, charged them with great spirit : in an instant the greater part of his company and Major Trotter were killed, but the gun was saved. The Brigadier-General was now obliged to confine himself to the defence of the convent, from which the riflemen kept up a well-directed fire upon such of the enemy as approached the post; but the quantity of round shot, grape, and musketry to which they were exposed, at last obliged them to quit the top of the building; and the enemy, to the number of 6000, bringing up cannon to force the wooden gates which fronted the fort, the Brigadier-General having no communication with any other columns, and judging from the cessation of firing that those next him had not been successful, surrendered at four o'clock in the afternoon. The result of this day's action had left me in possession of the *Plaza de Tauros*, a strong post on the enemy's right, and the *Residencia*, another strong post, on his left, whilst I occupied an advanced position opposite his centre. But these advantages had cost about 2500 men in killed, wounded, and prisoners. The nature of the fire to which the troops were exposed was violent in the extreme. Grape-shot at the corners of all the streets, musketry, hand-grenades, bricks and stones from the tops of all the houses. Every householder, with his negroes, defended his dwelling, each of which was in itself a fortress: and it is perhaps not too much to say, that the whole male population of Buenos Ayres was employed in its defence. This was the situation of the army on the morning of the 6th instant, when General Liniers addressed a letter to me, offering to give up all his prisoners taken in the late affair, together with the 71st regiment, and others taken with Brigadier-General Beresford, if I desisted from any further attack on the town, and withdraw his Majesty's forces from the river *Plata;* intimating at the same time, that from the exasperated state of the populace, he could not answer for the safety of the prisoners, if I persisted in offensive measures. Influenced by this consideration (which I knew, from better authority, to be founded in fact), and reflecting of how little advantage would be the possession of a country, the inhabitants of which were so absolutely hostile, I resolved to forego the advantages which the bravery of the troops had obtained, and acceded to the annexed treaty, which I trust will meet the approbation of his Majesty.

I have nothing further to add, except to mention, in terms of the highest praise, the conduct of Rear-Admiral Murray, whose cordial co-operation has never been wanting whenever the army could be benefited by his exertions; Captain Rowley,

APPENDIX.

of the royal navy, commanding the seamen on shore; Captain Bayntun, of his Majesty's ship "Africa," who superintended the disembarkation; and Captain Thomson, of the "Fly," who had the direction of the gun-boats, and had previously rendered me much service, by reconnoitering the river, are all entitled to my best thanks.

As his character already stands so high, it is almost unnecessary to state, that from my second in command, Major-General Levison Gower, I have experienced every zealous and useful assistance. My thanks are likewise due to Brigadier-Generals Sir Samuel Achmuty and Lumley, and to Colonel Mahon, and to Brigadier-General Craufurd, commanding brigades. I cannot sufficiently bring to notice the uncommon exertions of Captain Fraser, commanding the royal artillery, the fertility of whose mind, zeal and animation in all cases, left difficulties behind. Captain Squire, of the royal engineers, is also entitled to my best thanks. Nor should I omit the gallant conduct of Major Nichols, of the 45th regiment, who, on the morning of the 6th instant, being pressed by the enemy, near the *Residencia*, charged them with great spirit, and took two howitzers and many prisoners. Lieutenant-Colonel Bradford, Deputy Adjutant-General, has likewise a great claim to my approbation, as a gallant and promising officer. The officers of my personal staff, Lieutenant-Colonel Torrens, military secretary, Captains Brown, Foster, Douglas, and Whittingham, aides-de-camp, must also be mentioned by me in terms of just regard. The knowledge which the latter possesses of the Spanish language has been eminently useful to me.

This despatch will be delivered to you by Lieutenant-Colonel Bourke, Deputy-Quartermaster-General, who has afforded me that assistance which might be looked for from an officer of his military talents and attachment to the service; to whom I beg to refer you for any further particulars respecting the military operations in this part of the world.—I have the honour to be, &c.

(Signed)   JOHN WHITELOCKE,
Lieutenant-General.

The Right Hon. W. Windham,
&c. &c. &c.

APPENDIX.

Copy of Letter from Lieutenant-General Whitelocke, to the Right Honourable William Windham, dated July 10th, 1807.—Private.

BUENOS AYRES, *July 10th*, 1807.

SIR,—I have the honour to inform you, that immediately after my arrival at *Monte Video*, on the 10th of May, I began to make every possible preparation for the attack of this place, as the first and most essential step towards the reduction of the province. For this purpose sloops of war and other light vessels were sent to reconnoitre the southern bank of the river, in order to fix upon the precise point of debarkation. It was found that the water was too shallow to admit of a landing, under cover of the ships of war, anywhere to the westward of the town of *Buenos Ayres*, nor nearer to it on the eastward than the *Enseñada* of *Barragon*. This bay was, therefore, fixed upon as the point of debarkation, and every arrangement that could previously be made was pressed forward with expedition, whilst I waited anxiously for the arrival of Brigadier-General Craufurd's corps, and the fleet with which I had sailed from England.

On the 27th of May, Rear-Admiral Murray and Brigadier-General Craufurd arrived at the mouth of the river; but owing to a prevalence of contrary winds, the expedition did not reach Monte Video until the 14th of June. I immediately determined not to wait the arrival of the convoy from England, as by the general voice of the inhabitants, and of those officers who had passed the winter in the province, the months of July and August were represented as most unfavourable to military operations, on account of the heavy and continual rains which prevail at that season. Having fixed upon *Colonia* as the place of assembly from which the expedition was to proceed, I sent the troops upwards, in small divisions, on account of the intricate navigation, leaving at *Monte Video* the 47th regiment, the detachments of the 20th and 21st light dragoons, two companies of the 38th regiment, and a corps of militia, formed by the British merchants, in all composing a garrison of about 1300 men, under the command of Colonel Browne, of the 40th regiment; and after much delay, caused by contrary winds, Rear-Admiral Murray and myself arrived opposite the point of debarkation on the 28th ultimo.

APPENDIX.

In the morning the fleet stood into the bay, and before night the whole army, consisting as per margin,* was landed, without opposition, on the enemy's coast. The greater part of the next day was occupied in landing artillery, horses, and stores. Immediately on the landing of Brigadier-General Craufurd's brigade, and the 38th and 87th regiments, I detached Major-General L. Gower with this force and two 3-pounders, to occupy the heights in my front, about five miles distant; and the next morning I proceeded to join him with the rest of the army, four 6-pounders, and two 3-pounders, the remainder of the artillery not being landed. The same day I directed Major-General L. Gower to precede my march with his advanced corps, substituting the 36th and 88th regiments, under Brigadier-General Lumley, for the 38th and 87th regiments; and I left Colonel Mahon, with four troops of the 17th light dragoons, and the 40th regiment, to protect the guns when they should come up, and cover the rear of the army, being principally induced to break my force into these divisions, for the purpose of more readily procuring cover and fuel. On the 1st of July the advanced corps drove a small party of the enemy from the village of *Reduction*, and took post about two miles beyond it, whilst I occupied the village with the main body. I was now distant about nine miles from the bridge over the *Rio Chuello*, on the opposite bank of which I understood the enemy had constructed batteries, and intended to make a stand. I determined, therefore, instead of forcing the bridge, to turn the enemy's line of defence, by marching from our left, and crossing the river in two columns higher up, where it was represented fordable, and continuing to march until I should have got completely to the westward and northward of the town, appuyed my left on the river *La Plata*, and opened a communication with the fleet. On the 2nd instant, at nine o'clock, Major-General L. Gower marched with his corps, which should now be considered as the right column, and I marched myself at ten, with the intention of uniting our forces that evening in the suburbs of the town.

---

* 3 brigades artillery.
5th ⎱
38th ⎰ Brigadier-General Sir S. Achmuty.
87th ⎱
17th dragoons.
36th ⎱
88th ⎰ Brigadier-General Lumley

95th ⎱ Brigadier-General
Light battalion ⎰ Craufurd.
4 troops 6th dragoon guards.
9th light dragoons.
40th ⎱
45th ⎰ Colonel Mahon.

Major-General L. Gower having crossed the river, his leading brigade fell in with a considerable corps of the enemy, under General Liniers himself, which he attacked with great vivacity, completely overthrew it, taking ten pieces of cannon and some prisoners. The Major-General halted on the ground from which he had driven the enemy, waiting my arrival, and sending, at the same time, a summons to General Liniers (No. 1), which was refused on this occasion, as well as the following day, when I sent to him myself (as per No. 2). Owing to the ignorance of my guide, who conducted me by a considerable detour, I did not reach the Major-General until the next day, when I formed my line by placing one of my brigades under Sir Samuel Achmuty, on the left of Brigadier-General Lumley's, extending it towards the convent of the *Recolleta*, distant about two miles; and another under Lieutenant-Colonel Guard, on the right, towards the *Residencia*, whilst Brigadier-General Craufurd's brigade occupied the central and principal avenues into the town, being distant about three miles from the great square and the fort of *Buenos Ayres*. In pursuance of my original design, I intended to march the next morning by my left to the convent of *Recolleta*, which standing on high ground immediately over the river, I could have communicated with the fleet, and landed heavy guns for a vigorous attack of the town, should General Liniers obstinately refuse to surrender it. Upon consulting, however, with Major-General L. Gower, he submitted to me another plan of attack, which as it promised a more expeditious issue, inasmuch as it obviated the necessity of marching to the left, and the delay which would be occasioned by landing heavy guns and erecting batteries, a delay which I the more dreaded on account of the rains having, to all appearance, set in, and the men being in a great degree exposed to the severity of the weather, from the impossibility of conveying camp equipage. I consented, for these reasons, to change my plan, and adopt what seemed to be generally approved by the general officers under me. Besides, the measure of bombardment, or any other measure which might occasion an indiscriminate loss of life, ruin the town, and irritate the people, appeared to me, upon reflection, contrary both to the letter and spirit of my instructions. I hoped also, by this plan, to be able to dislodge those who opposed the progress of his Majesty's arms, and by driving them to the bottom of the town, there make a number of prisoners, which might be, in our hands, so many pledges for the return of the 71st regiment and the other troops captured with Brigadier-General Beresford, whilst the peaceable inhabitants, and those best disposed towards us, by remaining quietly in their houses, might escape the danger of the attack. The nature of this attack can be best explained by annexing the General Order (No. 3). The result was successful in the principal points, as I obtained possession of the *Plaza de Tauros*, a strong post on the enemy's right flank, 32 pieces of ordnance, and a large depôt of ammunition and provisions, as well as the *Residencia*, another strong post on the enemy's left, and four pieces of cannon which defended it. But these conquests were purchased with the loss of 2500 men killed, wounded, and prisoners, and amongst the latter Brigadier-General Craufurd and other officers of rank. The conduct of both officers and men in this action has been gallant in the highest degree, and the severity of the loss occasioned solely by the obstinacy of the defence. The enemy had dug ditches across the principal streets, and placed cannon within them: he occupied the flat roofs of all the houses in commanding situations, and from thence, and the windows, poured a destructive fire of musketry, hand-grenades, fire-pots, &c. upon the columns as they advanced; having likewise had the precaution to barricade the doors in so strong a manner as to render them very difficult to force, though the troops had been provided with instruments for that purpose. Every householder, with his negroes, defended his dwelling; and it is, perhaps, not too much to say, that the whole male population of *Buenos Ayres* was employed in its defence, which very population in the field would probably not have withstood the attack of two British regiments.

On the morning succeeding the attack I received a letter from General Liniers, offering to give up all prisoners taken in the late affair, as well as those taken with Major-General Beresford, if I condescend to relinquish the attack, and withdraw his Majesty's forces from the province. A correspondence upon this took place, which ended in the treaty I have the honour to transmit.

My reasons for acceding to this negotiation were briefly these:—I had lost in the preceding attack —— men, although I had gained a strong post on the enemy's right flank, from

APPENDIX.

which I communicated with the fleet, and from which it might be possible to fire heavy cannon on the town, and otherwise annoy it. Yet the enemy's chief defences were too remote from this point, and too much covered by houses to allow me to hope that I could, in any given time, destroy them by cannon alone, even if the nature of my instructions had not militated against such a measure. General Liniers had likewise acquainted me in his letter, that he could not answer for the lives of his prisoners, if the attack was persisted in; and from everything I have since heard from the officers themselves, I have reason to believe they would all have been sacrificed to the fury of an exasperated rabble. Nothing, therefore, remained to be done offensively, but another attack on the town, conducted in a manner similar to the last; the event of which must have been doubtful, as my force, when collected, did not reach 5000 men; and, if even successful, my loss would probably have rendered that force insufficient to keep the place when taken. If it was deemed fruitless to attempt another attack, there yet remained two modes of retreat, either by treaty, or re-embarking in the face of the enemy. The latter measure would certainly have been attended with additional loss, and the wounded and prisoners of the late affair, as well as the 71st regiment, in all 4000 men, lost for ever to Great Britain. In return for which I should have possessed but a nominal command at *Monte Video*, a post which can never be considered of any advantage whilst the capital of the province and the great entrepôt of commerce remained in the hands of the enemy.

I determined, therefore, to accede to this treaty, by which I shall be enabled to bring off my own army almost entire, and recover the 71st regiment, a point which my instructions has taught me to consider as of the first importance; and I shall evacuate a province which the force I was authorised to calculate upon could never maintain, and which, from the very hostile disposition of its inhabitants, was in truth not worth maintaining.

I shall dispose of the army in the manner pointed out in my instructions, the particulars of which I shall detail to you from *Monte Video*, by another man-of-war that will sail from thence with duplicates of these despatches. Trusting that the conduct I have pursued in this difficult situation may meet with the gracious approval of his Majesty,—I have the honour to be, &c.

(Signed)   JOHN WHITELOCKE,
Lieutenant-General.

This will be delivered to you by Lieutenant-Colonel Bourke, to whom, as well as Sir Samuel Achmuty, I refer you for further particulars.

(A true copy)   E. COOKE.

Right Honourable William Windham,
&c. &c. &c.

TREATY.

A Definitive Treaty between the Generals in Chief of his Brittanic Majesty and of his Catholic Majesty, as per the following articles:

1st. There shall be, from this time, a cessation of hostilities on both sides of the river *Plate*.

2d. The troops of his Brittanic Majesty shall retain, for the period of two months, the fortress and place of *Monte Video;* and, as a neutral country: there shall be considered a line drawn from *San Carlos* on the west, to *Pando* on the east, and there shall not be on any part of that line hostilities committed on any side, the neutrality being understood, only that the individuals of both nations may live freely under their respective laws—the Spanish subjects being judged by theirs, as the English by those of their nation.

3d. There shall be on both sides a mutual restitution of prisoners, including not only those which have been taken since the arrival of the troops under Lieutenant-General Whitelocke, but also all those his Britannic Majesty's subjects captured in South America since the commencement of the war.

4th. That, for the prompt despatch of the vessels and troops of his Brittanic Majesty, there shall be no impediment thrown in the way of the supplies of provision which may be requested for *Monte Video.*

5th. A period of ten days, from this time, is given for the re-embarkation of his Britannic Majesty's troops, to pass to the north side of the river *La Plata*, with the arms which may

APPENDIX.

actually be in their power, stores and equipage, at the most convenient points which may be selected, and during this time provisions may be sold to them.

6th. That at the time of the delivery of the place and fortress of *Monte Video*, which shall take place at the end of the two months fixed in the second article, the delivery will be made in the terms it was found, and with the artillery it had when it was taken.

7th. Three officers of rank shall be delivered for and until the fulfilment of the above articles by both parties; being well understood, that his Britannic Majesty's officers who have been on their parole, cannot serve against South America until their arrival in Europe.

Done at the Fort of *Buenos Ayres*, the seventh day of July, one thousand eight hundred and seven, signing two of one tenor.

SANTIAGO LINIERS,   JN. WHITELOCKE,
CASER BALBIANI,   Lieut.-Gen. Comm&.
BERNARDO VELASCOS,   GEO. MURRAY,
   Rear-Admiral Comm&.

(A True Copy)   E. COOKE.

Major-General Gower to General Liniers, July 3.

CORAL DE MISERALA, BEFORE BUENOS AYRES,
July 3, 1807.

SIR,—Captain Roache, of the 17th dragoons, whom I had the honour of sending unto you this morning, having informed me that you wished to communicate with me on the subject of terms, I beg to acquaint you, that his Excellency Lieutenant-General Whitelocke has ordered me (from his sincere wish to spare an unnecessary effusion of human blood) to intimate to you, that in the present situation of affairs, if they do not proceed to further hostilities, he will grant terms to the town of *Buenos Ayres:* that the following must be the basis on which they are to be granted; but that any trifling alteration which may make them more favourable, without altering their original fundamental stipulations, may possibly be agreed to :

1st. All British subjects detained in South America must be delivered up, and sufficient hostages placed in the power of the British Commander till their arrival at *Buenos Ayres*.

2d. That all persons holding civil offices dependent on the government of *Buenos Ayres*, and all military officers and soldiers, become prisoners of war.

3d. That all cannon, stores, arms, and ammunition, be delivered up uninjured.

4th. That all public property, of every description, be delivered up to the British Commanders.

5th. That the free and unrestrained exercise of the Roman Catholic religion be granted to the inhabitants of *Buenos Ayres*.

6th. That all private property on shore shall be respected, and secured to its owners.

Our force is so considerable that I believe, in candour, you cannot doubt of the ultimate result. I trust you will believe me when I assure you that a wish to avoid so dreadful a scene as that which a town taken by assault always presents is the only thing which has induced his Excellency Lieutenant-General Whitelocke to permit me to address you.

(Signed)   J. L. GOWER,
Major-General.

His Excellency Gen. Liniers,
&c. &c. &c.   (A true Copy)   E. COOKE.

Major-General ELLIO's Answer to Major-General GOWER.

July 3, 1807.

SIR,—By orders of the Spanish General, *Don* Santiago Liniers, I answer to the letter brought by your flag of truce respecting the surrender of this capital, by saying that nothing relative to laying down our arms will be attended to—that the Spanish General has a sufficient number of brave troops, commanded by brave chiefs, full of desire to die in defence of their country, and that this is the moment to show their patriotism. —I remain, &c.

(Signed)   Major-General CALL. ELLIO.

Major-Gen. Levison Gower.

APPENDIX.

Plan of Attack.—Circular.

HEADQUARTERS, CAMP BEFORE BUENOS
AYRES, *July* 4, 1807.

SIR,—Herewith I have the honour to enclose instructions for the attack of Buenos Ayres. The refusal of the Spanish General to listen to terms, and the state of the army from fatigue and bad weather, leaves but little choice as to the mode of accomplishing our purpose; otherwise I should assuredly be disposed to adopt one *equally calculated* * to secure to us possession of the place without the probable chance of so much blood being spilt.

I therefore have to desire that you will impress upon the minds of all officers acting under your immediate orders, the necessity of preventing, in as great a degree as possible under such circumstances, acts of violence on the persons of those who do not carry arms, as well as women and children.—I have the honour to be, &c.

(Signed) JOHN WHITELOCKE.

To Brigadiers.

COPY OF GENERAL ORDERS,

4th July, 1807.

Sir Samuel Achmuty to detach the 38th regiment, to possess itself of the *Plaza de Tauros* and the adjacent strong grounds, and there post itself.

The 87th, 5th, 36th, and 88th regiments to be divided into wings, and each wing is to penetrate into the street directly in its front, in a column of sections right in front.

The light battalion to penetrate by wings into the second street, on the right of that leading up from Mr. White's house, and the next to it, followed by the 95th regiment.

The left division of the 95th is to receive its orders from Colonel Park, the right division from General Craufurd; two 3-pounders to follow these columns, one each. The 45th to advance by wings, left in front, up to the two next streets beyond the light battalion. The carabineers to move up with the cover two 6-pounders, which will be advanced up the street from Mr. White's, and remain with them.

* . The *Italics* are the author's.

The 9th light dragoons to move to the left, and take the ground of the light battalion, at five o'clock, where they will receive further orders.

Each officer commanding a division of the left wing, which is from the 88th to 87th inclusively, to take care that he does not incline to his right of the right wing, that is, light brigade and 45th regiment to the left.

The cannonade in the centre to be the signal for the whole to rush forward; and each division to go, if possible, straight down the street before it, till it arrives at the last square of houses near to the river *Plate*, of which they are to possess themselves, and on the tops of which they are to form: if they find that they suffer by any interior defences, to lodge themselves as far in advance as they can. Two corporals, with tools, to be attached to the head of each column. The whole to be unloaded, and no firing to be allowed on any account.

When the business is over, the utmost exertion to be used to keep the men collected and formed.

The regiments may leave their packs in their present cantonments, with a subaltern's guard, if they wish.

The cannonade will commence at 30 minutes past six o'clock precisely.

(A true copy)   E. COOKE.

Major-General Gower's Orders.

Major-General Levison Gower, as second in command, will be occupied in making the necessary arrangements relative to the executive duties and localities of the situation, aided by Brigadier-General Sir Samuel Achmuty; whose able assistance will also be brought in aid of what may appertain to the many other points to which the attention of the Commander of the forces must of course be directed, in a command in its nature new and intricate.

The other appointments to the Staff will be communicated to the army on the arrival of the additional force.

The 9th light dragoons to march to the left, and take the ground of the light battalion at five o'clock, where they will remain till further orders.

Lieutenant-General Whitelocke to General Liniers.

HEADQUARTERS BEFORE BUENOS AYRES,
July 4, 1807.

I beg you will do me the justice to impute to the principles of humanity only, the information I give you of my arrival, having joined the troops under the command of Major-General Levison Gower with the principal column of the army. I dare say it is not unknown to you that another column awaits my orders within little more than a league from your capital.

I beg, therefore, only to be informed, if, after this faithful communication, you still adhere to the answer given to the Major-General in your letter of yesterday, who was authorized to address you on this subject, in the event of his arrival before me.

The bearer, Captain Whittingham, has my orders to deliver this, and to wait half an hour from that time for your answer, yes or no.

J. WHITELOCKE.

To General Liniers, &c.

General Liniers to Major-General Whitelocke.

SIR,—I have just received your Excellency's letter of this date, to the contents of which I have the honour to reply, that whilst I have ammunition, and whilst the same spirit which now animates this garrison and people shall continue to exist, I shall never think of delivering up the post which has been confided to me: and I am perfectly convinced, that I have more than sufficient means to resist all the efforts which your Excellency can make to conquer me.

The duties of humanity of which your Excellency speaks, will, I conceive, be more wounded by your Excellency, who is the aggressor, than by me. I merely do that duty which is prescribed to me by honour and the just right of retaliation.—I have the honour to be, &c.

(Signed)   SANTIAGO LINIERS.

July 4, 1807.   (A true Copy)   E. COOKE.

APPENDIX.

CORAL OF MISERALA, *July* 3, 1807.

SIR,—I have the honour to report to you, for the information of the Lieutenant-General Whitelocke, that the advanced corps under my command, consisting of three companies of the 95th light battalion, 36th and 38th regiments, with two 3 and two 6-pounders, advanced from the position I had taken up in front of the village of Reduction; and, after making a considerable detour from the badness of the roads, I crossed the *Chuello* at the *Chico* Pass; from thence I continued my route, though very strongly enclosed, and difficult ground, till the head of the column arrived at the junction of two roads, about 500 yards from the Canal of *Miserala*. At the same moment that we discovered the enemy, they commenced a heavy, though, after the first round, not well-directed fire of shot and shells, my artillery having been left in the rear, under the protection of three companies of Brigadier-General Lumley's brigade, owing to the inability of the horses to bring it up at the same rate at which the infantry marched. I directed an immediate attack to be made on their left flank with the bayonet, which was executed by Brigadier-General Craufurd in the most perfect manner, with his brigade, and he was so well seconded by the gallantry of Lieutenant-Colonel Pack and Major Travers, the officers and men of the 95th, and light battalion, that in five minutes the enemy's force, though strongly posted behind hedges and embankments, gave way, leaving about 60 killed and 70 prisoners, with all their artillery, consisting of nine guns, one howitzer, three tumbrels with limbers complete.

I beg to state that the conduct of every officer and soldier engaged was admirable; and that I am also under great obligation to Brigadier-General Lumley, for his exertions to take a share in the action, but which alone the very exhausted state of his regiments, from the severity of the march, prevented. Immediately after I formed, I found that he had taken a good position on the right of the light brigade, to support it in case of re-attack.

I am happy to add our loss has been but trifling, not exceeding 14 rank and file killed, 5 officers, and 25 rank and file wounded. The exact returns I have not been able to obtain.—I have the honour to be, &c.

(Signed)   J. LEVISON GOWER,
Major-General.

Lieutenant-Colonel Torrens,
   Military Secretary.

II.

Extract of a Letter from Sir S. Achmuty to Mr. Wyndham.

THE escape of General Beresford, an event as pleasing and important as it was unexpected, has put us in full possession of the views of the leading men, and the real state of the country. He had been ordered, immediately after the fall of *Monte Video*, to a town 300 leagues inland, and was already between forty and fifty leagues from *Buenos Ayres*, when two Spanish officers, in the family of the Governor, who had been endeavouring to enter into some political negotiation with him, proposed to assist and accompany him in making his escape, which, with great difficulty, was effected; and the General, after being three successive days secreted in *Buenos Ayres*, fortunately reached the ship with our despatches.

Letter from General Liniers to Admiral Stirling and Sir Samuel Achmuty.

BUENOS AYRES, *March 2d*, 1807.

SIRS,—I am very sorry that the first time I have the honour to write to your Excellencies, is on the unpleasant subject of complaining of proceedings of officers of your nation. Major-General Beresford and Lieutenant-Colonel Pack, of the 71st regiment, forgetting every sentiment of honour, and in violation of their word, and the oath which they had taken on the 6th of September last, have absconded, and the first with the infamy of having fomented an insurrection in this county, where the greatest part of his vile accomplices, now under the lash of the law, will soon pay for their horrid crime.

This violation of public faith and the law of nations, has, however, only increased the enthusiasm of all the inhabitants of this city, ever ready and disposed to bury themselves under the ruins of their edifices sooner than give themselves up to any other dominion than that of their lawful sovereign.

The pretext which Mr. Beresford makes use of, in alleging that there was a pretended capitulation, your Excellencies will

APPENDIX.

see by the enclosed prints is without foundation, and it only remains with me, conformably to the laws of war, to reclaim those two prisoners; and I trust to your integrity that you will order them to be given up: at all events I fulfil my duty in reclaiming them, and the military world will decide on which side justice is.

I do not answer Mr. Beresford, not having anything to add to what I now express to your Excellencies; and I have only further to observe, that the determination of the people, as has been represented by their magistrates, is irrevocable: they are resolved to defend themselves to the last extremity, and prepared to make their defence memorable.

Your Excellencies will, therefore, avoid making any further offers; for be assured, that no answer will be returned, and that nothing but force can decide our fate.

God preserve your Excellencies many years.

(Signed) SANTIAGO LINIERS.

To their Excellencies Sir C. Stirling
and Sir S. Achmuty.

CORAL DE MISERALA, *July* 2, 1807.

SIR,—I had the honour to report to you, for the information of the Commander of the forces, that the advanced corps of the army now occupy a position, the centre of which is across the prolongation of the centre street of *Buenos Ayres*. I have taken most of the cattle intended for the consumption of the city for this day, and occupy the principal *coral*. I have secured 20,000 lbs. of biscuit, and my corps is fully supplied with it; spirits I am searching for, and I have hopes that I shall be able to secure some; to what extent I do not yet know. I sent to report to you, yesterday evening, immediately after the action, in which I stated we had taken eight pieces of cannon, I now find it increased to ten, many prisoners, and a great quantity of arms and ammunition. General Liniers and Colonel Ellio were both present. Supposing that a considerable impression may have been made by so complete a defeat as this considerable portion of their force has sustained, I have sent in a summons to General Liniers, at first verbally only, to discover how they appeared to feel in the town. Colonel Ellio met Brigade-Major

APPENDIX.

Roache who went with the flag, and requested that they might receive a written proposal. I have now, therefore, sent one, founded on the instructions I received yesterday by Colonel Bourke.

I believe it will not be difficult to, nearly if not entirely, invest the town by placing about 1000 on my right towards the *Chuello*, and all the rest on my left towards the Recollata, having that in the rear. The centre of the town makes a salient angle; it appears to me, therefore, that our centre should be a little refused, and our flanks thrown forward, as the right will be rested on the *Chuello*, and the left secured by the *Plata;* but this of course must be regulated by the better judgment of the Commander of the forces.—I have the honour to be, &c.

J. LEVISON GOWER,
Major-General.

Lieutenant-Colonel Torrens,
&c. &c. &c.

Sentence.

The court-martial having duly considered the evidence given in support of the charges against the prisoner, Lieutenant-General Whitelocke, his defence, and the evidence he has adduced, are of opinion that he is guilty of the whole of the said charges, with the exception of that part of the second charge which relates to the order that "the columns should be unloaded, and that no firing should be permitted on any account."

The court are anxious that it may be distinctly understood that they attach no censure whatever to the precautions taken to prevent unnecessary firing during the advance of the troops to the proposed points of attack, and do therefore acquit Lieutenant-General Whitelocke of that part of the said charge.

The court adjudge that the said Lieutenant-General Whitelocke be cashiered, and declared totally unfit and unworthy to serve his Majesty in any military capacity whatever.

www.ingramcontent.com/pod-product-compliance
Lightning Source LLC
Chambersburg PA
CBHW030737230426
43667CB00007B/749